MW01484621

IN HOSPITAL
AND CAMP

A WOMAN'S RECORD OF THRILLING INCIDENTS
AMONG THE WOUNDED IN THE CIVIL WAR.

SOPHRONIA E. BUCKLIN

WITH AN INTRODUCTION

BY S. L. C.

1869.

Contents

BIOGRAPHY.

Sophronia E. Bucklin was born March 5, 1828 in Cayuga County, New York, making her 33 years old at the outbreak of the American Civil War, two years younger than the required age to enlist as a nurse. Yet, since no one asked, she enlisted in 1864. Before and after the war, she lived in Ithaca, New York, in her later years in a home that she owned there.

Sophronia never married and it is unclear when she left the home of her parents. At the time she enlisted her services to the Union cause, she was either working in or visiting at the Orphan Asylum at Auburn, New York. Black, white, Union, and Confederate—she treated them all. She did not take leave once during her service.

Little else is known of her except that she appears in the 1883 Ithaca city directory and the 1900 federal census. In October of 1892, she applied for an invalid pension as a Civil War veteran. She died in November of 1902 and was buried in Ithaca. Her obituary in the local paper noted that she was a famous Civil War nurse and that she had written this remarkable and compassionate book. Her home and estate were auctioned off by her executor, L. H. Van Kirk, the following May but it is uncertain to whom the proceeds went, as she had no surviving relatives listed.

INTRODUCTION.

Amongst that band of noble women, who served their country in hospital and camp during the late gigantic struggle with rebellion, the heroine of the following pages justly deserves a foremost place. Others went out with like patriotism warming their hearts, but the toils and hardships, which made the position of hospital nurse anything but pastime, sent many of them back to their comfortable homes—the romance of soldiering sadly crushed out of their hearts.

Yet sickness, nor starvation, nor daily contact with loathsome diseases, and hideous wounds could alter the purpose of our heroine to stand by the boys in blue, till the bloody conflict was ended. Not till the heart of the nation beat free from the coils of the serpent which enwrapped it with such deadly persistence, did she feel herself at liberty, and willing to go home.

For nearly three long years she led the life of an actual soldier. She partook of their rude fare, lived under unsubstantial tents, shared their weary marches to new hospital grounds, from the transports on which they had been borne over river and bay, starving through long days and nights of waiting, sick from exposure to the sun and dews: in all things, save the wild, deadly charges of battle, A TRUE SOLDIER OF THE UNION.

It has been said, when the work of those women who came out under the patronage of the Commissions was placed in contrast with that of the Government nurse, that, while the former worked voluntarily, the latter had her pay and rations. Pay and rations!— twelve dollars a month and soldiers' fare—themselves to clothe from the bountiful allowance; and, withal, the privilege of attending upon men sick with putrid wounds, their torn and filthy uniforms in worse condition than that of the saddest beggar who crawls in the by-ways of a crowded city! So did the common soldier receive, for his chances of the dangers of active warfare, a price and his subsistence; but who questions the loyalty or bravery of those men in their worn shrouds of blue, around whose shattered bones to-day the tangled grassroots of Southern battle fields weave their intricate net-work? Who says, because they were paid, the sacrifice which

2

they laid on their country's smoking altar was not a voluntary blood-offering? Who says, because they were furnished subsistence, and were clad, that they died not to save the glorious Union, interposing their mangled, bleeding bodies to hold back the tide of anarchy and destruction, which else would have rolled in one resistless wave over the hills and valleys of the North?

Many women, possessed of independent means, were enabled, under the patronage of the Commissions, and under pretence of aiding the work in the hospitals, to behold the grandeur of the Capitol, and gratify a taste for romantic adventure. But how many of these slept for nights under the white cover of a tent, on the bare ground, and suffered the pangs of starvation for days, while they bent over the festering wounds of dying men? How many endured the horrible sights of mangled bodies, just brought in by the ambulance trains from the gory sods, whereon they fell when the foe met them?

The well-ordered hospital, in which every sight which might shock a sensitive nature was carefully hidden—where lemonades, and jellies, and fruits, and flowers could, at fixed hours, be distributed by their fair hands—was not the field hospital, into which men were brought direct from the awful place of carnage, with the dirt of rifle pits mingling with their own gore, unable to meet nature's demands, with worms rioting over the putrifying flesh. Yet, it was in the field hospitals that Miss Bucklin did her greatest work. One of the first at Gettysburg; the first at White House Landing, before the white wings of a single tent fluttered over the grass-grown field, so soon to be a trampled waste, and haunted by the ghosts of agonized men, whose souls went up from its sod; and with the first at City Point, when the open field lay waiting its transformation into one of the grandest hospitals which was established during the war—she shrunk from no hardships if, thereby, she might minister to the wants of some who were very nigh to death, and whose feet seemed upon the brink of the soundless river.

In the long transit from White House to City Point, when the passage of the Grand Army of the Potomac, at Charles City, obstructed their journey up the river—on board a boat, without

3

shelter or rations, for days she endured the excessive heat of the June sunshine, and the chilling dews of the Southern nights, with no thought of availing herself of the privilege, which she had at any time, of returning home to comfort and plenty.

While in the service, the insolence of shoulder-strapped officials, and their tyranny, was borne in silence, lest, at a murmur from her lips, the work which was in her hands would be taken from her, and she be shut out from her good work among the boys in their wretched need. But now, ho personal fear of censure, or craving of favor has induced her to speak of such officials in any terms but those of strictest truth. She witnessed the perpetration of outrages which filled her soul with horror, while the perpetrators, oft times, continued in position as well as in favor. Men were only men in the army as out of it, and the consciousness of holding a little brief authority made many a little soul a tyrant on his narrow beat. It was not in the power of Government to regulate this evil, and it was endured in sullen silence by the soldiers, and with indignant -but suppressed rage by the women, who were powerless to stay the unbridled brute force. Over the imbittered memory of many scenes of such inhumanity, it is impossible to wrap the mercy of utter silence forever.

Not once during the term for which she served did she avail herself of the offer of a journey home to recruit and rest. Her life was there, where so many yielded up their lives; her heart could not separate itself from the wounded men in blue, whose number increased alike with victory or defeat. She could not have fallen back into the old life of comfort, knowing that noble men were suffering and dying for the need of woman's help. Her patriotism was of that obdurate nature which could have crowned the offering with her own life, if, in yielding it, her country's cause might be the better served.

At all times a faithful and consistent worker, she won the esteem of the Superintendent of Women Nurses, and endeared herself to those who, in their weakness, but for her willing hands, must have gone untended and uncomforted into the shadows of the dark valley. Waking from needful slumber, at Gettysburg, we find her busy through the night preparing a lunch for a squad of convalescing

4

men, who were to be sent off on the morrow. Again we find her taking from her own tent even the bare bedstead, on which she had slept, to exchange it with the Sanitary Commission for a cot, on which one of the maimed heroes of that great fight might be borne in comparative comfort to another hospital.

And her interest in these men went not out even after she had carefully arranged the pads and pillows under their aching limbs— placed a lunch close at their hand, and amidst long and repeated protestations of gratitude, answered the farewell wave of the hand, and heard the scream of the locomotive as it sped out of the battle town, bearing them to new scenes and new mercies; for letters were constantly received and answered— on the one hand giving the details of the journey, and telling the faithful nurse, in homely but expressive words, how comfortable her provisions had made the otherwise toilsome transit; on the other, expressing solicitude and prayerful concern in behalf of their speedy recovery. Scores of letters now lie before me, written out of the gratitude of noble hearts, thanking Miss Bucklin again and again for the kind care which had proved the salvation of their mortal bodies. One illiterate scrawl, thanking her for her interest in obtaining a furlough for the writer, and blessing her for the happiness which was then resting over himself and wife and the new born babe, on consultation, was found to be the effort of one of her colored patients from Point of Rocks.

But it is impossible to make anything like a satisfactory selection from them, when all are alike expressive of gratefulness, and alike invoke blessings on the unselfish heart which could so crucify itself for the welfare of the boys in their worn and faded blue. A volume would not suffice to hold them in full, and mere fragmentary extracts would unfairly express the feelings pervading a letter, when the writer's heart is surcharged with thankfulness. Like the diamond dew-drops which are threaded over the grasses in early summer mornings, the expressions of gratefulness pervade every line, and like the quivering dew-drops when shaken together into a chalice, though bright and sparkling still, yet they lose the scintillant radiance of the slender grass stem, making it worth the ransom of a king.

I find confidential notes from Miss Dix [Dorothea Dix, Superintendent of Army Nurses for the Union, activist for the mentally ill], showing that she knew the value of the hospital nurse she had trusted; letters from sister nurses, who had shared her tent, and knew from their own experiences, the hardships which beset her pathway like jagged rocks and thorns; long communications from her soldier boys, who, transferred to other hospitals, still languished on sick beds, and yearned for her willing care, and epistles from fathers, and mothers, and sisters, and wives whose beloved ones had with their lives gone to meet the common enemy. Each is stamped with the writer's individuality, some evincing scholarly polish, some written with hands unused to the pen, hardly legible, yet bearing upon it the sincere feelings of the full heart which indited it.

Thus we leave them, well knowing that all over the land brave ones will rise up to say, "She saved my life, I can never forget her; she was my sister when friends were far away—my mother when the bosom that nourished me was torn with anguish for her son, yet could not stand beside him. All honor to the noble self-sacrificing women who endured hardships and privations for our sake, that we might be strong to save the Union."

The records are few of that undaunted band, who, as Government nurses, gave themselves just as truly to their country as did those who fought and died, and found a sepulchre under the bloody sods of the South. The many humble women with brave hearts and stout hands, who, having little beyond the ordinary means of subsistence, themselves offered their services to assist in the gigantic work of mercy, are at times passed carelessly by, and others—dainty women, whose hands were bejeweled, whose garments were of fine texture, who could afford the luxury of horses and aids in distributing the stores which had been poured into the bosom of the Commissions— these are among the lauded of the Nation. The women, used to toil, counting privation and hunger as the price of their devotion to their country's cause and its heroes, stand in the same relation to these fair women as do the common soldiers to the well- eared for officers who lead them into the swift combat to die, or to escape with bloody wounds and maimed bodies. When work, solid, terrible work was to be done, the well-worn hands were put to the task. When men groaned under the first torture of the knife, when the tents were insufficient to shelter the agonized multitude, there was no shrinking from contact with the bare awful reality, and women's nerves learned the steadiness which controls the surgeon's hand, when bone and muscle and flesh feel the rasp of his remorseless instruments.

All honor to the women who, in their unpretending garb, saved to us our fathers and brothers and sons and husbands. We owe them a debt second only to that which is due the fallen heroes who sleep in unremembered graves, and whom we must not forget, although nature hides away the little patch of earth enclosing them. And let us hope that, alike with those who survived the battle and the prison pen, the constant nurse, who wiped the death damps from the brows of those we could not reach, and witnessed the grateful smile as the light of life flickered away, may be remembered and rewarded in substantial testimonials of gratitude.

It is said that republics are ungrateful, but in the progress of events, when the claims of the common soldier have been more fully considered, then will these noble women, who saved thousands of common soldiers to fight again for freedom, find their names also inscribed on the long Roll of Honor. America can well afford to be grateful to every class of her defenders, when from the pure patriotism of her striving millions she draws the life blood which makes her a power amongst the nations of the earth.

No partizan feelings actuated these workers in the cause of humanity. When all over the length and breadth of the land the flag of our Union floats free in the azure air, no bitter thoughts shall rise up to taunt them with neglect to the grey uniformed Confederate, groaning on the hard hospital bed, a prisoner of war. Alike with our boys in blue, they shared the mercies which made the hospital nurses seem angels in disguise. In many a Southern home, when they tell the tale of the fight, and how the Yankee bullet had well-nigh found the source of life, they speak in tones of gentleness of the untiring nurse who watched and bent pityingly over them as over a tenderly loved brother.

The full and clear descriptions of places and incidents in the following work, and the readiness with which incident succeeds incident cannot fail to convince all of its truthfulness. The imagination was neither drawn upon to create pictures, nor led to other works for details and facts. The scenes are minutely and carefully given, and it has been the aim of the author, rather to condense than to enlarge them. The book cannot fail to absorb the minds of those whose hearts were with their dear ones in the long perilous marches, and in the awful battles where thousands were slain, while to any one whose soul is open to the sufferings of humanity it will prove a narrative of intense interest.

Believing that a correct knowledge of life in the military hospitals, can be better attained through this impartial work than any other yet published, we close a task which from its nature has been one of an absorbingly interesting character.

Trusting that no one will be disappointed in its careful perusal, and willing to submit it to the fair criticism of each and all, we leave in the hands of a discriminating public this record of the HOSPITAL AND Camp. S. L. C.

CHAPTER I.

WHEN, in the complexity of national affairs, it became necessary for armed men to assemble in multitudes, to become exposed to the hardships and privations of camps and the deadly peril of battle fields, there arose the same necessity for woman to lend her helping hand to bind up the wounds of the shattered soldier, and smooth the hard pillow of the dying hero.

The same patriotism which took the young and brave from workshop and plow, from counting-rooms, and college halls, making up the vast army of the loyal North, and sending it forth to conquer, after months of conflict, lent also to our hearts its thrilling measure, and sent us out to do and dare for those whose strong arms were to retrieve the honor of our insulted flag. Because we could not don the uniform of the soldier, and follow the beat of the stirring drums, we chose our silent journeys into hospitals and camps, and there waited for the wounded sufferer, who would escape with vital breath, from before the belching flames which burst forth amid lurid clouds of battle.

We claim not the meed of high-sounding praise; we ask not crowns of laurel for our brows, while the thousands and thousands who suffered and died in the same heroic service, and who were, laid in their gory blue shrouds under the blood moistened sods of the South, have raised their story above the common atmosphere of army life, and made it a tale to stir the blood in every loyal heart to a quicker flow.

Our work was among every class of men who wore the uniforms of soldiers, and they represented almost every household in the land. They were mainly the bone and sinew of the country, and they counted life no loss if in the giving the nation's glory could be preserved. Many such an one we saw close his eyes in death, while our own moistened for those who would never see their valiant soldier again.

With the picture of horror-strewn slaughter- grounds laid vividly before me; with the well- wrought details of hospital suffering brought to my mind in strong, truthful colors; with sickness and possible death made plain to my vision, when

I thought it was my duty to go, if the Government needed me to care for its wounded defenders, I said, "I might die if I remain here, if there they will give me decent burial, and such care as a soldier has—I do not need more."

And when the question was put if I thought myself strong enough to endure all the hardships which were inevitable, I said, "If any woman has done this, I can," and felt the warm blood surging through my heart, every throb of which was beating for my country, and urging me to add my mite in comforting her sworn protectors.

From the day on which the boom of the first cannon rolled over the startled waters in Charleston harbor, it was my constant study how I could with credit to myself get into the military service of the Union.

I made inquiries, and studiously examined the public journals, but no ray of light dawned upon me. "It is no place for women," was the cry on every hand. Hospitals were as the houses of death, in the minds of respectable and virtuous communities. Still the steady streams of youthful valor flowed into the red shambles of war, and were sacrificed at the streaming altars.

In the ravines of Bull Run the remains of our murdered men lay rotting in the sun of the second summer, and the swamps of the Chickahominy had opened their wet bosoms to make room for thousands of graves. Richmond was still in the gloomy distance, and the people groaned in the heaviness of sorrow, which lay like a funeral pall over city, town, and hamlet.

The trickling streams of Manassas were again stained with the gore from human hearts, and, amidst the trampled greenery of its shadowy ravines, dead men lay close to the whitened skeletons of the last year's fight.

The dread suspense which followed every battle's thunder, hung like a dense cloud over the whole stretch of our darkened land. Pale faces looked into pale faces, which dared not open their white lips to speak the fear that was knocking at the trembling heart.

While this dread fear lay over us, I was led by Providence into the right channel. Sitting at a window in the Orphan Asylum at Auburn, New York, conversing with Mrs. Reed, the kindly matron, and watching the newly enlisted soldiers of the adjacent country, at a game of ball near the camp, I said, "I wish I knew of some way to get into the military service to take care of just such boys as those, when they shall need it." Assuring herself of my sincerity, while laying all the hardships of such a life in reality before me, she said, "The Board of Managers for the Soldier's Aid Society meets to-morrow, and you can ascertain from them just what is necessary for you to do in order to secure a situation."

I met the board, stated my errand, and as they had a pass for one nurse, I was nominated, recommended, and voted upon, receiving the appointment, subject to the approval of Miss D. L. Dix, Superintendent of Women Nurses in the Military Hospitals of the Union.

In due time, under the cover of "Official Business," my appointment was confirmed, and accompanied by circulars, which served to define clearly the requisites for service.

One is signed by William A. Hammond, Surgeon General, marked No. 7, and dated Washington, D. C., July 14, 1862, and reads as follows: "In order to give greater utility to the acts of Miss D. L. Dix, as Superintendent of Women Nurses in General Hospitals, and to make the employment of such nurses conform more closely to existing laws, and orders of the War Department, the following announcement is made for the information and guidance of medical officers, and all concerned:

"Miss Dix has been entrusted by the War Department with the duty of selecting women nurses, and assigning them to general or permanent military hospitals. Women nurses are not to be employed in such hospitals without her sanction and approval, except in cases of urgent need.

"Women nurses will be under the control and direction of the medical officer in charge of the hospital to which they are assigned, and may be discharged by him, if incompetent, insubordinate, or otherwise unfit for their vocation.

"Miss Dix is charged with the diligent over sight of women nurses, and with the duty of ascertaining, by personal inspection, whether, or not, they are performing their duties. Medical officers are enjoined to receive her suggestions and counsels with respect, and carry them into effect, if compatible with the hospital service.

As it will be impossible for Miss Dix to supervise in person all the military hospitals, she is authorized to delegate her authority as herein defined, to subordinate agents, not to exceed one for each city or military district u Women wishing employment as nurses must apply to Miss Dix, or her authorized agents.

The army regulations allow one nurse to every ten patients (beds) in a general hospital. As it is the expressed will of the Government that a portion of these nurses shall be women, and, as Congress has given to the Surgeon General authority to decide in what numbers women shall be substituted for men, it is ordered that there shall be one woman nurse to every two men nurses. Medical officers are hereby required to organize their respective hospitals accordingly.

"Medical officers requiring women nurses will apply to Miss Dix, or to her authorized agent, for the place where their hospitals are located.

"Sisters of Charity will be employed, as at present, under special instructions from this office." The other is signed by Miss D. L. Dix, approved by William A. Hammond, Surgeon General, marked No. 8, and dated Washington, D. C., July 14, 1862, and reads as follows: "No candidate for service in the women's department for nursing in the military hospitals of the United States will be received below the age of thirty-five, nor above fifty.

"Only women of strong health—not subjects of chronic diseases, nor liable to sudden illnesses need apply. The duties of the station make large and continued demands on strength.

"Matronly persons of experience, good conduct, or superior education, and serious disposition, will always have preference. Habits of neatness, order, sobriety, and industry are pre-requisites.

"All applicants must present certificates of qualification and good character from, at least, two persons of trust, testifying to morality, integrity, seriousness, and capacity for the care of the sick.

"Obedience to the rules of the service, and conformity to special regulations will be required and enforced.-

"Compensation, as regulated by act of Congress, forty cents a day and subsistence. Transportation furnished to and from the place of service.

"Amount of luggage limited within small compass.

"Dress, plain (colors—brown, grey, or black), and, while connected with the service, without ornaments of any sort.

"No applicants accepted for less than three months' service; those for longer periods always have preference."

I was not of the requisite age, but no special inquiries on that subject rendering it necessary for me to testify to my years, I resolved not to be kept from the great work because no wrinkles seamed my face, and no vestige of grey hair nestled among my locks. I could, and did, bring all other testimonials, and within eight days, with the regulation supply of clothing in a small trunk, and Miss Dix's letter of instructions in my pocket,

I was journeying alone from the city of Auburn to the beleaguered Capital.

Antietam had just been fought. The battle ground was yet wet with blood, and fresh sorrow had been added to the grief of the people.

It was a novel thing to journey on a military ticket—car passengers stared as though a Government nurse were a nondescript, and public curiosity a cardinal virtue. Thanks to the kindness of Miss Dix, to whom I was to report on my arrival in Washington, my journey was -planned, and no accident of note occurred to break its perfect working.

The lovely September weather seemed profaned with the news of death by slaughter, which was borne on every wire along the route. The intense excitement of the scenes, to which I was so rapidly hastening, thrilled every fibre of my being, and the golden haze, which wrapped wood, and meadow, and grain field, seemed only a floating mist, veiling my new life from my eager sight.

The blue sky and the soft hush of the perfect day came to my senses like a fleeting summer breeze, borne on the wings of a November blast, and the rollicking and plunging of the iron steed, the swinging of warning bells, the rush at the stations —all were the passing scenes in a drama, of which I seemed to be ah uninterested spectator.

A few thoughts were given to the report that the railroad track was not in order from New York to Baltimore, but the cars moved on with no break in their usual time. At Baltimore, failing to meet Col. Beiger, to whom I was referred by Miss Dix, relieved of the necessity of venturing out into the blank darkness of the depot in that midnight hour, I retained my seat in the cars, and waited for them to move.

The lonely night ride was wearisome in the extreme. With neither travelling companion on whom to rely for a word of cheer, nor the kindly questionings and remarks that relieve the monotony of silence and fatigue, I could but muse upon the probabilities and improbabilities locked up in the storehouse of that exciting future, towards which I was now rapidly hastening. I pondered upon my situation—a Government nurse—alone amidst strangers—a novice in scenes of suffering and death—swiftly driving along to meet that from which my soul would recoil in terror—and thus the daylight greeted my eyes. The streaks of crimson flushing up the East, revealed to me the first warlike sight in a camp of soldiers just waking from sleep.

My heart began to sicken. There they lay with one blanket over them, on the bare ground, knapsacks for pillows, rousing from dreams of home to a sense of their actual condition. Alas! how many of them would never see home, or dear ones again!

The soldiers who had arisen were busy with the labors of the morning. Some were dipping water for their coffee from a little brook, which ran merrily by, some performing their morning ablutions, others washing their pocket handkerchiefs, and all in the same stream. I noticed that, man-like, the washing was going on above those who took out the water for their coffee.

One man lay sleeping on the ties so soundly that he never moved as we thundered down past him. Poor fellow! I wondered in what pleasant dream his senses were chained, and if he would ever realize the thought of a meeting when war was done, and the laurels of battle were gathered thickly around him in many an honorable scar.

While waiting, a cavalryman came hurrying into the cars, shouting, "Have you any papers for a poor soldier?"

His arms were full in a moment, and he retreated to read over, with brother comrades, the news from the homes which they had left to preserve. For days I thought of his heavy eyelids, which seemed to droop for long want of refreshing sleep, and the chill that struck me while looking at the frost glittering on his coat and cap.

We whirled on, past pleasant farms, and delightful country-seats, and soon entered the great cavernous depot at Washington. It was dark as though the smoke from a thousand grim throated furnaces had settled upon its walls, and thousands of soldiers had shook there the dust from their feet, brought from every State in the Union.

I stood alone in the city of strangers, vainly waiting for the appearance of Col. Belger, whom the conductor had promised to find, and accompany hither. Every carriage had disappeared, and still I waited for Col. Belger's coming before seeking conveyance to the house of Miss Dix.

There was not a seat, or tank of water, or civilized convenience of any kind whatever, and tired, thirsty, and hungry, after two days and nights of travel, I stood wretchedly surveying the situation. A dim sense of what was before me struck upon my understanding, and I began to realize that a soldier's life was anything but pastime.

I accosted a dirty ragged little girl, who was passing through the depot, staring vacantly at my motionless, solitary figure, and asked her if she could procure me some water. With a prolonged stolid look into my face, she hurried away without a word, soon however returning with a battered tin tumbler filled with dirty-looking water. Although so filthy as to be revolting, I took a swallow to quench my feverish thirst, and used the remainder, by pouring it on my handkerchief, to wash the dust of travel from my hands and face.

I was in a sad plight to appear before the superintendent, but there was no alternative, and acting on the suggestion of a passer-by, I took the street cars, and went out to seek her residence.

Dust was flying thickly through the murky air of Washington. Officers were riding at the topmost speed, up and down the avenues, and a train of supply wagons, with from four to six mules attached, stood solidly packed together for two miles in length.

Everything was bustle and excitement—the bright new uniforms of the officers—the glitter of military trappings were all new sights to my wondering eyes. It had not entered my heart that the army had reached such gigantic proportions, and consumed such marvellous supplies.

But what most interested me, in the great moving panorama of war, was the sight of wounded men, lying on blood-stained stretchers, under fly tents, being borne in at every hand where a sheltering roof made it possible to establish a hospital. The Capitol, Patent Office, city churches, and private dwellings even were turned from their legitimate usage into hospitals.

These sights, which especially recalled to mind the errand on which I had come, made all the courage in my soul recoil at one dread bound. A strange sense of suffocation oppressed me, as if the air by which I was surrounded was filled with poisonous vapors, and for a few minutes I doubted my own strength.

I have since wondered, when I looked hack on all these wretched self-abnegating sensations, and then remembered that I did labor with reward amongst men torn in the conflict, bleeding and dying, whether the many daring spirits, who have climbed to the very

16

pinnacle of fame, ever experienced in the rough upward path any of these despairing feelings, which, while they perhaps did not turn the feet from the onward march, yet clogged them as with the heavy mire and clay of earth, making the triumphant end seem distant.

At Fifteenth street I left the car and set out on foot to reach Miss Dix's residence. Up and down the street I passed, and repassed, unable to find the number designated by my orders, as they had been read. Prompted by feelings of despair, I made inquiries, and found that the numbers did not range so high, and that I was misdirected. On producing her letter the mistake was rectified, and I was very soon at Miss Dix's door.

There I was kindly received by her housekeeper, who said, pityingly, "Why, you poor child, I have seen you running up and down here all the morning."

Miss Dix was absent on the battle field of Antietam, directing and organizing the force of women nurses who received orders from her hands. My appointment, however, awaited me, and also a letter of introduction to Dr. Charles Page, the surgeon in charge of Judiciary Square Hospital, to which I was assigned for initiatory duty.

After a comforting cup of tea, and generous slices of solid bread and butter, with some sauce, I found the ambulance in waiting to convey me to the scenes of my introductory labor.

CHAPTER II

IN the sinking of heart which fell upon me, as I saw the great stretch of low unpainted buildings, which filled the space at my side, it was necessary to summon all the latent courage in my soul before I could gain courage enough to enter. Somehow I knew I must be sustained, I should not be forsaken for doing my plain duty, and I gave myself up to the drifting current.

It was of my own seeking; I had been eager to lend myself to the glorious cause of Freedom, and now, on the threshold of the hospital in which gaping wounds, and fevered, thirsting lips awaited me, telling their ghastly tales of the bloody battle, my cheek flushed, and my hand grew hot and trembling. Weak flesh and timid heart would have counseled flight, but a strong will held them in abeyance, and the doors opened to receive me.

I was shown to my quarters, and kindly welcomed by Miss Clark, the woman nurse from whom I was to take my instructions.

Urging me to occupy one of the two beds which were in the room, and remarking upon my tired worn look, she left me with an injunction to try hard to rest, while she must hasten away to the bedside of a dying man in our ward.

I had never been so near death before. The horror of its nearness had never chilled my heart till now. I could not sleep. My brain seemed on fire; the groans of suffering men echoing on all sides, aroused me to the highest pitch of excitement.

Was it any wonder that mortal weakness shrank from confronting the hard cold realities of sharpest anguish like this? Would you question the courage of the soldier who braved death, charging intrepidly upon the enemy's works, if you knew that in his heart, a moment before the blow met it, was the wild thought, "o, why did I leave home, wife, friends and children for this?"

The human heart is a complex thing. It may lie bare and quivering at your feet to await the stroke, and yet give no signs of the terror with which it awaits the transfixing blow.

Sounds of woe resounded about me, mingled now and then with hilarious laughter. I wondered if ever in this bare room, with only the length of an unpainted board for the partition walls between wards, halls, nurses' quarters, and all other officers, I should ever close my eyes to such sleep as used to come to their lids before they beheld grim-visaged war catch up the death dealing weapons.

A shuffling past my door started me to my feet, and when Miss Clark returned with the information that the man was dead, and carried to the dead-house, fancy painted the picture of the stark stiffening corps, as careless feet walked through the hall, bearing the dead out from amidst the living.

The porter's call of, "Dinner for the ladies— turn out for dinner— all things are ready—turn in to dinner," was a welcome cry, for I had eaten nothing substantial for two days.

The dinner consisted of a leg of beef, not very well dressed, dry beans, and bread in which the grit set my teeth on edge. The Potomac water furnished our beverage, and sufficed to wash down the morsel which rebelliously stuck in our throats.

There was no duty for me that day, and after dinner was over, I went with Miss Clark to the dead-house to see the man who died in the morning.

Could I ever suppress the shuddering that passed over me, as I entered the low wooden house, in which on rude benches lay the cold white corpses of three men? Miss Clark uncovered the face 4 of the man who died last, and told me his story— of the wife and three children in the far West, who were yet to know how it had gone with their soldier. He was wounded in the second battle of Bull Run, and had been under her care for ten days.

A cloth saturated with blood lay over a bench, and I was so wrought upon by the sadness of the scene, and the echoing of many groans coming from the wards, that I only desired to hasten away from the dreadful place, and forget that it was man against his brother man, who was causing this awful destruction.

I clung to Miss Clark with the tenacity of long established friendship in these first experiences of hospital service. She was a New England woman—whole-hearted, and ready to sacrifice her own comfort at any time, if by so doing she could ease the pain of any sick or suffering soldier. She was a Christian woman, sending the light of real consolation into the darkness to cheer the dying, and lift up those on whom, in the throes of agony, despair was preying.

And many such women, with true hearts, went down to be the soldiers friend, regarding privations, and sickness, and toil as of little consequence, if some eyes over which the film of death was stealing, could look upon them and die in the calm belief that a mother, or wife, or sister was standing by the bedside, smoothing the pillow, and moistening the parched lips.

At the usual time we were called to a supper, consisting of the same dark, dirty bread, with dried apple-sauce, and tea which was black with strength. An introductory visit to the wards, in which my labors were to commence so soon, ended the long, strange day. I looked upon the narrow iron bedsteads furnished with bed of straw, one straw pillow, two sheets, one blanket and counterpane, three rows of which ran the length of the long room, forming narrow passage ways through which we walked, and I said to myself, "I will do this -work—not of myself have I strength, but the Lord being my helper, I shall be enabled to do that good labor for which my hands have been so long waiting."

The night, dragging its weary hours along—for they were not winged by sleep—came to me with visions of battle fields strewn with horror; sounds as of blood trickling from many wounds; green grass and waving grain trodden by artillery; and the woods made the hiding places of ten thousand deaths. Lovely plains stretched out before me, on which the harvest, just mown, was not yet prepared for flesh, and blood, and muscle. Then the scene changed to home with its peaceful pleasures; friends greeting each other in the hazy September mornings; work, which at this distance seemed mere pastime; the quiet woods, the meadows ankle deep with their rich food and the well-rounded cattle ranging over them; the blue lake lying like a gem in the loveliest of vallies.

All these came to my pillow that night, and haunted me with a strange restiveness which drove slumber from my eyelids.

The morning of the nineteenth of September dawned over the long low hospital, and my duties began. With silent prayers for courage, and struggling with the beating at my heart, armed with wash bowl, soap and towels, I went into the ward, and entered upon my first work as a hospital nurse, amongst those who had been wounded in fighting the second battle of Bull Run.

It was no small matter for me to apply the wet towel to the faces of bronzed and bearded men; it ' was no slight task to comb out the tangled hair and part it over foreheads which seemed hot with the flash of cannon. I had been nurtured in quietude, and had little conception of the actual state of things when the timid heart preferred to remain in that state, though the brain and hand were in rebellion to it, and held it down to the servitude.

I did not fancy it would wear off so soon. I did not think when, shudderingly, I first looked into the dead-house, and saw the three icy corpses, that these feet would ever stumble over stiff mortal clay, and hardly pause to note what lay within their path.

But this strange feature in human mechanism is incomprehensible, and will forever remain a mystery with successive generations.

It was wonderful to me to see the universal childishness with which each threw himself upon our sympathies, and related, as to a mother, the history of the fight, the position in which he was shot, the length of time which he passed on the battle ground, the final removal, and, most of all, the deep thankfulness with which he received our attention.

Woman's help had not been counted upon, when, in the first tumultuous rush of excited feeling, the citizen enlisted to serve under the banner of the soldier. And when her hand with its softer touch pressed on the aching forehead, and bathed the fevered face, words failed in the attempt to express the gratitude of a full heart.

For several successive mornings one poor fellow, whose eyes were both shot out, with his head badly shattered, lay silent while his ablutions were being performed. I thought he had perhaps lost his speech in the untold terror of his sightless condition, but by-and-by he said, "Thank you," when the process of washing was completed.

I could not comb his hair, for the bandages were bound tightly over it, and, as he turned away after the simple recognition of thanks, I passed on without questioning him. A few days went by, then he said, "Did you notice that I never talked to you, as other patients did, when you first came to take care of us?" I replied, "I did."

"Then I will tell you why," he continued; "I was so thankful, that I had no words for speech —to think the women of the North should come down here, and do so much for us, being exposed lo all kinds of disease, and to so much work and hard fare, all to take care of us poor soldiers, when we lie as I do."

I inquired how he came to be a soldier, he seeming so young, and barely of the requisite age to serve his country. He told me the same old story of enthusiastic desire to do for his country in her hour of peril, and it seemed a cowardly thing to stand back, and let others share all the dangers, when he, too, had a land to save. When those, who were reared among the same hills, were going out to the beat of the drum to fight, and die if God so willed it, he felt like a craven to linger behind.

While at the place of enlistment, in the very act of signing his name, his father appeared, and forbade the act, took him home, and confined him within the house. But the patriotism in his boyish heart grew beyond all bounds, and he eluded his jailor in season to go out amongst the boys, with whom he had hunted squirrels, and roamed the woods in search of autumn's dropping nuts, to be hoarded up for winter.

It was all over now. He had done all that he could for the dear old flag—he had been shattered, and left a useless thing to die among the numerous dead around him on that terrible field. He had lain for eleven days amongst the rotting, putrid throng—the horrors shut out, indeed, from his sight, but with his other senses, sharpened by the sounds of pain, revealing to his ears and imagination the real nature of the scene around bum.

His only food during that time was two hard tack, which he shaved down with his pocket knife, and moistened with a few drops of water, that remained in his canteen. Then, too, this had to be drawn into his mouth with his tongue, for he could not move his jaws.

Another soldier, wounded in the limbs, and unable to move away, made himself known to the blind man, and, to avoid starvation, they agreed each to help the other, one having the eyes, and the other the limbs. Thus staggering under the weight, the exhausted soldier started from the awful spot, where death was holding high carnival. o! the soul sickens at the thought of the sights shut out to the one, but to the other only too palpable — the horrible flow of blood; the putrid masses of human flesh; the gleaming bones, from which everything had fallen clean; but over the despair—the sickness almost unto death—the love of life fluttered like a prisoned bird, and would not let them droop.

Then, like hyenas snuffing the scent of prey in the hot air, in the likeness of humanity, but void of its soul, vampires came upon the ground, rifling the bodies of the slain. To these creatures, many of the wounded turned, imploring them to convey them from that place of death, to prison, anywhere away from the horrors, which hourly grew greater and greater.

Some were taken to a rebel hospital, and their wounds were there dressed by Union soldiers, who were also held as prisoners of war. Soon after they were exchanged, and the gratitude in the soldier's heart, when he heard a woman's step about his bedside, and felt the touch of her hand upon his pillow was indeed too great for utterance.

A father came after a while to see his son, and as he looked upon the sightless eyes, he groaned in bitterness of spirit, "o, my son, if you had only obeyed your father you would have been spared this affliction. Now you can never look upon the world again, henceforth and forever darkness is over your vision!"

"But," said the patriotic boy, the loss of my sight is nothing in comparison to the sufferings which filled my soul, when I thought how they needed me to help fight the battles for freedom, and I was held from going!"

He recovered his health, and went forth into a darkened world; and though his eyes shall no more behold the fair land for which he has made so terrible a sacrifice, his name is inscribed upon the lists of Fame as one of earth's demi-gods,

"Ennobled by himself, by all approved."

CHAPTER III.

FORTY-SIX wounded men LAY helpless on the iron bedsteads in our ward at Judiciary Square Hospital, and from out the hall enough more had gone into the convalescents' room, to swell the entire number under our care to eighty. Each of the fourteen wards, which projected in wings from the long central building, held also its full quota.

Amongst the wounded were many hopelessly shattered, who would henceforth drag useless members through life, and some who would miss forever the good stout limbs which lay in the trenches of Manassas.

A minnie ball had passed through both ankles of one—another had a fractured thigh—the arm of one had been amputated—a shot in the head destroyed the senses of another; and one with his back bone severely injured was compelled to lay upon his face through the tedious hours.

Every case was different, and nearly all seemed suffering to the greatest extent of human endurance. Only that first strong hope in life which is implanted in all our species kept up their sinking courage, and enabled them to bear bravely the throes of pain.

Our duties here were to distribute food to the patients, when brought up from the kitchen; wash the faces and hands, and comb the heads of the wounded; see that their bedding and clothing was kept clean and whole, bring pocket handkerchiefs, prepare and give the various drinks and stimulants at such times as they were ordered by the surgeon.

I dropped into my desired sphere at once, and my whole soul was in the work. Every man wore the look of a hero in my eyes, for had they not faced, the red death from thundering artillery, and braved the deadly shots of the "minnies?" Had they not stood fearlessly, when like leaves of the autumn before a howling blast, they had fallen thick and fast—bronzed and dripping with gore—faces forward in the black mud of the trenches?

25

Home, with its joys and peaceful pleasures, was well-nigh forgotten. I remembered them all as the faint sounds of music are remembered, when the being is wholly wrapped up in new and intense thought. The horrors of the first day had faded from my vision—wounds and suffering " became habitual sights, and the absorbing nature of hospital labor gradually hardened my nerves to the strength of steel.

Surgeons and officers were very kind to us, but they gave stringent orders which we were sometimes almost willing to disobey. The red tape, as the soldiers termed it, required too much official ceremony in the untying—we would rather break the string, and in serving the wounded hurriedly throw away the pieces.

Women nurses were not allowed to go into the kitchen for articles of any kind; consequently the patients were many times obliged to go without the countless little comforts which a sick fancy craves. We devised many ways to relieve their wants, begging tea, sugar, and other luxuries of loyal ladies—of Miss Dix, of State agents, 'and of Sanitary and Christian Commissions, and when these failed us, the boys took the hard earned pay of soldiers, and sent out for the articles themselves. We would prepare it for them by slipping a basin of water into the stove in the ward, and by dropping the tea into it when boiling.

It was then taken to our quarters, and carried thence in a bowl, having all the appearance of official ordering, if a surgeon or the officer of the day chanced to pass through the ward. The men had for their food whatever the surgeon chose to order for them while on his daily rounds. Their meals usually consisted, for the severest cases, of tea, toast, rice, milk, eggs, gruel, and chicken soup. Others generally had a tin cup two-thirds full of tea or coffee, and sugar and milk, with potatoes, meats, soups, bread and butter often for dinner.

It was Miss Dix's wish that we should learn to dress wounds, but we were peremptorily ordered from the ward, when that process was in operation. One day I was sent out with an abrupt, "Nurse, we can dispense with your services now," and, retiring to our room, I stretched myself upon my little iron bedstead to ease my weary feet and limbs.

While, in this position, I lay thinking of my work, a tall woman, habited in black, came in with noiseless steps, and appeared before me. She put various questions to me, with an authority which I was too startled to dispute. She gave me instructions in regard to duty" lectured me roundly on this seeming neglect, and when my lips opened to plead my defence, an admonitory, "hush," from the strange figure closed them again..

I was altogether too young for a nurse, she said. Then came visions of disgrace—of the shame which would overcome me, if Miss Dix should send me home for this grave fault, concerning which I had no conception but that of innocence. My pride rose at the thought, and when an order came, summoning me to appear before Miss Dix at seven o'clock on the following morning, I felt like the culprit, who is about to be led into court for sentence, for I had discovered, on inquiry, that my strange visitor was no other than the Superintendent of Women Nurses.

I found her busy with letters, and, after watching her in uneasy nervousness, as she dashed off two or three, I gathered courage enough to say, "Miss Dix, I should like to return as soon as possible to my duties."

She replied, "You can go, dear," at the same time she opened a drawer in her table, and took therefrom a five dollar bill, which she handed me, saying, "This is not pay—only a little present from me."

I took it in confusion, and, as she bade me a kind "Good-morning," I hastened back to the hospital, feeling like the prisoner, who has unexpectedly received his acquittal, and finished the duties of the day with unwonted cheerfulness.

Mine was only a temporary assignment for instruction. Miss Clark had been there only four weeks on my arrival, and neither of us knew that our true rank was next to the surgeon of the ward. Consequently, when the head nurse imposed upon us the washing of dishes for the whole ward, although with demurring among ourselves, and considerable questioning as to the duty, we wielded the dish cloth for days, soiling our clothing, and often busily employed when we knew we needed the hours for rest.

But a change soon came over the spirit of this dream, brought about by my usual unsophisticated manner. One of our convalescents said to me one evening, while standing in the hall, "Miss Bucklin, there's a letter for you in the office," and my reply, "I wish you had brought it down," drew forth the offer to go and fetch it. Our nurse, seeing us in conversation, roughly ordered the boy into his room, I protesting mildly that "he was doing no hurt out of it a moment."

The man repeated his command, at the same time pushed the boy violently through the door, ' and closed it. Presently there appeared a pair of red pants, a blue jacket above, and the whole surmounted by a red cap, with the usual tassel pendant—the garb of a soldier, who, stalking out, demanded to know what was the matter? "Why he was thus badgering the women? he had heard enough of it; it had been going on ever since we had been there, and now must be ended."

He sent a blow at the nurse, which, overreaching him, pushed me backward into the scullery, and cut off my escape, while they struggled each to reach a knife from the shelves their hands clenched with murderous intent. A guard was summoned, and the zouave stated the case, while the crest-fallen nurse hurled defiance at him from his scowling visage.

"And we both live in New York," the soldier said, "and we may meet some day; but for fear we won't, I will give you the rest now,"— jumping at him, and dealing heavy blows thick and fast, the men looking on calmly till it was ended. He then went quietly away with the guard, and the nurse was invisible for two days at the end of that time, after due inquiries by the proper officials, he received his relief papers, and our dishwashing was ended; a boy having been detailed for that purpose, as was the regular method.

A young New York captain, named Stephens, received a box full of tempting things from home one day, and the generous fellow could not enjoy it alone; no selfish hoarding of the dainty bits for his own palate would satisfy the whole-hearted soldier, and he gave the contents into my hands for distribution in the ward.

In my eagerness to give each one able to eat it a slice of the cake, and a bit of the buttered bread, I lost all thought of its being forbidden to give such articles without the consent of the surgeon, and cutting the several loaves of cake in pieces, and nicely buttering the slices of bread from the contents of a little tin can also in the box, I went round with the loaded tray in triumph.

While in the midst of the excitement, the officer of the day came into the ward; and before I was aware of his presence, laid his hand heavily on my shoulders, saying distinctly, "Nurse, what are you doing?"

Had a thunder-bolt fallen at my feet I could not have been more startled. My heart leaped into my throat, and almost suffocated me with its throbbings. I had been doing an extraordinary thing; an act strictly forbidden by the officials of the hospital, and in my terror I expected the doom of utter disgrace and dismissal from the service.

My relief came from the captain, whose bounty I was dispensing, as he said quickly, "Doctor, the ward surgeon gave her leave to distribute these things."

"Oh, it's all right then," was the reply, and the empty tray soon was laid aside. The contents of the captain's box was a day's treat to the soldiers of the ward.

I sat one evening, after my duties were over, thinking how happy I would be to see every man in the hospital sent home, recovered in health and spirits, and wondering if death waited for any amongst them. My meditations were broken in upon by the appearance of an orderly, commanding me to report to Miss Dix without delay.

I obeyed forthwith, but instead of written instructions, verbal ones only awaited me from her housekeeper. The matter being somewhat mixed, instead of being assigned to permanent duty at Judiciary Square, and Miss Clark going to Thirteenth Street Hospital to take care of a nurse who was down with the measles, I was sent to the latter place, and the change came like a blow upon me. I had become so much interested in the welfare of each patient, had made each one's history the story of a brother, and how could I leave them, without feeling pangs of the regret, which comes not at the severing of common friendships.

I hesitated at the thought of the new faces— the new ways which I must learn—but as I was under military control, nothing remained for me but to obey without a murmur. The soldier may not chose in what ditch he will die; he may not say under whose generalship he will be led out to battle; he is only one little part of the giant machine which is to crush out wrong by its resistless might—and why was I better than our boys in blue?

CHAPTER IV.

ON arriving at the hospital I found it established in the Baptist Church—a branch from the Epiphany Church Hospital, and in charge of a Dr. Miller, whose home was near my own. I learned soon after, to the comfort of my heart, that the steward, general ward master, and cook were also from that region.

How the senses waken to everything, however remote, over which our native sky has bent, and look with favor upon hearts which retain the image of the same familiar flowers that spangle the dewy meadows about our homes. Although too much absorbed in my work for genuine homesickness, yet the thought of familiar Auburn, Cayuga, and Ithaca sent a momentary longing to my brain, after which, with unabated strength, I took up the thread of toil again.

The sick nurse's work—the care of the linen room, fell to my hands in addition to the charge of nursing. I began the task of mending, and laying the clothes properly away.

Our accommodations were very good, the purified linen occupying the shelves about the room, which had evidently been a session house. We had each a bedstead, a bed covered with a white counterpane, and a chair with a stand which we used in common. A stove with a stew pan, a frying pan, and a quart cup sufficed as utensils by which we were to cook our food, and boil our coffee— both being furnished raw from the kitchen, as we preferred to prepare them ourselves.

Some trunks holding jellies, wines, and other delicacies were in the room, and we were told to take from them whatever we required for our comfort.

One day, at the steward's request, I went with him to the yard where the clothes were hanging to dry, and, to my utter consternation, found the ground covered with garments lying in the dirt, and badly mildewed. This sight led to an investigation into the wash-room, where five hundred pieces more were found in the same condition— wet and mouldy. In one portion of the room was a tub of bandages, with a green scum over the putrid water; in another corner a huge pile of flannel shirts, drawers, blankets, bed quilts, and stockings lay on the floor, wet with the dirty slops which had run underneath, till they were rotten at one- end, and burned at the other by the heat of the laundry stoves.

Seven contraband women were still toiling among this condition of things, and yet I was told that there was not a single change for the men, neither had the beds been cleansed for two weeks. It was a sad state, where the comfort of so many men was at stake, and I asked permission to undertake a revolution in the department.

The steward replied that I could not confer a greater favor on the hospital than to obtain a change for the men and beds by Sunday, adding, "But it is an arduous task; I do not wish to impose it upon you."

I said, "It is my work, if I can do it, for I came out to put my hands to anything which my strength and ability made possible, if it would add to the soldiers' comfort." And I thought myself capable of attending to my patients, and this task also.

Permission was willingly granted, and I set myself about planning the unclean labor. With the promise of Sunday for a day of rest, when hitherto it had been like the long six days of the week just ended, I enlisted the interest of the colored women, and laid out the work.

I went into the room after dinner, had the garments brought in from the yard, sorted and folded those which would answer for ironing, and sent the remainder to the wash. Three of the women I took to wash, three to iron, and one to make the fires, fill the kettles with water, and fold the clothes. Having thus divided the labor, I remained to see that the work was properly done, now ironing a garment at the table, then going to the tub, and washing a piece, talking to them all the while about the necessity of doing their work well..

They were illy inclined to be taught, and somewhat morose about it, but soon recovered their equanimity of spirits; and Saturday afternoon found us with the clothes washed and ironed, and the stoves and floors cleaned for the first time since the hospital had being. Those seven women had a day of rest on Sunday, and the soldiers a supply of clean clothing, and clean beds.

Unused to work where order was to be observed —-just loosed from the bonds of slavery, it mattered little to the naturally indolent dispositions of the washerwomen whether the bedding rotted in the dirty slops on the filthy floor, or whether the mildew left its blight upon scores of garments—the supply from Government was inexhaustible—and, if it was not, it mattered little to them. So they had toiled on, the work never done, and what was done only fit for another washing.

They wanted a directing spirit. The long use of a lifetime—the overseer and the lash must be represented in some shape, even if they came in the person of an humble hospital nurse, whose visions of Monday's purified garments, fluttering in snowy whiteness over a strip of green sward, bordered with currant bushes, was hardly comparable with the tawny complexion of the wash hung out into the shifting dust of a hospital yard.

Officers now and then threw out hints that women were a nuisance in war. We cared little when we saw them button their dress coats complacently over their lofty forms, and only smiled as we saw them draw up the white paper collars which surmounted their bright uniforms, as though conscious of inspiring respect by the show of seeming linen.

We knew that many a poor wounded fellow' blessed in his heart the women who provided sheets, fresh from the purifying scent of water, for his beds, and it was enough for us to know that we were wanted and appreciated by the very soldiers—the heroes of the fight—whom we had come especially to minister unto, especially when their shadows were lengthening out into the valley that leads to a new life.

It was something for all to remember that the poor pittance of forty cents a day and soldiers' rations constituted the pay of an army nurse. That consideration certainly could not have allured us from homes of comparative ease and luxury, whereas the charge of serving for the one hundred dollars and upward a month was brought with a show of justice against many a shoulder-strapped fellow, who proved unfit to lead men with souls into a fight.

No man of generous heart wished women shut out from the doors of either field or city hospitals —none with a single thought for the comfort of those who missed by a hair's breadth, the death which met scores of comrades in rifle pits, and in the face of the deadly sweep of columns, charging across the open plain. It was only the ruffians who feared the just censure of compassionate women, who wished to exclude these from performing the labors, which kept our feet on the round from early morn to the setting of the sun. Such were not fair exponents, however, of manliness in the army, while thousands of brave men, who aided us in the duties devolving upon our hands, cheered us on with appreciative words.

Only one death occurred during my brief stay in Thirteenth Street Hospital—a young man of such interesting character, that he was mourned over by surgeons, nurses, and patients alike. He passed to his rest while his father stood by the bedside, and saw the triumphant smile which lingered on the pale face after angels had talked with the ransomed spirit.

I remained in this place for four weeks, when Miss Clapp, recovering from her illness, was again on duty. Just as I was becoming interested in the hospital patients, I was ordered to report to Miss Dix again, and my newly planted affections were wrenched, root and branch, from the soil.

Another battle was to be fought. The preparations were rapidly going forward to meet the demands it would make upon humanity.

On the first of November I reported to the superintendent, and was given my letter of introduction to the surgeon at Hammond General Hospital, at Point Lookout, Maryland. Miss Dix met me with a "Good morning, dear," and an urgent request to come in for a cup of tea. How I revered the hand which never withheld from lowly hospital nurse, or suffering, starving soldiers! Age may have wrinkled that brow, but in its placid look of peace was a beauty such as youth may not boast—the serene sunshine which breaks over a life well-spent in doing good to its fellow creatures.

34

"Go in the spirit of my Master—God bless you, and good-by," she said, as she gave me my final orders, and I left her hospitable roof in her own carriage, and went to the wharf to board the steamer which we both thought would soon be pushing down the blue Potomac.

All day, with Miss Ella Wolcott, another Government nurse, I waited in the captain's office, but the boat still lay at the wharf. Weary and hungry we walked the long two miles back to the house of the superintendent and reported. I was sent to my old quarters in the hospital, so recently left, while Miss Wolcott found shelter elsewhere. For seven days in succession we reported nightly; every morning we went to the wharf to remain through the long dull hours, and again back through the dust, which was ankle deep in the busy streets of the Capital.

Faint with anxiety and weary with waiting, on the sixth day my companion, noticing that we were attracting attention, proposed to go over to Georgetown, where three other nurses were waiting to join us on the steamer. Without any knowledge of the route, we walked across the country in the direction in which we supposed the city lay, and went miles further than necessary, getting burned with the heat, choked with the heavy dust, foot-sore and discouraged, and arrived a few moments after the dinner hour was over.

Tears were well-nigh forced up, by our vexation of spirit, when one of the new nurses, taking a liberty which an old nurse dared not, went into the kitchen and brought up a generous supply of turkey, chicken, and other of this life's good things, which, bountiful as it was, hardly sufficed to appease our ravenous appetites. We, however, had a few crumbs remaining from the lunch with which Miss Dix had supplied us for the anticipated voyage.

As day after day passed, the packages which were to give comfort to hospital patients accumulated in unwieldy proportions. I was charged by the superintendent with their exclusive care, and with strict injunctions not to let them go from under my hands.

Finally we were driven to the wharf for the last time, and Miss Dix pressed her carriage shawl upon me, deeming my wrappings insufficient for the inclement weather of November, which for two

35

years I carried from hospital to hospital, only to return it to the benevolent owner when at last I directed my steps homeward. I had neglected to take a heavy garment of the kind with me only because I believed that in going to the sunny South, I was passing beyond all need of that sort of protection.

We were at last going—there could be no doubt of that—and with all our luggage stowed away we stepped on board the Keyport, and swung away from the wharf.

CHAPTER V.

It was an Indian-summer day, and the smoky light hung over the wood tops, while every sound echoed hollow from the near hills, where the cricket's chirp was loud in the tufts of grass yet beautifully green; where the landscape was colored so brightly with beauty, that it was deeply recorded in the writer's heart as a picture of peculiar loveliness. And yet the shores of the Potomac are beautiful at all seasons—the herbage growing beautifully green down the gentle slopes, even into the mellow water.

We passed the home and tomb of Washington. The historic interest attached to the place drew all eyes thitherward. In quiet beauty it stood, as yet respected by the hand of war—a monument which the women of the nation have been striving to hand down, in its perfection, to the generations in the future. The winds stirred the clumps of verdure, which were touched with the evidences of decay. The ripples roughened up into billowy proportions, as the great wheels of the steamer plowed steadily on and on.

All day we journeyed, till our eyes grew familiar with the changing beauty of the shores; and then, as these receded, and the river widened into the broad expanse of bay, new and grander loveliness lay spread out before the red sunset.

At nine o'clock in the evening we reached Point Lookout, and reported to Dr. Wagner, surgeon in charge of the hospital. We were assigned comfortable quarters for the night, and after partaking of supper, were only too glad to lay our weary selves to rest after the toilsome voyage.

We woke in the grey of the November morning to look about us, and find that our lot had been cast on one of the loveliest points which reach their slender green arms out into the shimmering waters of the Atlantic. On one hand the broad Potomac lay in its beauty, on the other the Chesapeake Bay smiled in placid brightness. I here indulged in a walk upon a sand bar, that reached so far into the waters, that, with one hand, I dipped into the Potomac, and sprinkled its contents into the bay.

37

Away back the lovely shores sloped with gentle undulations to the narrow strip of white, pebbly sand. Cottages, light-house, and all, looked like the creation of fairy hands, being diminutive in the distance, but broad and expansive in their beauty before and around me. No wonder this place was sought as a summer resort by those who preferred to lie under outstretched branches of the nodding trees, and 'dream away the passing days within sound of the lashing waves. To those who had made it such a resort in the summers gone, we were indebted for the little row of cottages, covering a full square, for the spacious hotel, the light-house, and one other building, all of which were surrendered for hospital purposes.

Just back of the cluster of cottages a grove of graceful pines towered up, lifting their dense, needled leaves into the upper air. Underneath the shadows lay dark and oppressive. No blossoms broke the mould over the dry, dead leaves of many summers, and the feet, hurrying through the gloom, were buried almost ankle deep in the dead foliage. A long, unfinished building stood in this pine wood, and in it were fifty men, occupying iron bedsteads, who were at once assigned to my care. It was evident that the place had been used by the Southern aristocracy as a bowling- alley, and within it they had passed many hours and days at one of their favorite games.

In this place, shut out from the genial rays of the autumn sun, the patients seemed to gain strength slowly. They needed the healthful face of a smiling sky, and the soft air, through which the sun's golden-tipped arrows had been freshly sent therefore, after some days, the building was vacated, and the patients were removed to the cottages. After this change, to where the free sea breeze and bright light of heaven could wander at will about their hard pillows, new life seemed to enter their sluggish veins.

In the November weather, sometimes chilly and raw, my mind, at times, wandered back to the happy summer days, while at others, I seemed to drink in the full beauty of the spot, and snuff the sea air, while watching the placid flow of the river. My thoughts soon, however, ran out to the men who were to be brought, bloody, pale, and suffering, from the impending battle of Fredericksburg.

To me it was a sad as well as a delightful place, and I at times fancied how smoothly life would glide with me then, if the dear old friends, who were there garnering up the fruits of summer, preparatory to the bitter winter, could only be with me, and war be unknown. But preparations were on every hand. A battle was inevitable, and to our hands they would be borne when the deadly work was ended, and the awful harvest-field had done its work.

The patients being mostly convalescent, there was but little for us to do, but to mend their clothing, and look after their food to the full extent allowed. A close supervision was kept over us at this hospital, but we found it a trifle better than the one at Washington.

Our corps of women nurses numbered seventeen. Miss Heald, a Quakeress from Boston, was at the dignified post of matron. The number of patients reached nearly three thousand. Six surgeons were in our medical corps, who each had a round of patients, such as would have astonished the country practitioners, who trundled over hilly roads in an old-fashioned one-horse shay, before a civil war brought to the knife and the pill box its tens of thousands of brave men. Of men nurses, we had the usual liberal supply. A general ward master had supervision over all the wards, and each ward had its master.

Twenty-five Sisters of Charity with their priest and Sister Superior had supervision over the patients in a part of the cottages previous to the finishing of the new wards, and also over the freshly wounded from Fredericksburg, who were assigned to the new quarters after their wounds had been once dressed.

But our duties were entirely separate from them. They had charge of the linen room, however, which was on the lower floor of the hotel, and there we sometimes caught a glimpse of a sweet placid face from under the long white bonnets which they wore. They were ceaseless in the work of mercy amongst those poor suffering soldiers. They, however, did not prove entirely impervious to the wiles of those passions which belong to this earthly state, for by-and-by one of them was wooed by, and fell in love with a Union officer. She renounced her faith, and they went to Seven Pines, and were united in the holy bonds of matrimony. Another died, and was

39

buried in the wave-washed cemetery, surrounded by the graves of the soldiers.

Of course, to supply daily food for establishments like ours, it required the labor of many hands. For the general cook-house the convalescent soldiers were detailed to perform the work, superintended by an overseer, styled the general cook. From this kitchen came up the food for all the patients, in full diet, extra diet, and low diet, with the exception of the little delicacies which we had the liberty of having cooked over our mess stove.

Surgeons, stewards, and nurses, each had their own mess—the rations being drawn from the commissary. The dining-room for the patients was built when the hospital was first established on this point, in 1862, and was capable of seating about nine hundred persons. The bugle-call sounding for dinner was a welcome strain to many of these poor fellows, whose sharpened appetites brought visions of bountiful dainties, which, like the sparkling waters forever glimmering in the unseen distance to the traveller on the desert sands, was but an illusion of the brain.

I could not but pity them as they fell into long lines, and stood shivering at times in the chill rains and winds OF November, waiting for the call "FALL IN TO DINNER" Perhaps there was NO other way for them but to wait through the long half hour, exposed to the storms, and with insufficient clothing; but busy woman's brain fancied that in the inexhaustible regions of contrivance some better way might be discovered.

Our dairy was supplied from the milk of nineteen cows that grazed upon the autumn pastures on the adjacent plantations. Beautiful butter was said to be made from the rich cream which rose to the snowy surface of the contents of the pans—indeed I think a few times we saw sample rolls, but not often. Officials in charge believed butter an indigestible article of food, and therefore it was kept for the use of those whose stomachs were supposed to be in sound condition.

Sometimes we caught glimpses of the animals as they ranged the pastures in frosty mornings, and it was something like a look at peace to see them quietly feeding amidst the dewy grass and clover.

A steam-engine, with its strong tireless arms, wrought for us the work of scores of men. It sawed the wood for the entire hospital, including kitchens and offices, baked the bread, boiled the water for washing, dried and ironed the clothes. One of my patients, formerly a railroad engineer, controlled its huge strength, and kept it at its varied work, forever tireless—its great heart throbbing forever free.

Our quarters were in one of the cottages—and 6 there, through the cold dreary weeks, till midwinter, we endured the cold without sufficient bedding for our hard beds, and with no provision made for fires. On bitter mornings we rose shivering, broke the ice in our pails, and washed our numb hands and faces, then went out into the raw air, up to our mess room, also without fire, thence to the wards to begin the distribution of the rations before the warmth of a stove was allowed to reach us.

One blanket each was allowed us, and in the chilling atmosphere of the cottages it was but little protection against the raw sea wind which swept about us. If I had not been favored with the carriage shawl loaned me by Miss Dix, I do not care to think what my condition would have become we often went to the quartermaster to urge him to hasten along the stoves for the patients, and for ourselves; but he was intemperate in his habits, the fire-water seemed to render him insensible to our needs, and when they finally did arrive from Baltimore, after repeated attempts they were with difficulty matched in pipe and elbows. On the first day of March we had enjoyed the luxury of a fire for about two weeks in our quarters—the patients having been supplied shortly previous.

The cottages stood on the very edge of the bay, high from the ground, with only one layer of boards to the floor, and when the bitter cold weather came upon us, in long nights, under our 'scant bedding, on a straw tick, we lay sleepless, and thought of the cosy rooms which were unoccupied at home, and the bright fires which gave out their genial glow without stint.

41

Had it been necessary we would have endured this without a murmur, but it was hard to think that one drunken inefficient man was the means of withholding from us what the Government was willing to supply for our comfort while doing its work.

Our food was hardly what we had a right to expect under the circumstances. For breakfast, we had bread and coffee, and occasionally a savory hash, that did much toward reminding us of better days. For dinner, roast beef, bread, potatoes, and sometimes boiled onions, with water for drink. For supper, bread and tea, browning our bread occasionally before the fire in lieu of butter, and, as a rare treat, a molasses cake.

Sanitary stores were collected here at that time, but, being a novice in the art of foraging, I hrid not learned the way to compel them to disgorge for me. They were, therefore, appropriated by those having the advantage of seniority in the military service.

Our hospital camp was guarded by a regiment called the "Independent Battalion," or the "Lost Children." Fourteen different languages -were spoken amongst them; and to this strange admixture of foreign element, it had been impossible to issue intelligible commands in battle. In the Shenandoah Valley they were lost from their corps, and were taken for guard duty at Hammond General Hospital.

Their dress was a picturesque costume of blue, somewhat like the zouave's in style, trimmed with gold cord—the long leggings buttoning closely up to loose-flowing trowsers, and altogether presenting a novel and pretty uniform.

Their quarters were in rear of the pine woods, and their rough shelters, leaning against the sombre ground-work of the dark trees, served to enliven the scene.

Within these woods, after the bowling-alley was vacated, the contrabands were sole denizens. Amidst the dense, dark pines they burrowed like beasts of the field in half-subterranean dens. A hole from three to four feet deep was dug by them in the black soil, and roofed over with boards, on which turf was closely packed. An opening, which admitted them on their hands and feet, and one for the escape of the smoke, which went up from an exceedingly primitive fireplace, were the only vents for the impure air, and the only openings for light.

In these dens men, women and children burrowed all winter, and to one of them I went one day to see a dead infant, only surprised that the dusky father and mother still breathed the breath of life. Bare as the barest poverty could make them—my heart grew sick at thought of the terrible straits to which human beings could be brought.

Government was doing all it could do for these people—feeding them, and giving them protection within our lines; but would there ever be a time when they should emerge out of the darkness which enveloped them like a thunder-cloud, and be a self-reliant, self-supporting people. When the thoughtless indolence of the generation, which has been burthened with no care for the morrow, shall pass away, then perhaps into the souls of a new generation the lessons of industry and self- reliance will be instilled, and the race be redeemed.

CHAPTER VI.

THANKSGIVING DAY came and went. The little incident of preparing mince meat for eighty pies, a day or so previous, receiving in return half of the baked pies from the cook-house, and distributing from an eighth to a quarter of one, according to patient, marked it from other hospital days.

With the forty pies, I received the following characteristic note from the commissary:—

Thanksgiving Day, November 27th, 1862.

Miss Bucklin:—Be thankful for all you receive, and if more is needed write me. Take care of the plates that I may return them to whom they belong.

Let your thanks arise, as you swallow the pies,

And be sure that you eat enough;

And if more of such feed, you think you will need,

Let me know, for there's plenty of stuff.

Will R.

That day we thought in silence of groups gathered around bountifully spread tables, at which those who sat missed our faces, and we turned to our work, striving by a show of cheerfulness, which it was impossible to feel, to cheat these poor fellows of the sad task of brooding over home scenes, and home comforts, which so many were never to know.

December winds howled through pine grove and leafless tree tops. The white billows ran upon the shore and broke in their mad reckless course. The shock of battle came at last in the sudden upheaval of the volcano of war. From out the hot crater lurid fires flamed, and the admonitory quakings, and far-off rumblings of internal struggling had ended in the earthquake.

'Molten lead had been poured into the living ranks until there ran streams of blood. From out the quivering mass, they brought to us eleven hundred men, with tangled hair, and begrimed faces, whose

44

uniforms were covered with the dirt of the rifle-pits and barricades, and were reeking with the smoke of the battle. They were landed while we were busy with our duties in the respective wards, and one cold afternoon the call of the steward, "TURN OUT TO HELP DRESS THE WOUNDS," sounded to me like a death-knell. Men fresh from the gory field had never been under my hands as yet, and with a quaking at my heart I went out with the hospital force, to do my duty toward the suffering and shattered men.

Beds were to be made, hands and faces stripped of the hideous mask of blood and grime, matted hair to be combed out over the bronzed brows, and gaping wounds to be sponged with soft water, till cleaned of the gore and filth preparatory to the dressing. I busied myself with everything save touching the dreadful wounds till I could evade it no longer. Then with all my resolution I nerved myself to the task and bound up the aching limbs.

Before ten o'clock the wounds were all dressed, and the soldiers comfortably in beds, occupying the new hospital for the first time. Then oh! with what fidelity in times of sore distress the troubled heart turns in memory to the sacred altar of Home! When danger and death have been faced, and from the long fierce struggle the brother, or husband, or son has been borne to the hospital seared and bleeding, to thee, oh! father, wife, mother, or sister that wounded soldier turns, and gives his first uttered thoughts!

"Bring pen and ink and paper, that I may let them know at home that I still live, though I lie weak, maimed, and helpless on a hospital bed!"

Oh! mother if you had a son who has given you cause to weep bitter tears over his erring ways— who spurned your counsels when you warned him of the result of his evil deeds, be assured that on the battle field he remembered your kind admonitions, and would have given worlds had he heeded them.

Oh! wife, did coldness creep between you and the husband of your youth? did he neglect you for the company of the ungodly, and send your little babes with profane words from his side. Be comforted, for in the hospital he repented of the wrong he did your faithful heart, and when excruciating pains racked his wounded body, he knew how soft the touch of your hand would be on his fevered face, and how you would move, heaven and earth to minister to his many wants.

Home would appear to these men in fair and living colors. It might have been a low, humble shelter by the lonely roadside, where only few passed to feel an instinctive pity for the dwellers within it; but he thought, when the summer weather had wreathed its roses over the small window-panes, and the old apple tree was hanging its leafy boughs over the well-sweep, and the garden patch was giving promise of good dinners to come, that it was a pleasant spot, although so far away from the bustle of towns, and the din of cities.

On the hard beds, how many thought of some snug little room, with pillows of down resting on high soft beds, over which lay the spotless white quilt, wrought in flowery patterns by loved fingers, and sighed to be within its narrow walls, with doors and windows open to the woods and hills, every nook of which was familiar to their sturdy feet.

Many a poor fellow so set his heart on these beguiling visions of home, that from sheer home-

sickness alone he died. Care, medicine, diet were at times of no avail, so long as the one sharp pang of absence cut at the sinking heart, and so they passed beyond the veil. For them to-day many eyelids droop over wet eyes, as the lips speak of the soldier who died in the hospital when the battle was ended, and after he had lived to tell the story of the tight.

How their eyes seemed to sparkle, when they talked to us of home. They would often ask us to come in and sit by them, while they told us of the dear waiting ones; and at times smiles would illumine their pale faces, as they spoke the gratitude of full hearts, that they were spared to return perhaps to the loved ones within the far- off family circle.

The upper story of the hotel, with two halls running at right angles, and crossing in the middle, and from which forty-one rooms opened, was assigned to my care for the winter. In these rooms ninety-six men were lying, mostly wounded, and my duties were to give the medicines; distribute the food on plates at the scullery, designating to whom, and into what room it must be taken; comb heads, and wash the faces of those unable to do so for themselves; see that everything about their beds and clothing was in right condition; prepare what delicacies I could procure for their comfort, and dress wounds.

At this date, although there was a special time, and a special nurse appointed for wound-dressing, there were so many, and of such an aggravated character, that some of us were kept busy at that duty nearly all the time. And many preferred the lighter, the gentler hand of a woman.

In this hospital we were allowed to do much of this work at all times, it being optional with the ward surgeons in the different hospitals what duties should be assigned to the nurses. Perhaps it may be well for the reader to understand that on this surgeon depended also, in a great measure, the quiet or discomfort of our situations.

It was in his power to make our paths smooth, or to throw disagreeable things in the way which would make our positions extremely unpleasant, and subject us to no ordinary annoyance. Yet no murmur or complaint dared pass the lips of a hospital nurse, for disgrace and dismissal only awaited the beck of his authoritative hand.

At that time it was a question of tolerance with him whether she remained or not, for it was in his power to procure her relief papers at any moment. Happily, this arbitrary method of disposing of persons, which, although they might be personally obnoxious, yet were good and efficient nurses, doing a valuable work for the Government in saving her soldiers for duty and alleviating the sufferings of the wounded heroes, was done away with a little later in the progress of the war, when it was officially ordered that the reasons for the discharge of any woman nurse should be endorsed upon the certificate of her removal.

Previous to this order, which was not issued ' until October 29th, 1863, Miss Dix was subject to much annoyance by the frequent appearance of her competent nurses, who had been ordered to report to her by some domineering surgeon, whose love of power had been thwarted in some manner.

The surgeon in charge of this ward, when I first entered it, was a fine, generous-hearted man, who was interested in everything pertaining to the welfare of his men, and he gave me unstinted orders for sugar, butter, eggs, and other articles, with which I could prepare delicacies for the faint appetites, which revolted at the food sent up from the general cook-house.

The word master also had it in his power to give us a world of annoyance, but, fortunately, the one in charge of my beat was a co-worker with the surgeon in all efforts to promote the comfort of the men. When, by daily contrast with other overseers of other wards, I was congratulating myself on my good fortune in being placed where such generous men held control, an order came, sending them to another beat, and strangers stepped into their places.

It was but a short time before I learned, to my regret, that I had men of an entirely different stamp with whom to deal, and, with envious eyes, I looked over to the new hospital, where the Sisters of Charity were enjoying the rule of our lost surgeon and ward master.

Instead of the kind, "Nurse, what would you like for your men to-day," if I made a request for butter, sugar, eggs, or milk, I was met by a volley of oaths, and a loud, "Didn't I give you an order for a pound of sugar yesterday?" A pound of sugar for ninety men, when each was entitled to a large spoonful a day from Government supplies, and we must be content with a pound to distribute for three or four days amongst ninety men!

Some one was living on the rations of these poor men, who were suffering and starving for the want of them. It seemed enough to soften a heart of stone to hear them beg for their rightful food, and be denied when others feasted on the stolen supply. I could do nothing but take the food frequently, which I needed myself to keep up strength and courage, and give it to them, which was also a forbidden thing, but we did it often and again, and for a whole day I have gone with wretched hunger gnawing at my healthy stomach— glad to do so, if not detected—that some poor fellow's hunger might be satisfied.

Often the extra rations were taken from the tray, as they were being sent up to the men, which, being once sent, were all that could be obtained till the next meal, and if that chanced to occur again, the men had to remain in a starving condition day after day, unless, by some strategy, we could elude the vigilance of our wretched overseer, and substitute something for what had been lost.

The stimulants often went the same way, and woe to the unhappy being who crossed the path of the official creature, when throwing off the effects of his debauch.

There were various ways by which we strove to obtain possession of things to make up for every lack of supplies. Many letters were written to the friends of soldiers from the North, and boxes were forwarded, the contents of which rejoiced our hearts, and made our patients glad indeed. We took thence just what the sick soldiers wanted, and saw the joyous sparkle of the eye, which a moment before was languid with hope deferred. Often we begged of the Sanitary Commission— sometimes were repulsed like street beggars by the very men who were fattening on the choice things sent by many a kind-hearted mother, with tearful hopes that her boy might taste a share, if, by the chances of sickness or war, he was sent into the hospital.

We have begged ofttimes in vain, while those who were sent out to distribute the stores sat in their tents, and used the Sanitary tobacco, and drank the wine, and ate the canned fruit and meats, until, with bitterness in our hearts, we returned to meet pleading eyes, and hungry, pinched features. I do not wish to be understood as casting any reflections upon the good mission which the Sanitary Commission performed, for many noble-souled men were with it at times, engaged in dealing out from its abundance with commendable honesty and manliness, and then the duty was done without withholding from the rightful owners to adorn the tables of their own tents.

An Irish family lived half a mile from us who kept a cow, and employed themselves at gathering oysters. They furnished those of us, who walked that distance, with dried apple pies—the crust made of flour and water—for twenty-five cents. A Northern housekeeper may know to what straits we were reduced, when we say that we eagerly walked to the place through rain and shine, the mud over shoe deep, to gratify the homesick wants of some poor fellow, who put little value on his currency when he was starving.

We cooked the oysters for them, when we could accomplish that feat without danger of the scent of the smoke reaching the wards. I thought it a trying thing, to be thus circumscribed in privileges, when they had cost no one but the soldiers and ourselves either money or time, but it was only my initiation into hardships. I was just striking the stormy waves of humanity. The bufferings, and rude jarring against the sharp rocks of military law were new to me then. I hardly thought I should grow so callous as to fling back word for word, and almost dare a blow for a blow.

CHAPTER VII.

An incident of an unpleasant character occurred to me while Miss Ella Wolcott was absent in Washington, during which absence I had charge of her ward, in addition to my own duties—an incident which pointed to a disgraceful dismissal from the service, when I was unconscious of having committed any wrong, but, on the contrary, fully convinced that great injustice was being done to me in some shape, and by some one.

The ward surgeon had given me the key of the cupboard, in which the delicacies and stimulants were kept, and requested me also to distribute the rations to the patients, I consenting to the arrangement. A few days passed when the ward master, getting hungry, entered complaint to the steward that I had usurped his position, and taken his duties from out his hands.

Shortly after, I was engaged one morning on my accustomed round, when the ward master entered, saying, "The steward wishes to see you." I replied, "I am here, he can see me," not dreaming that I was expected to go out into the drenching rain, then falling, to suit his pleasure. Presently I was accosted by his sharp voice, in which' there was an evident leaning toward severity, with the question, "Yat for you don't give up de key to de cupboard?"

I said I was unaware of its being required, that it had been given me by the surgeon, on complaint of the patients that their choicest food had been appropriated by the ward master, and male nurses.

"You had no right to de key," the Dutch steward insisted; "give it up dis moment, you shall be relieved for dis," he added.

I retired to my quarters, and in an hour my relief papers were handed me by an orderly. Stung by the injustice, I went directly to our good matron, and laid the case before her. She was troubled, and determined that the order should be countermanded. The surgeon in charge of the hospital being absent at that time, Dr. Gardner was acting surgeon, and to him Miss Heald sent her orderly. I was soon summoned to appear before him, and give a detailed account of the affair.

I was in the kitchen making ginger cakes for supper, and when the summons came my hands were deep in the dark dough. But military law 7 knows no delay, and I went, with doughy hands and sleeves pinned up, while the desperation of despair nerved me with unusual courage.

I explained away the charge to his entire satisfaction, and he said, "Miss Bucklin, you may go 'to your quarters, and to your duties in the morning—for I countermand that order."

With a load taken from me, I returned to finish my work. At tea time I noticed an unusual commotion around our quarters—an orderly with papers going in and out, and when I repaired thither, I found my second relief papers lying conspicuously on my bed.

I could hardly believe my senses—to be thus plunged, for the second time, into the depths of disgrace. I repaired to Miss Heald at once for counsel, while nearer and nearer the boat was approaching the wharf, and on its return trip, I was ordered to leave for Washington to report to Miss Dix.

In sorrow we saw no way of escape. The surgeon in charge was absent, and there was no one to whom we could appeal. I sorrowfully returned to my quarters, thinking of those to whom I could not even speak the good-by, and, getting up my limited possessions, I prepared to leave Point Lookout.

The steamer touched the wharf—the surgeon in charge on board. Miss Heald's orderly conducted him immediately to her quarters, and, indignant at the relief of one of his nurses, by those who had no authority to do so in his absence, he countermanded the order, and again I breathed free. Things moved quietly along for several days, when one morning, while busy in my quarters the steward passed the door, and halted in 'surprise.

"Why you not go to Washington as ordered?" he said, flushing up with feeling at finding his commands so disregarded.

"Because I had orders to remain," I replied.

"Orders from whom," he questioned.

"From one who had the authority to give them," I said, and he left me, muttering to himself, and wondering who "the d—l" it could be.

From this hospital steward, who assumed as much dignity as a major-general was entitled to, we often received much annoyance. Patients and nurses alike grew to dislike the sound of his voice, and the tramp of his feet. Nothing could be found about the bed of a patient without subjecting the owner to -some punishment, either lying stripped of clothing, in bed if ill; or a diet of bread and water; or the guard-house, if able to be taken there.

For one patient, who craved eggs dropped into boiling water for his daily food, and whose stomach could not bear them cold as they were brought in from the nearest cook-house, I procured a stew-pan, and cooked them on the stove which stood in the hall of the ward. Our steward coming in unexpectedly one day, found the pan

sitting by the stove, waiting to be washed. He called out to me, "Vat isk dis?"

"A frying-pan, sir."

"Vat you use it for?"

"To cook eggs in, sir."

An order was immediately issued to the effect that not a single article of food should be cooked on the stoves in the wards. The surgeon under whose orders I had acted in preparing the eggs for the sick man, however, highly resented this interference, and said, "Jam everything you want to cook into the stove, there isn't an order against that." So into the stove the eggs went, and they were cooked and eaten hot as before.

An Italian, an official from the regiment doing guard duty at Point Lookout, was a patient in my ward, receiving from the mess table little attentions in the shape of coffee, and articles of food of a somewhat relish able character. The coffee-pot was put on the stove in the hall for the purpose of warming its contents. Our steward found it there one day, and straightway ordered the officer to bed, on a diet of bread and water. Resistance was made—for the officer outranking any one in the hospital, was furious at the insult—and he

53

stalked away to headquarters, where a great commotion was kept up for some time. It was so far away, however, that wrathy words could not be heard by us. He never returned to the ward— the storm of indignation swept all illness away, and he went to his regiment, no doubt entertain- mg a poor opinion of hospitals, and hospital stewards.

The question of rank was at that time before Congress, and this steward, in advance of its being settled, required and insisted on being saluted with military honor whenever he appeared, or was met by us in the ward. By most of us the burly figure, inspiring anything but respect, was passed time and again without an ordinary effort at recognition, which brought, of course, a whole train of his indignation thundering down upon us.

Men died on the transports while seeking the hospital, only making port to be transferred to Government coffins, and be interred on the wave- washed shore. It seemed a hard necessity which demanded this removal, but the stem military law had a granite heart, and the piteous moans and beseeching voices pleading to be left to die rather than to be tortured by the slow process of travel, had no more visible effect than the rain washing the stony front of a mountain.

If individual officers, with human hearts, were actuated by pity, as they ofttimes were, they were powerless to be generous. True to themselves in this, the dead men were brought to us, and coffins were furnished to cover the poor clay from further exposure.

One boat brought five corpses, and while the order for the coffins was being filled, another one died just as the boat touched the shore. Our inhuman Dutch steward, in his perplexity, could not understand why he had not died before, or, at least, waited till within the hospital limits. He went capering about, undecided how to dispose of the stiffening body, and muttering to himself, "lie pelongs neither to de boat nor de hospital —what for he die now— what for he die now?"

Sad as the event seemed to us, we could not resist a smile at the ludicrous manner of the obnoxious steward, who, in his dull

54

comprehension of the mystery of death, could not understand why the man had chosen this unfavorable opportunity to succumb in the struggle for life.

We sighed over the dead soldier, and watched them bear his uncoffined remains to the dead- house, to join his pallid companions, while the steward was constrained to order a coffin.

In the daily routine of our life time sped. Sometimes on swift wings—sometimes slowly creeping through dull damp days, when air and earth, and sea, were of the leaden hue of despondency. Our hearts occasionally sunk in the presence of a misery, and consequent home-sickness, which we had no power to charm away.

Two snow storms occurred through the winter. The driving sea wind, which was brisk at all times, was then full of the wildly-sweeping flakes of snow which melted as they fell, until dark, deep, soft mud covered the feet of the throngs which turned out from quarters to ward, at the bugle-call. Once I was caught in the storm, and eight o'clock summoned me to repair to the nurses' quarters. With feet encased in a pair of boots belonging to a patient, I assayed the hidden path, which led to the cottages, but stumbled and blundered in my unaccustomed foot-gear—falling, and finding it almost impossible to rise in my over-exertion, and with limbs so weighed down. With the salt spray dashing into my face, with the sharp wind and snow blinding me, I reached at last a shelter, and crept shivering into bed.

The beauty of the Point was somewhat dimmed by the morning light, and my enthusiastic admiration of it somewhat dampened by the names by which homesick soldiers designated it, such as "Point of Misery," "Point of Despair." Hope deferred had clouded their vision. The yearnings after home, and home comforts, the restive heart throbbing, too, for the active combat; the dull routine of hospital life would have made a dreary, desolate place of the loveliest spot on earth, before the minds of those disabled men.

Deeds of foul import were sometimes hidden by the dense pines, and in the seething waters of the bay, although the waves did not always engulf the murdered dead, or the darkness of the woods conceal from the light of day the wretched men who were felled by robber hands.

A man was found dead on the beach, who had been missed for weeks, and was known to have had quite a sum of money in his possession, but nothing was found on his person, when, dripping

and swollen, the waves cast him upon the sands. No one may ever know what hand gave him the death-blow, but some unholy heart aches with the burthen of this awful crime, and seeks to cast it out, and rid the blood-stained hand of the foul spots that even a seared conscience must fix there.

Two men went to a house in the pines, purchased some little article, and handed a five dollar bill in payment. The change was withheld, and, before they had time to remonstrate, two shots were fired at them, one only scraping the temple of the one, but failing to take life. Reinforcements arriving for the villains from some unknown quarter, both men were knocked down, dragged away, and left to remain in the bitter cold through the wintry night, the oozing blood congealing into icy hardness, and freezing fast the cap of the wounded man. Both recovered, but had good cause to remember ever after the rebel inhabitants of Maryland, who were scattered over Point Lookout.

CHAPTER VIII.

IN bright days, when the raw winds were tempered by the genial smiles of the sun, the piazza, which ran on three sides of the hotel, and which was accessible from the halls, was an alluring place. I have often counted as many as thirty- five boats dotting the river and bay; and when the eye grew tired of the sea, there stood the lovely land, the pine woods through which the low winds swept with musical murmurs amidst the trembling of the leaves.

From this lookout I saw Burnside's fleet of seventy steamers gliding down on his North Carolina expedition. It was about ten o'clock in the morning when it passed our hospital. We knew that brave and loyal hearts beat upon those decks, and that proud, stalwart men were there, the embodiment of love and courage in many a waiting heart, which, in its Northern home, prayed for the safe return of its idol. We knew that disease and death lurked for them in treacherous swamps, and on pine-clad hill slopes, whither they were going, and that many a grave in that now unbroken sod was waiting to receive a bloody hero in its arms, and that ever after, far away from the place of his rest, his name would be spoken in tones of hushed sadness, and the evergreen garlands be woven in memory of the beloved soldier who died for his country.

While gazing out upon the billowy stretch of waters, and back again to the land, rich in its quiet loveliness, I could not but lift my heart upward in petition that all the sufferings of my country might speedily be healed. If all was but peace, what a rare life it would seem to live where the soft-lipped weaves kissed the white sands of that lovely shore. But groans would awake me to a sense of the terrible duty which brought me thus far from home. My heart held my country and its heroes dearest, and I turned from the bright, winding river to bend over the beds of some who had been very nigh to death, and give a little ray of comfort to others, who were fast drifting into the cold current.

A beautiful boy, whose home was in Philadelphia, was declining slowly—still declining. He had suffered an amputation, although he said to me, "I had rather die than lose my arm." Everything that

57

could be done to save him proved of no avail. He suffered intensely, and, during his wild flights in his delirium, he fancied that they had come to take me to the guard-house, for having cared too much for his comfort.

He would say, "It's too bad—too bad, to put you there for staying so long to take care of your poor little Shoe." (His name was Sylvester Shoe.) "You must go to your quarters, quick. Goodnight—come and see me first in the morning, and bring some of those nice oysters."

Morning dawned, but he was conscious only for a moment at a time, and I saw the end was nigh. That day he received two letters from home, but he was not in condition to know their contents. When I came to him, he said, "Put them under my pillow," which I did.

The letters were lying there when his spirit took its flight from the poor racked body of the beautiful boy. I procured, from' the stores which had been sent to us for distribution from home, the necessary clothing in which to shroud his body; had him properly washed, and arrayed for burial, and his corpse was taken to the dead-house, to await the hour of burial. (In the hospitals, dear reader, four o'clock in the afternoon was the hour for burials.)

The chaplain and myself, with a corporal and five soldiers, followed the ambulance accompanied by the fife and drum, and his remains were lowered into a grave amongst the pines, which grew so closely to the water's edge, that I thought, with a shudder, that at high water the breakers would leap sportively over that narrow bed. Yet I knew that no sound of their angry careering could awaken the dear boy, who was to sleep within it, to sorrow or pain again.

The chaplain repeated the burial service for the soldier dead—earth to earth, ashes to ashes, dust to dust; the sexton threw down the gravelly clay upon the coffin of my little friend; over the grave three rounds were fired, and then we turned away to the living who awaited us in the hospital, while the grave digger formed a little mound over all that was left of Sylvester Shoe.

I directed a friend, who came too late to see him, to that grave on the bank of the Potomac, beneath the murmuring pines, and to him I gave a lock of his auburn hair, and related the particulars of his death.

Two more deaths occurred soon afterwards from amputation of the arm. One of them seemed to possess an unusual appetite, craving the strongest food, and daily begging for that which I could not obtain. It so happened one day that we had the food each meal which he had so much wanted, when I supplied him, gladly fasting myself.

I shall never outlive the feeling that his was an unnecessary amputation, although I do not mean to censure or arraign the judgment of anyone;- but his wound was only that of a bullet through the fleshy part of the arm, and it seemed to be doing as well as could be expected. After the amputation, which did not discharge properly, his symptoms grew fatal, and when he died, seven or eight days afterwards, he was bloated to a misshapen, monstrous size, whilst his body was almost as transparent as glass. He left a wife and six children, and his latest thoughts and words were about the one who was so soon to be widowed, and the fatherless, and the little unborn babe which would come into his desolate home under the cloud of sadness.

The next man I visited about five o'clock in the afternoon, directly after the ^amputation had been performed, and I bathed his face, combed his hair, gave him an apple, and prepared him a nice cooling drink, and supposed him to be doing well. While preparing him for the night he expressed a desire to see his arm, and I took down the glass to gratify his wish. He looked long and earnestly at the bandaged stump, and then said, "I don't know whether I shall recover from this or not, if I don't, under my head is a nice new blanket which I lately drew, and which I want you to have." I promised to take it if he did not live, but saw no reason why he should not, and talked encouragingly to him, and said I would see him early in the morning.

The following day I was passing along, my duties already begun, when the ward master met me with, "Pennsylvania is dead, and gone to the dead-house." How my heart sunk within me, for this was the third death that had come so suddenly upon me. The surgeon was so much surprised that he ordered a post-mortem examination, and found death the result of inward causes, while the arm was doing well. I was not permitted to see him, although I begged for the privilege.

None can tell the sickness of heart which filled our souls when such stern realities confronted us. It was not the professional regret, which filled the heart of the nurse at the loss of her patient— higher and above all such feelings, which would at once reflect upon her capacity and integrity, the sorrow of the hospital nurse, as she grieved over each successive dead one, was as the sorrow of a sister over the fallen remains of a brave and true brother.

A mother came on to our hospital to nurse her fast sinking son. Nothing availed to fix a cure upon him, while home-sickness drank-low the fountain of his life; and she thought, if he were only at home, new hope and vigor would rise, and he would yet be spared to her. He had failed to receive a furlough, and the distressed mother saw him slowly but surely passing down into the dark valley.

She took the boat and went to Washington, to intercede with the President for his discharge.

She was ushered into his presence, but was so overcome by the rush of feelings that she burst into a flood of tears and was speechless with emotion.

The tender heart of the man before her, was melted at the sight, and he said, "Make known your request, madam, I promise to grant it, whatever it may be."

She told him of her dying son, and at once received his discharge and transportation home. The mother returned on the next boat, and reached Point Lookout at seven o'clock in the evening, and at eight the boy died. It was distressing to witness the grief of the poor, gray-haired mother, as she bent over the clay, which could return no more the many caresses lavished on pale lip and brow; but God alone could comfort her, we knew, and so we let the storm of grief sweep on in silence.

Back to her lonely home she went, bearing him a lifeless corpse whom she had hoped to take thence, and nurse into health and strength again.

An old man, who was brought in from another ward in a dying condition, was the last death which occurred amongst the ninety-six men under my charge.

Miss D. L. Dix, with Mrs. Gibbons, the former matron of the hospital, appeared to our wondering eyes one February morning, presaging some change in the even tenor of our life.

To Miss Dix's inquiry of Surgeon Wagner, whom she met on the sands, how her nurses were getting along, the reply of, "Splendidly, as well as I could ask," settled the fact in her mind that no removals were necessary, and Mrs. Gibbons signifying her intention of again assuming the matron- ship of the hospital, Miss Dix left for Fortress Monroe, whither she was bound, desiring to reach her destination before the impending storm should break over us.

Mrs. Gibbons was accompanied by five women, to whom she assigned places in the hospital, and as so many were not needed, amongst the fast decreasing numbers whose wounds were rapidly healing, she began the work of relieving Miss Dix's nurses, and assigning her own to their places.

I have no wish to speak disparagingly of any one. I wish to detail frankly and fearlessly the events as they occurred, and as Miss Dix was, by the authority of the War Department, vested with the power of full superintendence over all women nurses in the military hospitals, it was our duty and wish to report to her, and receive such situations as she saw fit to give us.

Mrs. Gibbons had not informed Miss Dix that the five young women accompanying her were to supersede her own nurses; they sat in silence, unmentioned, when she signified her intention of remaining, after being questioned by Miss Dix. Her strong Quaker sense of personal independence —her masculine contempt for all women not endowed with her energetic, unyielding will, rendered it exceedingly distasteful to her to recognize any superiority in the chosen Superintendent of Women Nurses in the Military Hospitals of the Union.

Miss Dix was unaware of her return from New York, and was only made cognizant of her intention to remain when at Miss Heald's headquarters, and this ignoring of Miss Dix's authorized position, in the opinion of her nurses, seemed a breach of military law without precedent.

It was impossible for me to attempt to see anything lovely or feminine in the character of the new matron. The sharp censorious scanning of the features of any woman, not so far developed in rugged strength of will as herself, was exceedingly annoying, and it was difficult for us to assume an air of indifference.

It was a mystery to many why she held the power she did—why she was not responsible to Miss Dix like other nurses and matrons, and ' why, although all in authority demurred, she still retained her position, and removed surgeons and nurses alike. Some subtle power of control she had attained—and all within reach of her sharp questionings bowed before it.

After being relieved from the Point, I received letters, and was cautioned as to what I wrote, and directed to burn what I received immediately, "For Mrs. Gibbons knows everything," the remark ran. She did seem, in her knowledge of 8 the disaffection of nurses and all other employees, to be almost omniscient.

Some spies she had, who, creeping about our quarters, obtained some information, doubtless receiving favor as the reward of their highly honorable services.

That a conscientious regard for the well-being of the blacks could be entertained, without taking them like pets into the bosom of one's family, I knew by long personal experience, and that due thought could be given them in supplying them with wholesome food and decent clothing, I was likewise certain.

That proper respect should also be shown to the feelings of the soldiers who were fighting for the idea of universal liberty—that they should be treated equally as well as those newly emancipated, dusky sons of the Republic, was more and more impressed upon my mind. Mrs. Gibbons had near her a circle of negroes, who, the soldiers in bitterness said, had cream in their tea and coffee, and were given hot beefsteaks, and, "That is where our rations go too," was the added exclamation.

Little lumps of ebony were occasionally carried about the ward, to the no little annoyance of soldiers who turned shudderingly from the contrast which memory suggested of fair Saxon babies in far Northern homes. Bitter feelings were invited, and instead of a sympathy toward the negro, in times so critical to his race, and in minds so wrought upon by sickness and wounds—in cases almost innumerable, a hatred was engendered which would have eventuated in a riot, if the soldiers had had the means and strength at their command.

A devotion of such character to the interests of the contraband, when wounded and dying heroes needed care and sympathy, evinced an evil judgment. The contrabands were fed and protected, while hundreds of brave white men were deprived of what would have been common fare at home. We knew them to suffer from want of ordinary diet, and saw better food distributed to negroes, with whom corn-bread and bacon had been luxurious living.

There is no one in this broad land, who, regardless of prejudice, can justify an unwholesome pandering after associations of this kind, or who can regard with favor this palpable injustice toward the men who stood between our homes and the guns of the enemy.

After a few days had passed, I was asked to resign my ward to one of the new comers, which I declined, believing that I could do more good where I knew the wants of each man, and recognizing no superior to the will of Miss Dix, or the surgeon in charge. I was asked, as the condition of being allowed to remain, to submit my correspondence with the superintendent to the perusal of the new matron of the hospital. This I also declined, firmly, but respectfully. After a few little annoyances, such as complaints of the beds being filthy on Monday morning, after having been changed on Sunday, I received my expected relief papers, and was ordered to leave on the first boat proceeding to Washington.

The evening brought the steamer, and the night was passed in making preparations for departure. I snatched a moment in which to bid "Good-by" to the boys, many—nay, nearly all, I never would greet again with my mortal vision. It seemed somewhat harder to go at this time, because a nephew had just arrived in Hammond General Hospital, detailed for duty, whom I had not seen for some time. I was not favored with so many kindred, that I could agree to the separation with indifference.

Only a moment was allowed me—I could not crowd the weight of sadness in that space of time —and I left them sorrowfully. While packing my trunk I found some lemons, which I laid down softly by the face of a boy, whose arm had been amputated after the Fredericksburg battle. He was sleeping so sweetly, that I could not disturb his peaceful rest, and took my silent farewell while bending over the brave young sufferer's bed, with a prayer for his safe and speedy recovery.

Tears were in my own eyes, and answering tears in the eyes of some, not too strong to betray the feelings of the heart, when I left the scene of the winter's labors, and went sadly away. I never met but two of the soldier boys from Point Lookout after that brief farewell.

Again I was upon the broad Potomac. The shores of the Point, which had seemed so lovely when autumn's verdure fringed them to the narrow margin of white sand, were now lone and bare under the March sun. Mud — the delayer of armies—the enemy about our weary feet—lay deep before our late quarters. The early springtime had sent its first signals, sounding from the adventurous throats on the edge of the pines, and I knew that green grass and dainty flowers would soon spring up, while we were far away, perhaps bending over sods, stained with the blood of those brave men, who were yet to yield up their lives, a sacrifice to the honor of their beloved country.

Miss Dix received us in unfeigned surprise. Five of her nurses, who, only one week before, she had been assured by the surgeon in charge, were doing as well as could be wished, were sent without warning to her house. Closely questioning us, she became convinced that our relief had only been accomplished to make way for others, and she proceeded to the Surgeon General with us, to inquire who had given Mrs. Gibbons authority to discharge her nurses.

He said she had not received it from him; and an officer was sent to ascertain what the charges were. He returned with the accusation of inefficiency." Most of us had served for months in the military hospitals, with the approval of the surgeons in charge, and sustained by Miss Dix, whose supervision was anything but nominal over her nurses in regard to character and usefulness. However, the charge was so unsatisfactory, that the Surgeon General ordered three of us to be retained in the service, and I went to the Sanitary Home for a few days of rest, and to allow Miss Dix an opportunity to find a fitting vacancy for me.

No battle since Fredericksburg had poured maimed and bleeding men into the hospitals. Old wounds were fast healing, and men were eager to leave the monotonous life which they led, to return to their regiments, ready for the renewal of the conflict in the spring. I enjoyed the rest at the luxurious Home, having something like the quiet of my old life, which had been so long broken, and filled with excitement.

I had leisure to think over what had passed, and gather up new courage for the future. Under no consideration was I willing to weary of my work.' So long as battles were fought, and the gory dead were hurled by the side of the quivering living, so long would be needed just such help as my hands could give, and I had no disposition to withhold it.

CHAPTER IX.

To Wolf-street Hospital in Alexandria, I was at last assigned for duty. Miss Dix accompanied me thither with a Miss Millar, a New England woman, who had been sent to the Mansion House, which was also a hospital.

Only one woman nurse beside myself, was on duty at Wolf-street Hospital. On inquiring what work was to be given to my hands to do, the surgeon in charge remarked, that there was very little to do; if I found little to do, do that—if I found less, to do that. Then we wandered aimlessly about, forbidden to enter the wards; the only employment presenting itself being the care of the linen with the ironing and mending—long and irksome tasks, which we felt were not the ones we had come out to perform.

The buildings which were occupied for the use of the hospital, were confiscated dwellings, in which all the rich furniture and table service still remained. These were used by the surgeons and their wives, who were staying with them. Our room, with those occupied by the three hundred patients, had been divested of the belongings, and contained nothing but Government bedsteads, and Government stands.

Beautiful grounds surrounded these houses, and I could not but think of those who had dwelt within their rooms, looking out upon the lovely villas and the frowning forts which guarded the city. I wondered if those wanderers from beautiful homes, with their hands raised against us, knew that sick and wounded enemies lay beneath their roofs.

Arlington Heights lay in the distance, and the Blue Ridge leaned against the western sky in solemn grandeur. Gen. Lee's home was in full view. Forts Lyon and Ellsworth, with the black muzzles of their guns toward us, seemed constantly to threaten these peaceful homes, so recently the abode of peace and comfort.

Though the exterior appeared faultless, I cannot, out of regard for truth, record as much for the interior. The surgeons messed together, and used the same room in which we took our meals.

Therefore our meals had to be prepared first, to allow them ample time to grow hungry, and about as much time in which to appease their hunger. Our breakfasts were usually made up of a distasteful hash, made of the bits of meat, bread, and potatoes which were left by the patients, and the slops of the mess table took the place of tea and coffee.

The surgeons were supposed to furnish their own board, while our rations were supposed to be supplied by Government. Yet, by a strange admixture of circumstances, it was hard to find out "what belonged to who, or who to which," and doubtless it was so when the bills came to be handed in for payment.

One thin slice of bread was laid by our plates —we could get no more until another meal. A nice roast would be served for dinner, and, when twelve o'clock arrived, the beef would be cooked only sufficiently for the blood to ooze out under the knife. From this raw material, thin slices were shaved, which were placed upon our plates, together with potatoes cooked in the patients' soup, another round of bread, and a draught of the filthy Potomac water. The roast went back into the oven, and, of course, was "delicious," when the surgeons' mess hour arrived.

Sometimes, for a change, we had codfish boiled in clear water— hunger being the only sauce. For supper we had another slice of baker's bread, some dried apples stewed, and a fresh supply of slops from the mess table, if there chanced to be any, and, if not, more water was added, till the cooks were able to turn out a cup full each from off the old grounds. Turning water through the spout of the tea or coffee pot, aided by a strong imagination, was sometimes regarded as having a fine effect.

Twice a week, a piece of butter, a little larger than a small-sized nutmeg, graced each plate, and we were absolutely almost starved. Although in perfect health and strength when I went there, before I left I found, it necessary to cling to the banisters to assist in ascending the stairs. As days went by I found myself growing weaker and weaker, with hunger gnawing at my vitals, and no opportunity to obtain food.

If we went out into the city, a soldier was every moment at our heels, and no one was allowed, by purchasing an article of food, to cast an imputation upon the character of the hospital —which, from its beauty, and the desirableness of the buildings, had acquired the reputation of a "model hospital." If visitors questioned, and complaint was made, the culprit was punished with extra diet. This was done with three soldiers who were thrust into the attic where no man could stand upright, and there forced, under a guard, to eat each three full rations at a meal.

During this time my dreams were troubled with visions of good things which seemed to pass in panoramic order over my sleeping hours—all disappearing with the light of the sun and leaving me hungry and wretched indeed. Our Government allowance was more than could possibly be eaten by a strong healthy man, and, when in a position to have it regularly served to us, the surplus material was turned over to the quartermaster to be sold, the proceeds creating a fund securing extras for both soldiers and nurses.

Sometimes a number of women were with us, on a visit to sick husbands, sons, and brothers, and with no means of subsistence. Such were fed from our full rations, and we had enough and to spare.

The patience of some natures forbids long indulgence in melancholy, whatever the outside pressure, and we sometimes felt so constituted that we could make merry in a dungeon, without the air or light of heaven. Therefore we at times forgot our sorrows, and beguiled the moments with cheerful conversations. The convalescents frequently called out in chorus at the ringing of the bell,

"O, don't you hear the bells a' ringing,

Down to Uncle Sam's hotel," when no prospect of a satisfying meal lay before them, thus throwing off, with careless show of merriment, the injurious effects of sadness and ill-treatment.

The steward often stood in the pantry adjoining the dining-room, to listen, and report in case we made complaint about our miserable food. Thus a course of espionage, unworthy of the dignity of hospital officials, was kept up among us all, and the weapon of relief from duty kept constantly suspended over our heads.

Taking a little stroll out into the country one day, in company with a woman attached to the hospital, we came to Fort Ellsworth, and, as I desired to go within it, having no pass, I asked the lieutenant of the guard, if it would be possible for us to enter without. He scanned us closely, and when told to what hospital we belonged, although against orders, he admitted us, and we were taken to the several points of interest.

On our return we called on an acquaintance of my companion's, and a plum pie was set before us. It was a tempting article of food at this time, and quickly disappeared before our voracious attacks. I have often thought of the satisfaction which I felt while furnishing the morsels rapidly to my palate, and the regret which filled my soul when the last mouthful was taken up, and only the red stain of the fruit lay temptingly on the plate.

Many surgeons, at this date of the war, were determined, by a systematic course of ill-treatment toward women nurses, to drive them from the service. To this class the surgeons in Wolf-street Hospital belonged, without any shadow of doubt.

Ten women nurses were here relieved within a year, many of them recognized and efficient helpers of the Government, which provided that one-third of its hospital nurses should be women. To the class of occasional nurses, who, with teaspoon and tumbler of jelly, passed through the ward giving a taste indiscriminately to every patient—the class who wrote long glowing letters of hospital life, and who never did a thing for the soldiers only what could be performed with gloves on jewelled hands—Wolf-street Hospital seemed an abode of plenty and comfort for all under its roof.

The glittering silver—the costly china—the easy chairs and mirrors, all giving evidence of care—the food which seemed all-sufficient, when seen in the raw material, inspired visitors with a great respect for the place, and few patients dared to brave the punishments sure to follow any declaration as to the insufficient, or ill-cooked food.

We were not cowered from any fear of corporeal punishment being inflicted; no thought of bearing a load of wood on our backs, and being marched around by a guard for hours, deterred us from speaking of the wrongs we endured; but rather thoughts of usefulness cut off, of the disgrace of dismissal, of being shut out where our hands could not minister unto the brave wounded—those considerations argued against all complaints, and kept sentinel over our tongues to their every utterance.

My work grew into a systematic round of tailoring—changing pockets, cutting down collars, and repairing coats and pants. One day the dispensary steward gave me a call, and requested me to mend a garment for him, which, in the debauch of the night previous, had been sadly rent. He sat down in the room, and said, after a few moments silence, "A man died in this room, in that very corner,

"Well," I replied, "his ghost doesn't haunt me. I never injured him."

"But I did," he continued, "I said if he didn't stop groaning so, I would strike him over the head with the broom stick, and I raised it over him, and he fell out of bed, and died in a little while."

I could not repress a shudder as the coarse man laughed in seeming satisfaction over the exploit, and I glanced furtively toward the comer, in which I seemed to see the pale ghastly face of the murdered dead, with glassy eyes fixed on his cruel murderer.

Was it true, that in the grossness of the soul in which this man was encased, no gleam of conscience could shed a ray? no compunctions stab at his selfish joy? He was a senseless clod, steeped in dissipation—a wreck with battered spars, and rotting hull, drifting to a swift destruction.

CHAPTER X.

THE spring of 1863 dotted the roadsides with dainty flowers, studding the grass like myriads of stars, and seemingly unconscious that the dust, which blew over them from the neighboring highways, was thrown from the advance of armies, which were to contend to the death for mastery.

In anticipation of a cavalry raid, the streets of Alexandria were stockaded—only at certain hours gates were opened, and carriages allowed to pass. Foot passengers clambered over the steps, and a feverish anxiety, by reason of our proximity to the rebels, kept us on the alert at all times.

When the magazine at Fort Lyon was blown up, feeling the shock, and hearing the bursting of shells, the throbbing blood hounded through my veins, causing a fearful commotion about my heart, and I went speedily to the highest lookout in the house, with the certainty that the rebels had come.

Visions of burning dwellings—of murdered women and children, of destruction and death— ran like lightning trains before my mind's eye, and when I learned the cause of the concussion, the terrible accident which had sent twenty-two men to their death without a moment's warning, and hurled as many more helplessly upon the sod, I could but feel a regret that they had not died while manfully resisting the foe—face forward.

Chancellorsville was fought. The dispirited troops had fallen back across the river, and our dead men filled bloody gaps in the long extended line of battle. I was eager for something to do— stitching aimlessly at tattered garments was not my work. The flush of indignation mantled my cheek, when I thought of the treatment to which loyal women had been subjected, when patriotic zeal had nerved them to leave home and its comforts to endure privation, sickness, hunger, and fatigue—and, after all, they were held from the good which they were eager to do.

When I could throw off these feelings, and get out into the free air, I found many places in Alexandria which interested me, because of the associations connected with them. The Marshall House, within which Col. Ellsworth fell, one of the first to die for his country, I explored to the very loft, from which he was bearing the rebel flag, when the traitor's hand directed at him his death shot. I also stood on the landing, where the avenger smote the murderer, and memory bore me back to that May day, when the tidings of the death of the lamented young Colonel "were borne through the whole land with electric speed, inciting others to catch up the fallen sword. It seems well, at times, to go back, even for a moment, in memory to the glorious acts of the brave men who gave their lives for the nation. It is our duty thus to honor them. History may write their names upon its pages—yet we, who are blessed through the sacrifice, should engrave their names upon the tables of our hearts, and be pleased to ponder upon their immortal deeds.

My mind was carried back to the recorded incidents of his life, to the hours of his death, and through the journey, when they bore the martyr to his native State, and a nation mourned over the victim to a cold and brutal murder.

The wife of Jackson returned to Alexandria, while I was there, soliciting alms, pleading the distress of unprotected widowhood, charging the citizens with making her desolate and penniless. They made up a generous purse for her, which she carried back into rebeldom, with all the information which she could gather relative to our forces, and the prevalent feeling in regard to the war.

A slave pen still stood within the city's limits, with auction block standing about it, and high stone wall surrounding it on three sides, the other wall made up of an old building, in which the human "chattels" had been thrust, in dirt and darkness, to await their transfer to new masters.

Blood spatters were on the wall of the house, and stained the auction blocks, suggesting horrible thoughts of lashings and agony, which were no sadder than the wrenching away of those dusky men and women from home, and children, and friends.

What sighs had gone up from that dreadful square; what cries and groans had appealed to hearts grown callous in the traffic in blood;

what unspeakable wretchedness of mind had these creatures endured, with the lash, the knife, and the blood-hound frequently their only reward for a life of toil.

The building was occupied by' ragged contrabands, huddled together in indolence, and filth, and poverty. They evinced a strange sense of freedom, and seemed perfectly secure while lines of men were marching in proud blue uniforms to drum-beat and bugle-call to guard them. They felt, where feeling was possible, where it had not been crushed out by life-long bondage, that they stood between the combatants, the prize for which they were contending. They had unbounded faith in "Massa Lincoln's soldiers."

This pen—degrading, disgraceful association— was used for the safe keeping of men who wore the blue uniform of Union soldiers, and who, for trifling offences, were put under guard in that loathsome pen, when the very dust was alive with vermin.

One man from our hospital was thrust in, but released in a few days, literally covered with vermin, and burning with rage at this insult to his manhood. He ran away to his regiment, well knowing that he could not be taken for desertion, and defying the keepers who used their brief authority to heap insult on men immeasurably their superiors.

When will the injustice of these things ever be wiped away? Many of the very men who exercised such contemptible temper while in their official capacity, know that, even though peace has usurped the din of war, they are hardly safe so long as soldiers, live, who, in putting off the uniform of their country's military service, did not put off the embittered feelings which were engendered by their insolence.

One amongst the little incidents which relieved the monotony of our life, was the rushing into town of the laborers who were repairing the Warrenton Railroad. They came in the utmost confusion—tent-poles, frying-pans, coffee-pots, tent- cloths, horse equipments jumbled together—with terror-whitened faces, and beating hearts, as if they had heard the bugle-call of the enemy ringing out on the air.

73

To the disappointment of many, it turned out only a scare, and they returned again to their work.

But time was drawing me near to the close of my labors in Wolf Street. One morning I went to the kitchen to make the biscuits for breakfast, the cook, who was from near the city of Auburn, and therefore seemed near to me, having promised me enough for my own meal in return. While waiting for them to bake, Dr. Stewart passed through, without saying a word. I was unconscious of committing any crime, and therefore gave no heed to the incident. When my relief papers were handed to me, in the forenoon, I had not the slightest idea of the charges brought against me, and went to the surgeon's room to ascertain.

I could get no satisfaction, only that there was no need of so many women in the hospital, but if Dr. Page was willing I might stay. Thus begging like a street vagrant for the privilege of remaining in Government employ, I went to Dr. Page, and was told that the accusation was doubtless a flimsy one, and if Dr. Stewart would countermand the order, of course I could remain. To Dr. Stewart again I hastened, smothering my pride, and choking down my rising indignation. I was told that I could consider the order countermanded, and could remain until after the anticipated battle, but I had better go and see Miss Dix first.

So, taking the steamer, I journeyed to Washington, to acquaint the superintendent of the state of affairs. She declared herself satisfied with the arrangement which had been made for the present, and returning to the hospital, my first greeting was in the shape of my second relief papers, ordering me to report to Miss Dix without delay. The boats left for Washington every hour through the day, from seven in the morning to the same hour in the evening.

Miss Dix was astounded, and met me with the query, "Miss Bucklin, what have you come for now?" In all my distress of mind—the fear of disgrace, the shame of being sent home—I could not suppress a smile at the ridiculousness of my situation in twice appearing, the same day; but as she listened to my detail of the circumstances, her surprise gave way to indignation at this treatment of her nurses.

74

There was no vacant place for me, she said; what should she do with me was the question of the hour. I was too young for field duty, and even if not, the battle was still delayed, and no more help was needed, for there were no freshly wounded soldiers. But I plead to remain—plead when boys in blue would have given half their life for the freedom of going, to escape the brutal tyranny of men whose insignia of office wa,s the solo indication of superiority.

And in this freedom lay the supreme blessedness of being , a woman. No compulsion of serving under hard human task masters when weary, with hands tired of the service which they had been eager to render; the enthusiasm and patriotic fire all turned, like the fabled apple, to ashes at the touch of real hospital life; chilled, hungry, browbeaten and driven out from hospital to hospital. Yet there is at times in the soul a feeling of love for one's bleeding country, and its suffering heroes, which makes it impossible to turn the eyes and feet homeward.

Thus, in the lull which followed a first series of conflicts in May, 1863, we waited for the next terrible shock. Determined to brave everything in order to be at hand, when, from the struggle, men should lie helpless on the field of battle, I remained in Alexandria, finding board at the house of Mr. Nichols, chief of engineers, whose family had come on with a few effects from Philadelphia, to be near him, and give him the comforts of a home. Here I sewed, and at times varied the employment by distributing Sanitary stores through some of the hospitals in Alexandria.

Sometimes, accompanied by one of the daughters, I made short excursions into the open country. One day I set out in search of a hospital patient, who had broken through the hard restraint, and gone without equipments or horse to join his regiment. We had heard that he was lying low in camp, a short distance from the city.

The camp presented a pretty picture, as the men gathered around the little circle of fires, over which the coffee was boiling, and by which, tethered to a stake, the faithful horse of each soldier waited for the breaking of the quiet. Steadily and persistently we made our way amongst the men; knowing them to be usually respectful men, we had no fear of insult; and at last drew near the house and grounds of a rebel woman, guarded by soldiers in blue uniforms.

Our request to be allowed to wander through the garden and admire the flowers was ungraciously refused, and we walked on, still uninformed in our inquiries after the wounded cavalryman. We had been only a few moments at the house on our return, when in stalked the soldier for whom we had made useless search—no wounds upon his person, and returning strength in his frame.

He gave us a little sketch of his adventures; told how, unmounted and unequipped, he had gone out in search of his regiment, and, soon after joining it, they had come in contact with rebel cavalry. During the fray, the horse of a rebel soldier, who had just fallen from his saddle, shot dead, galloped up to his side with a friendly neigh, and he accepted the ownership as providential. He had just come in—had driven down a stake, thrown off his saddle, and laid the reins over it, previous to searching for old friends at the hospital. There, missing me, he had inquired his way to my temporary home. After a friendly cup of tea, he departed on his way, leaving me thankful that the rumor of his wounded condition was unfounded.

The scorching sun appeared to catch with burning fingers upon the hills, and the languid leaves hung motionless in the hot air. Northward, the legions of rebellion were known to be sweeping, and somewhere—although our lips dared not utter our thoughts—we knew the Union army was in close pursuit. We knew, also, that this march could not be endured long without a conflict, and the breathless silence was ominous, of the dread horror which would soon paralyze many a heart with wretched woe.

At last, upon Pennsylvania's soil, the long lines of blue and grey grappled with each other in conflict. Through the streets, over lovely meadows, in tangled, rocky ravines, up wooded hill-slopes, along the edge of jagged rocks, and, alas! even in that silent resting-place of the village dead, where the inscriptions upon white tombstones told the names and virtues of those who had gone to heaven from the peaceful home, there they lay, as though an earthquake had upheaved them from thousands of graves.

Rolling into trickling rivulets, and dyeing them blood-red, foes strangled and smothered each other, while those who fell backward into the blood-dripping gorges died, howling curses up into the smoke-clouded air. Trees, broken and stripped of their foliage, were the only many silent witnesses to the death agony of men whom the deadly minnie sought out. Everywhere the grass had been moistened with blood, everywhere the grain had fallen under the trampling wheels of artillery, and everywhere startled horses were plunging in their harness. Everywhere the young orchards had given shelter to a contending soldiery, and over the threshold of every house wounded men had been borne, and pale-faced women had nerved themselves up to look upon the great agony of death.

In barns and under sheltering trees, where the shells and cannon balls and deadly bullets were at times flying, the surgeons plied their keen- edged saws, while the horrid rasps grated on ears, which would feign have shut out the dread sounds. Men were shot dead as they crawled away to seek a shelter from the storm, where they might die more peacefully from their fatal wounds. Hell seemed to have vomited up its legions, with its own lurid flames, and to have influenced many desperate souls to seek out their mangled victims.

Days passed, and we knew they needed help. We knew they needed more than could be gathered from the surrounding country, and we besought Miss Dix to allow us to go. I could make one, I thought, in the scores which were needed.

But, "No, you are too young for field duty," was the constant reply, and I chafed under the command which I dared not openly disobey. At last the gate was opened for me, and I passed through. Two weeks had gone by, and, one day, Mr. Knapp, of the Sanitary Commission, said to me, as I was tarrying in my restlessness at the Home, "Miss Bucklin, will you go to Gettysburg, and help distribute stores?"

I replied that I wished to go; more than that, it was in my heart to hasten there, but I had been positively forbidden to go, by the woman whom I acknowledged as my director.

"Go with Mrs. Caldwell," he said, "and I will stand between you and all blame."

"I will go," I said, and twenty minutes remained in which to gather up a little bundle of clothes, and roll them in a newspaper, to eat my supper, and go on board the train.

Friday afternoon we left Washington, and arrived at Baltimore in the evening, when the first person who met me in the hotel parlor where I stopped was Miss Dix, on her return from Gettysburg.

"Where are you going, child," she said, looking into my face with keen searching glances.

"To Gettysburg, madam," I replied.

"And did I not forbid you—why do you disobey my orders?"

Mrs. Caldwell related the persuasion which had been brought to bear upon me, and the kind superintendent, with no chiding, forgave me, and said, "Report to the Seminary Hospital for duty."

CHAPTER XI.

ON Saturday we entered the battle town. Everywhere were evidences of mortal combat, everywhere wounded men were lying in the streets on heaps of blood-stained straw, everywhere there was hurry and confusion, while soldiers were groaning and suffering.

Stripped of cattle and sheep—stores and houses robbed, still the people of Gettysburg stood nobly by their defenders. The women brought forth their contributions of bandages and lint, and poured out with unsparing hand their hidden delicacies, such as wines and jellies, like oil upon the sea of suffering humanity.

It seemed impossible to tread the streets without walking over maimed men, who had fallen in the shock of that July's fire, in which the sun seemed almost intent upon vieing with cannon and rifle in destructive heat. They lay like trees uprooted by a tornado, with summer's leafy crown upon them. With manhood's strength, and youth's vigor, and comeliness, they lay on the bloody ground, sick with the pains of wounds, grim with the dust of long marches and the smoke and powder of battle, looking up with wild haggard faces imploringly for succor.

In all their pride of health and usefulness— like the glossy leaved trees which sun, and rain, and air, and deep sucking roots had nourished— they were cut down, and lay upturned—their strength withering—their lives slowly ebbing away, the blood drops still oozing from deep wounds, their pulses intermitting, and their hearts fluttering in the spirit struggle.

I felt as if I could not be too thankful that I had been sent to aid with my well-nerved strength in the terrible work before us. Soon, rain fell copiously, washing out with its softly penetrating fingers the gory stains from among the grain and grass.

A carriage took us out from Gettysburg to the tent, which had partially been fitted up for Dr. Caldwell's wife,- but neither bed nor seat of any kind had been put in— only the rough-boarded floor lay under us, soaked through and through with the falling rain.

It was impossible to remain there in comfort— we were weary with travel, and needed rest to recruit ourselves for labor, so back to the town we were driven, where we found shelter in the house of a citizen, whose wife had been cooking for the Sanitary Commission. An elegant supper of chickens, biscuit, sauce, sweet-cake, and coffee made our appetites at peace with us under the roof, and our first night was passed within the little circle of a few miles, in which so many horrors had been lately enacted.

I was told, when asking to be directed to the Seminary Hospital, that I was not needed there, but that urgent necessity for woman's work existed in the field, and I must consent to go there for duty. Also that the patients from the Seminary were soon to be brought to the field and that that hospital was to be broken up. So on the following morning—a lovely dawning of the Sabbath— we took our way up to the hospital ground, where five hundred tents had already been erected.

It was the field on which the first guns were fired in that memorable battle. The sun shone brilliantly on the grass and leaves, wet with the rain of yesterday, and the round drops glittered like little stars wrought upon them by the swift embroidering fingers of the night.

I shall never forget that morning or that scene. Painted in truthful and glowing colors it still hangs on memory's walls unfadingly, and I have only to turn to that July, of 1863, to behold it fresh in all its glorious beauty.

The thousands of souls which had gone up from that grand circle of hills, within the waning and waxing of half a moon, the bloody dews which had dripped from the grass blades, and lowly flower leaves, and the too unmistakable agony of thousands of souls, had all made that spot a consecrated place.

I felt as though it were profane to speak with even assumed cheerfulness, while treading over it, although the long lines of white tents glimmering along the distant wood-side, spoke with a comforting earnestness of the many whom shot, and shell, and cold steel had failed to destroy.

A line of stretchers, a mile and a half in length, each bearing a hero, who had fought nigh to death, told us where lay our work, and we commenced it at once. I washed agonized faces, combed out matted hair, bandaged slight wounds, and administered drinks of raspberry vinegar and lemon syrup, while Mrs. Caldwell wrote letters to those who were waiting in dread suspense for news of their soldier, little knowing that he lay stretched on a narrow bed, weak with loss of blood, longing for the presence of those who were glad to be near him with their loving attentions when lying sick beneath the lowly roof among his native hills. Nor did many of the suffering brave ones know how the river of death flowed riplessly only a stone's throw before them.

The Sanitary Commission here did its work of mercy. Here it served its legitimate purpose with all the strength of its great humane heart. Without its generous supplies, untold suffering would have visited us, for Government stores could not be obtained, and in view of the host of wounded the ordinary hospital supplies were as a drop of water in the depths of the cool, silent well.

The hospital lay in the rear of a deep wood, in a large open field, a mile and a half from Gettysburg, and overlooking it, the single line of rail which connected the battle town with the outer world sweeping it on one side, and winding through the woods. In this open field our supplies were landed from Washington. Whole car loads of bread were moulded through and through, while for a time we were sorely pinched for the necessaries of life.

It needed only time to right this pressing want. We soon had a Government kitchen, a low diet, and an extra diet kitchen, with several large stoves, and large caldrons in which to make the soup which was always served for dinner. One set of men were detailed for soup-making, another for roasting beef, another for cooking vegetables, and when the great oven was prepared, the bread for the whole hospital was baked in its heated depths.

We were the first women on the ground, but the number soon increased to forty, including seven Government nurses. One woman superintended the extra diet, having several under her charge to do the cooking.

The hospital tents were set in rows—five hundred of them—seeming like great fluttering pairs of white wings, brooding peacefully over those wounded men, as though to shelter them from further evil. "Walks were thrown up between these rows, in order that they might dry quickly after the summer rains. The ground, now sodded —soon to be hardened by many feet—-was the only floor in the wards or in our quarters. The latter, with those of the surgeons, were set at the edge of the woods, where the sunlight broke through the green leaves and down upon the brown mould grown rich with the decay of years.

There was always a strange interest awakened in my mind by those grand old woods, wherein the screeches of shells had resounded, frightening the birds from their nest, and hurrying them away from the haunts of war and death.

My tent contained an iron bedstead, on which for a while I slept with the bare slats beneath, and covered with sheets and blanket. I afterwards obtained a tick and pillow, from the Sanitary Commission, and filled- them with straw, sleeping in comparative comfort. I soon found, however, that the wounded needed these more than I, and back I went to the hard slats again, this time without the sheets, which were given for the purpose of changing a patient's blood-saturated 'bed.

As time passed, and the heavy rains fell, sending muddy rivulets through our tents, we were often obliged in the morning to use our parasol handles to fish up our shoes from the water before we could dress ourselves. A tent cloth was afterwards put down for a carpet, and a Sibbly stove set up to dry our clothing. These were ofttimes so damp, that it was barely possible to draw on the sleeves of our dresses. By and by I had the additional comfort of two splint-bottomed rocking chairs, which were given me by convalescent patients, who had brought them to the hospital for their own use, and on departing left them a legacy to me. With these a stand was added to my furniture. I here learned how few are nature's real wants. I learned how much, which at home we call necessary, can be lopped off, and we still be satisfied; how sleep can visit our eyelids, and cold be driven away with the fewest comforts around us.

After all there seems to be a craving of the soul for unutterable joys, which keeps the restless body on its ceaseless round to find the means of gratification, in earthly surroundings; and we, poor blind spirits, grope darkly on in our house of clay for what we cannot find, while the soul will not cease its yearnings. After life's journey, with its perishable concerns, is over we can only hope to be satisfied.

Mrs. Caldwell and myself were soon only two amidst a throng of women eager to help in the good work. Women from Gettysburg, who were unnerved at the first sounds of advancing conflict, and whose houses had been rudely entered by some villainous Texan desperadoes, came here to help bind up the wounds of their defenders, and administer comfort to those whose hands had been turned against them for more than half of the wounded men in the hospital were rebel soldiers, grim, gaunt, ragged men—long-haired, hollow-eyed and sallow-cheeked. It was universally shown here, as elsewhere, that these bore their sufferings with far less fortitude than our brave soldiers who had been taught, in sober quiet homes in the North, that while consciousness remained, their manliness should suppress every groan, and that tears were for women and babes.

With the same care from attendants, and the same surgical skill, many more of the rebels died than of our own men—whether from the nature of their wounds, which seemed generally more frightful, or because they lacked courage to bear up under them, or whether the wild irregular lives which they had been leading had rendered the system less able to resist pain, will always remain a mystery with me. The truth of the assertion however is corroborated by army nurses all over the land.

Of twenty-two rebels who were brought into my ward at one time, thirteen died, after receiving the same care that was given to our men. Their wounds were severe, and their courage unequal to the despair which preyed upon them.

It was quite a study to see and ponder upon the contrast between the men of the two sections.

Those who were reared among the rugged hills, where they tilled the ground, and ate their bread by the sweat of their brows, were independent, self-confident, intelligent, and possessed of a quiet courage which could only succumb to the immediate presence of death. Those who were brought up in luxury and idleness were sullen and desponding, and groaned with pain. When convalescent the rebels were even too indolent to pluck from their garments the vermin that seemed to be swarming in every seam, while this employment formed the daily and apparently exciting pastime of our brave men, as soon as able to move about.

The rebels, who were prisoners of war, as yet had no reason to sink under the generous fare and kindly nursing they received; and the bare fact of capture could hardly have wrought any disadvantage in their condition.

Soldiers in blue, who had been in Southern prisons, told of the perfect discipline of the Confederate troops—how completely the leaders held in control the men who acknowledged the supremacy of wealth and culture long before the tide of war swept over the land. They endured hard fare without a murmur, and toilsome marches through midnights, when the steady tramp of the brigades roused the Union prisoners who were huddled together in the open air to sleep, and almost awed them into silent respect for the ragged soldiers of the rebellion.

The spirit which held them through all the long years of deadly peril seemed as enthusiastic as the spirit which fired a few of our troops, who in the first flush of enthusiasm went down to "whip them out in three months at most." Bitter complaints against Government, when Government was not responsible for their hardships; loud murmurs against long marches and stinted rations were seldom heard from the grey-clad soldiers, who silently endured on and almost depended upon their leaders for their thoughts.

Had the Confederate troops possessed the same spirit as our own, the rebellion would never have outlived its infancy. But instead, all through the South the full tide of patriotism swelled high, and women gave all they had to the cause, and made every sacrifice with heroic fortitude. When prisoners returned to us it was with a duller

84

confidence in the ultimate success of our arms, in view of this seeming united state of the South. They were not sharp-visioned enough to pierce the rind of the fair hanging fruit, and knew not that within it was filled with the ashes of error, because God and liberty had withheld their ripening agencies from it.

The strictest military rule could not utterly drive demoralization from our ranks. There was no complaint of this among the Southern leaders, and no signs of its working amongst those whom we held as prisoners of war.

A commendable spirit of devotion, generally unknown amongst our soldiers, pervaded the rebels, and while our men were singing and joking, morning and evening prayers were being said, and Old Hundred chanted by their lips.

Notwithstanding their hostility to us Northerners, I had much respect for them, and felt, when I watched their intense sufferings, that only an honest feeling could have driven them into such a conflict.

Perhaps some of these men died repentant, coming back in spirit to their allegiance to the old flag, and learning that Northern men and women, after all, were human creatures, capable of generously dealing with even a prostrate foe. That some appreciated the kindness done them I know, for I often received looks of thanks, and words of sincere gratitude.

They learned lessons in this close contact with the Northern element, which no doubt came to them as scattered seeds and have disseminated a clearer idea of our character amongst those to whom a portion of them returned. I knew that no estimate could be formed of the intelligence of the people of the South from the majority of their soldiers, in dirty, ragged grey—amongst whom a hydrophobic fear of water seemed to prevail.

I listened in considerable amusement to the questioning of one, who was interrogating a male nurse in long drawn accents of indolent helplessness, as he lay wrapped over with bandages:

"Am—I—so—very—black—nurse?"

"No, you aint so very black, nor you aint very d—d white," was the unsoftened reply.

"Then—what—do—you—wash—my—face for—every—day?" he inquired.

And herein lay a wide contrast between those so fearful of soap and water, and our men so eager to feel the splash of cool drops upon fever-heated face and burning brow. Habit may settle this feeling to some extent, but a naturally delicate sense shrinks from personal uncleanliness as from a fearful sin. A pure man will seek to be pure in body, and will be when not absolutely deprived of facilities for cleanliness.

Many of them died in prison pens, shut out from access to water, when, with its strengthening influence diffused through their starving bodies, they might have kept life and hope within them till the day of deliverance came.

And soldiers have told me how the simple process of bathing, after a long and weary march, renovated their frames, while others, who had neglected it, arose stiffened and wearied in the morning, their natural vigor seemingly impaired.

CHAPTER XII.

SWIFT organization characterized the movements of Dr. Goodman, the chief of hospitals, who marked out the plan under which ours should work. It was placed in charge of Dr. Chamber- lain. The original five hundred tents, spread in rear of the old woods, soon increased to many more; and each nurse was assigned her position, and work went forward with a will.

For several days our duties had been general. I did whatever my hands found to do, drawing" stores in food, bandages, and cooling drinks from the Sanitary Commission—administered alike to friend and foe—inditing letters to rebel mothers and union wives; finding my heart and soul engaged in the cause of bleeding humanity to an extent which banished personal discomfort from my mind, for the time, altogether.

Hunger gnawed at my vitals; swollen feet almost refused to support me; wearied limbs found but little rest upon the bare slats of my bedstead through the short summer nights. While the delirium of pain drove others from their beds, bewildered with phrenzy, with sleep banished from the hot eyelids, there was little opportunity for care of self. In one case, a man ran up and down the ward, with cries and groans, while we could but hear and sympathize—our thoughts asking us, why should we complain of hard beds and aching feet?

Hunger only made eatable the wretched food which was spoiled in its long heated journey over the dusty road from Washington. It was with much interest that we watched the progress of the new kitchen, the advent of the monster stoves, the filling of the huge caldrons, which set under the full glare of the sun—for out of their depths were to issue comforts for the many maimed heroes, and strength be given to others to do their duty by them.

The cook detailed for the nurses learned to forage with remarkable success, and we were soon well supplied with food, although the rations issued to seven Government nurses would have proved a scanty supply doled out to forty grown women—none other than Government nurses being entitled to rations in the hospital.

Citizens remembered us in the way of brimming pails of milk, of rolls of golden-hued butter, of luscious fruit, which had ripened since dead men lay under the shadows of the green orchard boughs in those July days. Chickens, which had escaped the hands of the many hungry ones, were poured into the hospital, and disappeared rapidly before the sharpened appetites of four thousand men.

The Christian Commission established itself on the ground, and did its work nobly. Both Sanitary and Christian Commission tents were located on the edge of the woods, in convenient proximity to our quarters. One woman, employed by the Christian Commission, daily took a team and scoured the country round for the solid things which only farmers usually possess in plenty. From her we obtained generous gifts of fowls, eggs, milk and butter.

One woman, whose house I afterwards visited— who, while on her way to Gettysburg to alarm the citizens on the last day of June, was caught in the grey lines of the marauders, and who, with great difficulty, escaped, and returned homeward—came 'to us, and pitched her tent with the nurses—and for four months worked for the wounded soldiers of her country. Many a pail of butter, and rich jug of milk she brought back from her home, after brief visits, and they were dispensed with a willing hand.

For two weeks, at the last, she lay a prisoner in the cloth-house, unable to return to her family, or to attend to her duties in the ward. I was awakened by her groans one night, and, getting up, went to her tent, which adjoined my own, and found her in great distress. A fire seemed to be needed, whereupon I split up a handful of wood, and started it into a blaze in my little Sibbly stove. I then went out into the darkness to— they were a great terror—the uncovered wells, which had been dug on the verge of the timber to supply the hospital with water. I drew a supply, and hastened back, heating it in a quart cup by holding it inside the door of my stove.

For the information of those who may not know, I will state that the shape of a Sibbly stove is that of an inverted funnel—the wide end being set over the fire, which is built on the ground, and the smaller end emitting the smoke. It is not a very convenient contrivance for heating water, especially when any one is in a critical condition, and requires prompt assistance.

I brought the doctor from his quarters, hastened to my ward for the camphor bottle, rousing many sleepers to wonder what the nurse wanted at that late hour, and did all in my power to relieve her. But, by the positive command of the surgeon, I was forbidden to attend to her after that night, as she had a family, on whom her claims were imperative. Her husband and daughter soon arrived, and ministered to her wants until she was able to be moved to her own home.

In the ward assigned me, after the first days of disjointed effort were over, there were three wives and two mothers, who had been prompted, by the solicitude in their hearts, to visit dear ones who lay helpless on hospital beds. One was the mother of a young hero—a volunteer from the city of Utica, who, in full possession of his senses, sat without a moan, while the surgeon took twenty- six pieces of shattered bone from his wounded shoulder. But his face was bloodless as that of a corpse, and cold sweat drops stood on his brow, in evidence of the terrible agony which he endured.

Another Pennsylvania mother, whose son had stood under the iron hail, and bore, in his quivering body, wounds from five minnie balls, was busy in the ward caring for his comfort. In cases of this kind, many eyes were attracted to the boy thus fortunate in having a mother's care, and many hearts longed to be where a fond mother's thoughts and prayers went up constantly for them.

We witnessed a happy meeting one day, when a father, who was also a soldier, came into the ward, and met his wife sitting at the bedside of their son. Many tears were shed around them, which they knew not of, nor could have regarded in the full thankfulness of their hearts that the life of the dear boy had been spared to them. This mother left us, and took her son with her, he being able to endure the fatigue of travel.

One soldier, in the presence of his wife, was striving to endure with calmness the pain of a fractured thigh and an amputated arm. No hand but hers could smooth his pillow, no other give him the nourishment to support life; no fingers were as tender as hers over the throbbing wounds, where worms were feeding upon the living, human flesh. But his life was spared, and the brave and anxious wife cared little for hardships, so long as his life could be saved to her, and she could look into his eyes, and know that she was a comfort to him in this victorious conflict with death.

As soon as he was able to be moved, he was transported to Baltimore, where she obtained a furlough for him, and carried him triumphantly to their New Hampshire home.

Another wife, clasping to her bosom a little child of eighteen months, sat for hours with bowed head, leaning over the prostrate form of her husband, whose frightful wound made it necessary to keep him stupified with morphine, so that his unearthly groans should not keep the whole tent in undue excitement.

A horrid fissure, through which a man's head might pass, had been made by a shot tearing through his bowels, and rendering it impossible to do anything to relieve him. He lay in this unconscious stupor, and the stricken wife waited in vain for some signs of recognition. A humane heart lay in the bosom of our surgeon, and he allowed the drug to exhaust itself, and consciousness to return, that he might recognize his wife and child before he died.

Slowly it passed away, and his mangled body was racked with intensest suffering. He lay on his face, with his eyes turned toward her, that, when his senses revived, she might he the first to meet his gaze. After a while he looked up—the wild glare of pain in his eyes— and said, as he saw whose face bent over him,

"Oh! Mary, are you here?" His groans were terrible to hear, and in mercy he was again given the opiate, and slept his life out in the deep breathing of unconsciousness.

How our hearts were pained for that wife, sitting motionless beside the body, holding in her lap the little boy who was so soon to be fatherless, tearless in her great agony, stricken as by the withering stroke of palsy—yet breathing and living. I brought her plates full of food from the Christian Commission, which never withheld its hand when sorrow like this was made known to them.

Broken-hearted she returned to the desolate home which should never know the sunlight of pleasure again, while her soldier's body rested under the distant sod on which was spilt an ocean of heroic blood.

Another wife, with only the devotion which true affection inspires, watched her husband through long days of pain, till danger was past, and had the satisfaction of knowing that recovery was rapidly progressing.

A widow, whose husband lay somewhere in his gory shroud of blue under the battle clods, tried to administer to the wants of th'e patients in the hospital, hut the sense of bereavement, and the shock it bore her heart, so wrought upon her that her heart was steeled against those who lay prostrate in grey uniforms, and she refused to give food or drink or aid of any kind to them. She persisted in regarding them as the wanton murderers of her beloved husband.

That instinct, which in the highest brute creation resents an injury to itself or its loved, was blindly rampant in her chilled heart, She had not yet learned that her noblest revenge was to do good to those very men; to bind up their wounds, and send them home to their wives that they might be spared a like desolation of heart.

She was necessarily discharged. Although good and faithful amongst our own men, the rules of the hospital rendered it necessary to treat rebel and union soldiers alike, in all things pertaining to care and comfort.

One woman worked with us through the whole period of four months, after she had taken the body of her soldier son from the trench in which it was buried, and carried it home to sleep with kindred dust. She had sought him out from the dreadful pit, and lifted him up with her own hands, her motherly heart yearning over the dead boy with unutterable anguish, nerving her to endure the horrible contact with the putrid corpses of the slain. Now, other mother's sons were stricken down, who with care might be restored to those who loved them, and her brave unselfish heart could work for that end.

Others would have perhaps taken the clay to its first resting-place, and sat down quietly to mourn over the desolation which death had wrought, but this heroic mother, with an unselfishness most commendable, sought to save sons to other loving mothers—a work which should make her name blessed forever.

Daily the sympathizing heart could here go out in deepest compassion to the many wretched sufferers who lay under our white hospital tents. One little fellow named Galagher, who in his bed looked like a boy of ten years, bore manfully eleven painful wounds in his slender body. Soon, however, he grew dull and desponding, and having lost his appetite, seemed rapidly going down to the grave. Such cases, where neither medicine nor food seemed to reach them, interested me deeply, and I studied over every available article of luxury which might be procured to stimulate the appetite, and induce the return of strength. I tried oyster soup at last, obtaining the material of the sutler, and "more! more!" was the feeble cry of returning life, till he began to rally from his despondency.

When it came his turn to be sent from the hospital, as all were, as rapidly as pronounced able, he could consume his rations with the strongest of them. A pot-pie was in the caldron, nearly ready for their hungry mouths, when the order came for them to go on board the cars and begin their tedious journey. How could they go without a taste of the nearly cooked dinner? I was determined they should not, and away I ran to the dish-house—the mud flying from my hurrying feet and my dress several inches deep with the clayey mass. Nothing could retard me, and going in, I grasped a pile of dishes, and started on my return, unheeding the hue and cry which was raised after me.

As I entered the ward, the pot-pie came in steaming hot, and was ladled out into dishes of every shape, and swallowed almost boiling with heat.' My little fellow said, "Oh, Miss Bucklin, let me have some to take with me," and I gave him a cup full, which he took into the cars, and no doubt relished considerably while on his journey.

CHAPTER XIII.

WHOLE wards were filled with rebels, who were attended by rebel nurses—one of officers only. A sharp contest often arose when the attendants met at the cook-house to draw food for their respective patients. Our men were often knocked down in the struggle, and the triumphant rebels appropriated all and everything upon which they could lay their hands.

According to their own version of affairs, it was not until they were sent to Baltimore, and confined in the West Buildings, that they began to realize themselves as prisoners of war. They had become sleek and fat, and the change from plenty to scarcity was a blow at their ravenous stomachs which they felt keenly.

Some of them were also scattered promiscuously through the other wards of the hospital. After a short time constant changes were being made, and rebel and union were put side by side. As fast as one bed was vacated, another wounded man seemed to spring up in the place, and we were always full to our utmost capacity.

Whence they came we could not tell; but doubtless, from the farm houses and the town, where they had been taken direct from the bloody field. They only seemed to be sent here as those who had cared for them thought the hospital a better place. Amongst others, who had been gathered into the rebel army, we found loyal men, who were only too glad to fall wounded prisoners of war into our hands. They presented quite a contrast to those who were bitter with hatred towards the North, and whose every breath was a curse on "Lincoln's invaders."

Three men with fractured thighs were brought in one day, and bound up with heavy bandages, in frames arranged for the purpose. For days they groaned in agony—the flesh decaying from their bones, and the putrid scent poisoning the very air they breathed. Two of them were taken out in a dying condition, and laid under a canvas, for their presence was unbearable to the other inmates of the tent. One lived only about an hour, while the other lingered till after nightfall before his spirit left its earthly tenement. I shudder, even now, as I think of the awful deaths, and realize that, somewhere, some poor souls mourn for them as dead—yet in blissful ignorance of the terrible manner of their death.

Oh! more welcome instant death on the field of battle—with face to the furious foe—than this long lingering, which saps the fountain of life, while the blood courses heavily through the blue veins, while corruption riots on the flesh, and the grave refuses to receive them until the breath of life is gone.

The third one of these awful sufferers died, also, in a few days—mercifully released from his pain.

A rebel, with a wounded knee, was brought in suffering acutely, and, the wound opening, a compress was put on, which, in a short time, cut through the dead flesh to the bare bone, when death gave him a welcome release.

Another little fellow, an orderly sergeant, only sixteen years of age, had a fractured thigh, the bone of which protruded some inches. It was cut off twice—the first time three days previous to his transfer to Little York Hospital, when three inches were sawed away, and, the day before leaving, four inches more.

He was worn to a skeleton—his thin hands seemed like the talons of a bird, and his sunken eyes looked with a strange lustre upon me, as I arranged the pads and pillows around him in the car, and saw his leg packed in the box, which the surgeon had ordered made for it. Again and again lie thanked me for my kindness to him; and then said, "I will try to write to you when I get there." The next news I received of him was from the hands of a soldier, who went away at the same time—and the little Ship had made port at last. His name was Ship. He died in three or four days after reaching the hospital, and when I remembered how helpless he would always be, and what a stormy ocean life was, I could but rejoice that he had anchored in the haven of rest in his youthfulness.

One of my number had a leg amputated very close to his body, and, suffering intense pain, steadily refusing to take the beef tea or stimulants, he rapidly wasted away to a skeleton. I tried to rouse him to realize his condition, and to converse with him about the future. He only said, in a short manner, "I will talk about that at a more convenient season."

A few nights later his stump bled, and reduced him to the very verge of the grave. One morning I asked him if he would like any letters written, for he was very weak, and life might not last long with him. After pondering a little while, he replied in the affirmative, and in feeble tones dictated an account of his wound, and of his general health—then paused abruptly. "And what shall I say of your prospects in the future, should you not recover," I asked. "Say nothing about it," he added, gloomily; and so the last message went to -tell the waiting ones that the sacrifice was finished, for he died that night, and I never saw his face again.

Another man, wounded in the elbow, lay for several weeks with his arm in one position, growing fleshy in the indulgence of a strong appetite, and when able to walk about, did so around the ward, remarking that he felt so much better, he believed he would often avail himself of the privilege. The same day he took another walk, and the weather being cold, raw and damp, he came in, had a chill, and the next day was dead.

He was intensely frightened, and gave himself up to die at the first symptom of the attack, and although many remedies were applied, all were in vain.

On one side of him, lay two Northern men, one wounded like himself in the elbow, the other with a fractured thigh, both had chills at the same time, in the same way, and recovered under the same treatment.

A great gaunt rebel was brought in ill with the typhoid fever; his mind was slightly shattered and we dared not cross him much, for he was a maniac in his passion. Soon, however, he gave signs of other affliction, and growing weaker and weaker every day, we finally determined to rid him of the pest.

He had not been able to endure the thorough cleansing, which it was the rule to give each patient on admittance to the hospital, and he was literally alive with the crawling vermin, which you could see working in his mustache and heard.

Determined to save him if possible, on the refusal of the men to cut his hair, or shave his face, which had not known a razor for three years, I took the revolting task upon myself. At arm's length, with sleeves pinned up, I severed his long hair, which bristled in unkempt disorder, and applied the lather and razor to his sharp sallow face, then saturated his head and beard with alcohol, to do its work at destruction.

The men nurses then took him, washed his body, changed his clothes, and laid him in a clean bed, so weak that he could scarcely lift his hands for days. But the cure was effectual, the blotches of raw eaten flesh healed up, and he recovered, being troubled no more from vermin than other patients were. It may seem strange to cleanly people, but it was impossible for soldiers entirely to avoid being troubled in this way. I have felt at times the discomfort myself—the keen hurt of pride, and the mortification—but by constant care and watchfulness have kept the number so few, as to give me only a temporary annoyance.

Many scenes transpired which drew tears from our eyes and filled our souls with pity for those who were still to live on after those they loved had gone. Death took the widow's son, and the aged father's staff. The remorseless bullets seemed vulture beaked, and tore alike into hearts throbbing with high hope, for whom earnest prayers were going up, and pierced as readily the vitals of those who knew neither kindred nor friends.

We were all much affected by the death of a young Michigan soldier, whose wound was in the back, and which discharged so fearfully that it was necessary to change both bedding and clothing twice a day, until, at last, the hope of recovery died out in his sick heart. Then the new life began to dawn upon his clouded sight. I entered the ward one morning, and found the men listening to the exhortations of the young Christian—many of them in tears. He said, "Come here, Miss Buck- lin," and, as I approached his bedside, he asked, "Ho you think I can live till my father can get here?" As he had been failing rapidly through the night, I thought it my duty to tell him the truth, and I said, "I fear you cannot?"

"If I take stimulants and beef tea in plenty, don't you think I may?" he questioned eagerly.

"We will do what we can," I answered, "I will telegraph for your father, and try the best to keep you up to meet him."

After a pause, he said, "I am not afraid to die. I have a bright hope that I shall soon meet my Saviour, where suffering is unknown, and where I shall be forever blessed. I thank you, and all of them for your long continued kindness to me, and I want to meet you in heaven—will you try to meet me there?"

I could only say, "I will—God being my helper." All day I gave him beef tea and stimulants freely, and left an abundant supply for the night.

Two days later his father came, meeting his son only to stand at his bedside in the night, and witness the flight of the triumphant spirit. The father said to me, "It was the brightest deathbed scene that I ever witnessed—and it was the happiest moment of my life, when I saw my boy pass so sweetly away from suffering into the arms of his Redeemer. It is all one can desire in this world."

And I could not restrain the words of gladness that fell from my lips, that the poor agonized soul had finished the sacrifice with such exceeding joy. As it was the duty of the women nurses to leave the ward at half-past eight o'clock, I was not beside him when death opened the gates of glory for his spirit to enter through.

For fifteen days, administering stimulants every few moments, I sat by the bedside of one of Pennsylvania's noble soldiers, named McMicken, who had lost his leg, and was prostrated nigh to the grave. The surgeon said to him often, "Me you wouldn't be here, if it wasn't for your nurse." But we could not save him. He died peacefully one night—receiving his summons, and going out silently to the land whence no traveller returns, and whither he goes burdened with no earth ills, to cloud the new life under heavenly skies.

His poor old father came to see him, but it was too late. We had seen him laid under the sod, and the withered fingers of autumn had strewn over his grave heaps of colored leaves, like a rude garland woven for the brave. He was the staff on which the old man had hoped to lean, when life's journey with him would near its close, and he wept tears which we could do nothing to check, and which, under the circumstances, we did not wish to check.

I collected together the few articles belonging to him, consisting of a comb and brush, a razor and strap, a looking-glass, a cigar, and a roll of bandages with which his limb had been dressed, and as he took them, he said, tremulously, "Oh! how much his poor mother will think of these things!" Surely, I thought, they will be a sorry comfort to the heart aching for the darling boy, who would never sit by their hearth again.

An interesting group, in one section of the ward, "was composed of five young men, who had each lost a leg in the battle. One was from Michigan, two from Massachusetts, and two from Pennsylvania. All of them recovered, and I often have the satisfaction of hearing from one and another of them.

A brother of Frank Ward, one of the five, came to Camp Letterman to take him to another hospital, hoping there to get a furlough—as none were given at Gettysburg, all being compelled to move before receiving them. We knew he could not be moved without a bed, and they could not obtain one, so I set myself about the task with the intention of succeeding. As we could not take a Government bedstead away from the hospital grounds, I changed mine with the Sanitary Commission. Thus I obtained a cot, with a spring head piece, on which we could spread blankets, sheets, and pillows, making it quite comfortable.

I received, on application, from the woman superintending the linen room, a Government pillow, having the appearance of having been used in a case of amputation. T threw it out of the door before her face, as an insult to the brave boy who had given so much to his country, and took a new hair pillow, regardless of the consequences, and made up the bed decently and in order.

He started on his journey in comparative comfort, and I learned afterward, therein feeling amply repaid for my trouble, that he arrived in Philadelphia, no more fatigued after his ride than would have been natural under the circumstances.

CHAPTER XIV.

The summer days glided swiftly away. The regular routine of hospital life was like the methodical operations of a thorough housekeeper. Men died, and in their empty beds others were speedily laid to recover or die also. Grain ripened in the Pennsylvania valleys, and fruit hung lusciously on the bending orchard boughs. Birds sung in the tops of the trees, under which, too preoccupied to drink in the momentary grandeur, nurses and surgeons took snatches of repose.

We grew familiar with sufferings of the in- tensest nature, for only those too badly wounded to be moved to other hospital points, had been left in Gettysburg, after the awful field had been gleaned. The hill slopes and wood front became the scene of busy hurrying to and fro. Nu' darted in and out with their bedraggled skirts and shaker bonnets, hither and thither from Christian to Sanitary Commission, and thence to the general cook-house, each one eager to secure for her patients the greatest amount of luxuries.

As only wounded men were in this field hospital, our duties were varied from what they had been at other points. The first round in the morning was to give the stimulants, and to attend to the distribution of the extra diet. After the thorough organization of the plan had been completed, we were not called upon to dress wounds, unless by special request, wound dressers being assigned to each section of the ward; but for a time, that duty had come next after the distribution of the extra diet.

.Beef tea was passed three times a day, stimulants three times, and extra diet three times— making nine visits which each woman nurse made a day to each of the two hundred men under her charge. This was done besides washing the faces and combing the hair of those who were still unable to perform these services for themselves, preparing the extra drinks ordered by the surgeons, and seeing that the bedding and clothing of every man was kept clean by the men nurses. We were not however responsible for any other neglect in the ward.

Each attendant had his work. First the surgeon in charge, next the hospital steward, then the ward surgeon, next women nurses, ward masters, men nurses, wound dressers, and night watch. The officer of the day made his round every two hours, day and night, ascertaining that no watchers were asleep, that they were performing their allotted duties, and to administer medical aid, if required.

There was no conflicting of duty—each knew the task assigned him, and was constrained to keep in utter silence the many thoughts, which, in civil life, would have been given forth without restraint. Yet, no doubt, this silence was best amidst so many conflicting opinions.

Each day, after the dinner hour was over, the kitchen was thoroughly searched for every scrap of meat, and any potatoes that may have been left. The nurses took their gleanings to their own quarters, with everything else out of which they could make a passable dish, and there the potatoes were peeled, and the meat cut in small bits. If we were fortunate enough to secure butter, eggs, sugar and milk, tempting messes were beaten up, and carried to the cook-house to be baked.

In the early morning, after reveille had awakened us from our slumbers, and the bugle-call summoned us to our duties, the frosty grass was soon thickly striped over with tiny paths, and the fallen leaves trodden into the ground. After a hurried toilette, we nurses hastened to the kitchen, and seized on frying-pan, or any other utensil in which we could submit our gleanings to the process of cooking.

On the hour, when the assistants, who had been busy taking up the regular diet to the wards, returned from that duty, our food was ready to go toward making up the meal, which to some, in their renewed strength, had been insufficient. The satisfaction with which they ate our extras repaid us for the scramble in obtaining them.

Often those poorly served by nurses, whose ambition was not like to ours, begged piteously of us for the food which they saw us carry by, but the distribution of it was strictly forbidden in this promiscuous manner, and we were obliged to deny them, hard as the necessity seemed.

One day, as I passed up by a ward, holding a freshly baked cake in each hand, I saw a soldier lying under a tent, which had been looped back to admit the soft air of the early autumn. He regarded me wishfully, and, as I neared him, he called out, "Oh, Miss Bucklin, do give me a piece." "I cannot," I said; "it is forbidden, and your nurse will bake you some." "No she won't; she ne er does any such thing for us," he replied. Again he begged for a taste, and again I was obliged to refuse him, although it was sad and harrowing enough to behold the pleading eyes, and surmise how he longed for it.

While the extra diet kitchen had been under the control of Mrs. Holstein, we had been forbidden this privilege of preparing extra food ourselves, and were not even allowed to go inside of the kitchen—she deeming it necessary to keep a guard, with fixed bayonet, at the entrance. Often she refused to fill the orders from our surgeon, remarking that he was the most unreasonable man she ever saw. When I reported back to him, after failing to receive what I had been refused, he often went to the kitchen himself, and, with his own hands, cooked the food, saying that what was the rightful property of the patients, that they should have.

His kindness to us won our highest respect, while it also made the contrast darker, when narrow-souled, selfish men, who held in utter disregard the wants of the wounded soldiers, were placed in authority.

My ward was especially" fortunate in being, for some time, under the charge of Dr. Jones, whose care for the well-being of his men was not delegated to under-officials.

Anything that it was in his power to do for us was ungrudgingly done, and many times he said to me, "I will give you orders for anything you want—only mention it to me."

To have known such a man redeemed one's faith, somewhat, in human nature, which, during these times, was often sorely tried. There were men, in whose presence you felt as if a whisky barrel was well represented, who had to be approached with all the deference due the insignia of office represented by their shoulder-straps. Often we felt that it was an insult to our womanhood to be constrained to give an outward show of respect when within there was nothing hut loathing and detestation.

When, in the darkness of midnight, a drunken surgeon staggered into the ward, and held at the tent-pole, swearing at the wondering patients, who were roused from their slumbers, and declaring he could not understand why the nurses had not uncovered the wounds for him to examine, he was generally confined until sober. It was difficult to see why, in the name of justice and common sense, he was retained, and why no punishment, or fine, or retention of pay was meeted out to him. For far less offenses men, wearing the uniforms of private soldiers, were put on bread and water diet within the dirty walls of a guard-house.

This surgeon, carelessly, and in disregard of duty, deputized to the wound-dressers all the care of the wounds. One fine-looking fellow, a son of Erin's isle, whose name was Peter Brock, was provoked by the neglect, and declared, with emphasis, that he would have his wounded shoulder examined by a surgeon—if he couldn't get one to look at it there lie would go where he could. He finally succeeded, by perseverance, in obtaining an examination.

He was found to be in a very critical situation, and one after another of the surgeons were called in, till a regular council of doctors was held over him in the ward. It was found necessary to take off a section of the bone, and the operation was begun in full view of the other patients.

After mangling him there for a time, partly holding him under the influence of chloroform, they removed him to the amputating room, where they paused awhile to have their photographs taken, the suffering patient lying in this critical condition. My blood boiled at the cruelty of the scene, but I could not avert the torture for a moment. For three hours he was kept under the knife and saw, and I was directed to hold my peace. He was brought back to his bed, as white as a dead man in his coffin, no semblance remaining of the ruddy-cheeked soldier who lay there three hours before, with strength in every part of his body, save the wounded shoulder.

"I give him into your special charge, Miss Bucklin," the doctor said, "and I shall be proud if you raise him." And raise him I did, although it seemed impossible when I first saw him, lying quite white and helpless before me.

I saw him depart for another hospital, wrapped in the grey overcoat belonging to the little rebel sergeant, who said he would never have any use for it again.

We were not forgotten by the people of Gettysburg. Day after day some tokens of their appreciation of us were manifested by them. Among other note-worthy incidents the choir came out twice each week to sing, in front of the wards, the old familiar hymns which these men loved.

From over the land generous streams poured down into field and hospital, and noble-hearted 12- men and women dispensed luxuries which were without prize in the incalculable good they did. Mrs. Brainard of Michigan, with her noble soul, entered into the work of distributing the supplies gathered up by the women of her State for the wounded and suffering. Mrs. Spencer, of New York, also aided in the good work.

Dr. Winslow, of the Sanitary Commission, did an impartial and generous work, and, as the summer passed, heavy drafts were still made on the constantly augmented supplies. The same generous Commission also sent cars each alternate day in which to convey the wounded to other hospitals —each time taking a certain class of wounds. To the cars each woman nurse went as her patients were being taken thence, her arms full of pads and pillows to adjust around the yet unhealed limbs of the departing boys, and taking a nice lunch for each to eat on his journey.

The making of these pads and pillows took away many a moment of mine, for I fancied I could fit them better than those 'who had never worked among the wounded. But I drew upon my devoted head, by thus doing, the severe displeasure of the overseer of the linen room, who reported me for taking hospital pillows, with which to stuff my pads. The surgeon in reprimanding me said, "Miss Bucklin, use all the pillows you want—you know they cost three dollars a pair, and that is more than a soldier's life is rated at here"—and I obeyed him to the letter.

Some moments of cheerfulness enlivened our clays—some light words were said even while the shadows of death lay thick about us. I remember being startled by a remark of the surgeon's, that he was going to recommend me for a pension, as having done more than any one man to put down the rebellion. On my puzzled inquiry as to his meaning, he referred to the death of the thirteen out of the twenty-two rebels, who had been placed under my charge.

Ladies came up to the hospital with bright flowers, which looked strangely on the hard hospital beds by faces so haggard and worn.

The old hero of Gettysburg, John L. Burns came up through our camp, with tottering steps, anxious to see live rebels. He gazed on them as though uncertain of their connection with the human species, and went hobbling away—his old wife following in his footsteps.

Sometimes we went, in our rambles, to various stores; at others, out into the surrounding country. In one of these I saw the hole in the door made by the bullet which struck the maiden, Jennie Wade, to the heart, as she stood moulding her bread at the table. At one of the stores I made the purchase of a hat, shakers and other head-gear being out of the market, and- this I hardly dared to wear, fearing the censure of the superintendent, who wished us to wear close shakers. When she came to make us a visit as she often, did, I threw it off in her presence.

CHAPTER XV.

On the discharge of a nurse her ward was given to me, and in it I found the man who had begged for the piece of cake and been refused. He was too ill to be indulged with anything of the kind now, else in my compassion I would have fed him with the best food obtainable. He died in a short time after; and in the six hours following, another one lay dead in the same section of the ward. My heart throbbed with pain to see them dropping off one by one, and look over into the full graveyard, where they lay sleeping in long unbroken ranks.

These soldiers were of the first who were buried in the new National Cemetery at Gettysburg, and they were laid to sleep under that dewy sod with military honors. At their burial the coffins draped with the flag preceded, the ambulances containing the women nurses followed, and then came the convalescents marching with reversed muskets to the plats of ground set apart for the dead of the particular State to which the deceased belonged.

In the hush of the lovely day, when the air seemed soft and bracing, we entered the cemetery, and reverently stood by the graves. Dr. Winslow, of the Sanitary Commission, officiated for the New York soldier, and the chaplain of the Christian Commission, for the one from Pennsylvania.

The bodies of our men, who had been buried, in the hospital cemetery, were afterwards exhumed, and each laid within the plat, appropriated-for the dead of his own State. But nearly two-thirds of the twelve hundred graves" which had been made there, were filled with rebel dead, who will sleep in their unknown resting-places until, the final awakening.

One of my boys, from & Wisconsin regiment, whom we called dim my, became convalescent, and hourly expected a furlough to go home. He had not yet been taken from the medicine list, and one morning, as usual, took the prescription, but was soon compelled to lie down. He was seized with a deadly coldness, and shivered incessantly; his muscles contracted with jerking movements, and great sweat-drops gathered on his cold forehead.

He sent for me, and, as I entered the ward, looked up and said, "It's all up with me now." I replied that we hoped yet to do something for him, but he shook his head doubtingly, and motioned for me to sit by his bed. The surgeon was summoned, but he could do nothing to break the chill of death, which was slowly stealing over him. He reached for my hand, and retained it, till one by one his senses left him. Just before the last convulsive shiver ran through his veins, one of the attendants took it from his grasp, remarking that it was a bad sign for any one to hold the hand of another when death came to the heart.

He was then too far gone to realize anything, and at eleven o'clock he died. The last prescription, by some awful mistake, was deadly poison, and nothing could have saved him. I had often heard him talk of home and friends, but do not know if they ever learned how he died, when he saw the dear prospect of soon meeting them in the near future.

Thus they perished; but the terrible weight of woe did not fall on any one soul, else it had crushed it into the depths of the grave. We sorrowed, but not as those who held those departed ones so dear to the heart; and the days came and went, carrying other separations in their train, and leaving their saddening influences.

One of the Ohio boys came to me one night, and said, "We expect we've got to go off in the morning, and we haven't any lunch; couldn't you fix us something to-night V

As I had prepared lunches often for the boys, when we knew of their departure long enough beforehand, I concluded to attempt a surprise movement, and told him if he would go with me to the kitchen, and help gather the articles together, I would make some fried cakes—it was the best I could do for them. We went over to the bakery, and got a large piece of light bread- dough; then to the store-house for eggs, sugar and spices; then to the tent, where the surplus fat was deposited, for the lard; and he built up the fire in the kitchen, while I mixed the seasoning into the dough, and commenced frying them. There was no time to let them rise again, but they were quite light, 'notwithstanding.

107

At daylight we had a huge basket filled, and when the cars were starting off with the Ohio boys, I saw it lifted up into their midst, and received with a cheer.

The tempting beauty of our grand old woods suggested the enjoyments of peace, and a picnic was projected, and carried into operation by the hospital, assisted by the people of Gettysburg. But we were disappointed in the result—the rebel convalescents rushed in upon the tables, driving our men away, and a scene of confusion ensued. They learned of our failure in Philadelphia, and one Sunday night took up a collection in three of the churches, and raised eleven hundred dollars for another. The tables were set in the shadow of the woods, and looked beautiful, after every preparation was completed.

This time the rebels were kept under guard until the Union soldiers had been served, and bountifully loaded trays carried into the wards, and the contents distributed amongst those who were allowed to eat of them. In due time all received an ample supply of the choicest food their condition would admit of.

We went to Round Top one day to plant a flag, and listen to a little speech from one of our surgeons. We clambered over rocks, up steep, mossy ledges, till the height was attained, and there, standing on the top of shelving, out-cropping stone of huge dimensions, Dr. May planted the American flag, its folds floating out over the heads of the little group of nurses, who sat on the rocks at his feet. It waved there till we were far away, and wintry winds tore it into shreds.

In the midst of my absorbing labors at Gettysburg, I came within a shadow of being relieved from duty, through my over-anxiety to secure for each patient the exact food adapted to his case. New orders were daily promulgated often relating to trifling things; sometimes they were in existence a day or so before every attendant was made aware of them by the head surgeon.

One order was issued stating that no nurse should receive from the milk depot more than one kind of milk, either cold or scalded— still, some of my patients were ordered scalded milk, and others cold milk by the ward surgeon.

Not knowing of this order, I went one morning to the milk depot, but no milk had arrived. It was raining in torrents—the ground was sodded, and not a dry thread remained upon us as we went about with dripping garments, gathering up our daily supplies. The forenoon passed away, when I again went to the depot to ascertain if the milk had come in, and learned that it had.

I said, "I will take so much cold milk, and so much hot milk, both morning and noon rations Many of my men had not tasted food for the day, I was informed that I could have only noon rations, and only one kind of milk. "But I must have it," I said, in my eagerness, "my doctor orders both kinds, and I must have them."

"There is an order allowing each nurse only one kind of milk," was the reply, and at that moment a rough voice startled me with the abrupt question, "What is your name, madam?" I answered correctly, when the same voice said, "I relieve you; go right out," motioning toward the entrance, where the rain seemed yet falling in wildest torrents.

I opened my lips to frame some sort of remonstrance, but the authoritative, "Go right out—go right out," shut them up emphatically, and I went up to my quarters. Hourly I expected my relief papers, but they did not come. My ward surgeon came in, and, with several others, advised me in the premises. I was told that if once sent out by the rough surgeon, there would be no countermanding my relief, and, for the sake of the boys, I had better go to Dr. Jaynes, who was then surgeon in charge, and tell him I was not aware of the last order being issued, or I should not have insisted on receiving milk of both kinds.

I smothered my pride of spirit, believing it would hurt me less to make the humiliating statement than it would to go, and thereby leave the boys to other hands, when I knew that I more thoroughly understood their wants. I went to the quarters of the surgeon in charge, but hearing the sound of voices within, hesitated at the entrance. Fortunately Dr. Jaynes came out of the door very soon, and I explained to him the nature of my visit. "Well, in the future, be more careful," he replied, and by that answer only, I understood that I should not be relieved at present, and I went back to my work with my opinion of the arbitrary powers of surgeons in charge not very much improved.

CHAPTER XVI.

I VISITED the battle ground on several occasions —the first time soon after the conflict, when the evidences of the horrid carnage which had ranged over it, lay on every hand in fearful sights. Shells had fallen without exploding, tempting some of the curious and heedless to their destruction; while everything that ingenuity could devise for the crushing out of human life seemed scattered promiscuously about.

Battered canteens, cartridge-boxes, torn knapsacks, muskets twisted by cannon shot and shell, rusted tin cups, pieces of rent uniform, caps, belts perforated with shot, and heaps of death's leaden hail, marked the spots where men were stricken down in solid ranks. Earlier in life it would have been almost impossible for me to walk over such a field of horror, but I had grown familiar with death in every shape. Yet, when right above my head, at one place, so close that it touched me, hung a sleeve of faded army blue—a dead hand protruding from the worn and blackened cuff—I could not but feel a momentary shudder.

Boots, with a foot and leg putrifying within, lay beside the pathway, and ghastly heads, too—over the exposed skulls of which insects crawled— while great worms bored through the rotting eyeballs. Astride a tree sat a bloody horror, with head and limbs severed by shells, the birds having banquetted on it, while the tattered uniform, stained with gore, fluttered dismally in the summer air.

Whole bodies were flattened against the rocks, smashed into a shapeless mass, as though thrown there by a giant hand, an awful sight in their battered and decaying condition. The freshly turned earth on every hand denoted the pits, from many of which legs were thrust above the scant covering, and arms and hands "were lifted up as though pleading to be assigned enough earth to keep them from the glare of day.

I could scarcely lay my hand upon the tree trunks but it touched an indentation made by a minnie ball—so thickly they had rained down among the products of these hills.

Round Top, Little Bound Top, and Culp's Hill were the spots around which our interest centred. From the slopes on their rocky sides thousands of brave men had gone to sleep when the battle clouds hung over them, and every grass-blade seemed to have been stained with blood.

Down in the ravines, where the water trickled cold and silently over slimy rocks, they had fallen—friend and foe—with death shrieks and cries, and the life stream had mingled with the flow of the little gurgling brook. Up rocky steeps, which seemed almost impassable to our unburdened feet, the artillery had been driven to where they belched forth the fires of death upon steadily advancing ranks of men.

Through dense woods they poured their streaming fire of death, and the long lines of entrenchments marked where two brave corps, the Eleventh and Twelfth, rolled back the grey tide which rose in fearful waves before them.

Every advantageous position was marked with torn turf, lopped tree boughs, and the graves of the slain. Indeed, our whole way was lined with the narrow strips of earth, which rested over forms gashed with the implements of carnage. It was heart-sickening to think of the deep agony which those few dreadful days spread abroad among the little groups at the firesides of fond homes all over the land. In fancy I saw the long procession of widows, and orphans, and kindred, who mourned for the slaughtered heroes. Every grave had its history, and thousands were there.

I went again over the field one hazy afternoon, when autumn began to cast its leaves over the graves—the many, colored glories, yet green and tender having drifted down into the hollows, and over the trenches where dead men lay rotting. Sometimes bodies were so completely wrapped up with the fallen leaves that, unconsciously, I stepped upon them—the quivering of the loose flesh making my feet unsteady, and the thought of the awful pit below sending me away with no little amount of nervous terror.

The paths leading along, with every evidence of the conflict hidden under the dropping foliage, were alluring to the feet of the nurses.

We had been shut so much within' the limits of the hospital grounds, that we heeded little the space over which we passed, as we went on, and on—gathering fragments of shell, battered bullets; mosses, which had held, among their tiny leaves, the lifeblood of a hero; scraps of curious stones, which had been loosened by the hail of shrapnell; and canister, solid shot, and tiny wild flowers, which sprung up in the rocky crevices.

The blue sky above us was flecked with white clouds, which seemed to be moving above the golden haze like the great expanded lilies-of snow, which I had seen swimming on the bosom of a mimic lake. The trees stood half-stripped, with here and there tufts of variegated leaves clinging tenaciously to the parent bough.

Amid all our buoyancy and interest in the things around us, at times the sigh of the wind grew unspeakably sad, as though ghosts haunted it, and burdened it with woe. No birds sang to us from the depths of the dismantling woods; solitary crows wheeled in awkward, dusky flight above us, the unmusical "caw, caw," echoing through the quiet air, while the cricket's chirp was loud in the clumps of rank grass.

No words can express the feeling of utter desolation, which will sweep over the human soul, at times, in spite of all philosophy. The very beauty and perfection of the mellow autumn day, when "finished," seems to be lettered on every visible thing, tends only to heighten the melancholy. We know the ermine robe of winter will soon wrap them up, and enfold them till the resurrection of spring; but when the mellow beauty is swung over a field like Gettysburg—where so many poured out the wine of life; where the very name of the field brings tears to the eyes of thousands of mourners—is it any wonder that, with feet standing upon the sacred sod, the very air seems haunted, as well as hallowed, and every wind the sigh of a ghostly presence.

We stopped to gather the ripened nuts from under black walnut and hickory trees to take back into camp, and so intently did we indulge in this new pastime, that we scarcely noticed the sun hanging low in the west. With feelings of consternation we found ourselves at sunset seven miles away, and a moonless night before us.

"We had come over the rough, rocky hill-sides, up which rebel and union infantry had swept under enfilading fires — had crossed the 'dark, sunless stream known as Plum Run, but knew it would be utter folly to attempt the return over the same path—and we took the old road leading to the little town. After numberless mishaps— so weary that any slight obstacle in our way seemed an effectual stumbling-block—we reached the hospital, and were met by some of our companions, in the capacious tent which I occupied, and which served as a sort of reception tent for all the nurses, besides accommodating Mrs. Johnson and her convalescing husband. There we cracked the gathered nuts, and enjoyed them all the better after the toil was over.

The hospital was at last to be broken up. No more need seemed to exist of supporting such a giant camp, away from the field of active operations, and we saw car load after car load depart, as comfortably arranged with pillows and pads as was possible. Amidst repeated shouts of, "Come to Ohio, Miss Bucklin, I will take care of you as long as you live,"—"Come out to Michigan, you shall always have a home with me," the "good- by was spoken, the last ones were gone, all excitement was over, and I lay down on my iron bedstead, too weak and ill to lift my head from my pillow.

All were gone—my occupation was gone; the strain of months was suddenly let go, and I found how much the strength of my hands depended on keeping them steadily employed.

The hospital tents were removed—each bare and dust-trampled space marking where corpses had lain after the death-agony was passed, and where the wounded had groaned in pain. Tears filled my eyes when I looked on that great field, so checkered with the ditches that had drained it dry. So many of them I had seen depart to the silent land; so many I had learned to respect, and my thoughts followed them to other hospitals, and to the fresh battle fields, which would receive them, when health was fully restored.

114

The dedication of the new National Cemetery, was to take place immediately, and the surgeon offered us our old quarters, and the privilege of keeping up our mess table, if we wished to remain until after the event. Miss Plummer, the only remaining Government nurse, and myself had been ordered to report to Washington, from whence after ten days of rest, we expected to be sent to North Carolina for duty.

The crowds began to arrive in the battle town, eager to be present at the great dedication. Gettysburg was full to its utmost capacity, and again the white tents were spread on the hospital ground, to accommodate the crowds of people, who had journeyed hither from all points.

We watched the surging of the human waves— secure in our tented home, and sewed at the garments which were to make us presentable to the superintendent—the long months having told considerably upon our wearing apparel. Our dresses had many times been mud-stained and stiffened five inches above the feet, and our shoes were often wet, till they dried upon the feet by the natural process.

Not a moment of active hospital life could be spared for mending purposes—too many rent bodies needed us—and all my effects, with which I had come to Gettysburg, were rolled up in a newspaper. I was therefore in a poor condition to appear before one whom we knew to be the impersonation of neatness and propriety.

We sat by the light of our lamps those autumn evenings, and sewed and talked of the brave ones gone. We could hear the rush of the officers' horses as they swept up into the woods, and the tramp of the orderlies seeking out quarters. Ours was a double tent, a smaller one having been attached to the main tent, and in that we had stowed away the many little contrivances which we wished out of sight.

The tent-cloth was tied down securely, and a bright fire burned in our little stove, close to which the stand was drawn. While the hurried feet went by us, one pair seemed to stop to reconnoitre.

115

"Halloo! there's women in there," we heard in surprise, while some one withdrew his head from the aperture.

In the morning we found that three or four little ebony waiters had slept under the wing of our tent, and we had been unconscious of the fact through the night. Our wash-dish was gone, and in fact every other movable piece of convenience which had been lying about. Some of the articles, however, were returned by gentlemanly officers, on learning from whom they had been purloined.

On the 19th of November the dedication took place. It was a clear autumn day, and the last leaves of summer were fluttering down upon the newly broken sod, and over the dense crowds of thousands, who seemed packed like fishes in a barrel. We stood, almost suffocated, for an hour and three-quarters, listening to the masterly oration of the lamented Everett.

The calm, honest face of the President at once exhibited a pride of country, and an affection for her fallen sons unusual among those high in authority. His soul was unconscious that he himself, ere the consummation of the great sacrifice, should be given up to the death by which martyred soldiers die.

We went out to the home of Mrs. Welty, who had been one of our faithful nurses since the establishment of the hospital, and whose sickness I have spoken of previously. The substantial farm house of brick had escaped the devastation of battle; rio shells had been thrown into its cool pleasant rooms—but the tramp of rebel feet had sounded by it for hours, as the long lines of grey moved by, unconscious that the field of conflict was so near. We enjoyed her hospitality in an excellent dinner, and returned to take the ambulance that drove to the town, thence to proceed to Washington in the cars.

We felt sorrowful when we left. Those hills had become familiar to our eyes, and as they receded from our view many parting tears were shed in memory of the dead who died upon them.

At Baltimore we visited the hospital; but were refused admittance to the west buildings, in which our rebel patients were confined—being told by the guard that he "could not admit his own mother."

116

From Washington we were sent to the Seminary Hospital for quarters, to enjoy a ten day's rest. We needed it sadly; we were sun browned and worn down from exposure; our clothing needed replenishing—after which we were ready for the work again.

CHAPTER XVII.

It was finally decided that we should not go to North Carolina, but a way nevertheless opened up to me for the resumption of labor. Mrs. Parker called for me one day, while I was at Seminary Hospital, to accompany her on a visit to Camp Stoneman—a cavalry post hospital situated six miles from Washington.

We found the men at that place in need of many things—the hospital having just been organized, and having only one woman to minister to the wants of five hundred. Mrs. Parker engaged herself at distributing stores, having been provided by Government with an ambulance, horses and driver for that purpose. A box of needed luxuries, which had been sent to me from the ladies of the Cazenovia Aid Society, while at Wolf-street Hospital, still remained at Nichol's house, and I proposed to Mrs. Parker that if she would call for me the day following, I would take some dried and canned fruit to the men.

She accordingly called for me, and we went over the rough road, the bitter November winds chilling us to the very bone, as they swept wildly by us. I did not remember having ever taken a colder ride.

We arrived half-frozen at the tented hospital, hardly able to put our numbed feet upon the hard ground. Government did not provide women nurses for post hospitals, but the surgeon in charge, Dr. Higgins, expressed a wish that Miss Dix would send him half a dozen, for the reason that be needed their help very badly.

I was sent for on the following day, and ordered to report to Miss Dix. In reply to an inquiry, I related to her the incident of my visit to Camp Stoneman, and the expressed wish of the surgeon for help.

"I had hoped to get you more comfortable quarters than a tent will be this inclement winter," she said. "You have been exposed to all kinds of weather for many months; but if you wish it, you can go to Camp Stoneman, and I will pay you"

I replied that I had not sought or expected ease in coming out to the army; yet I added that it was not clear to my mind why women nurses had not been paid in post hospitals as well as in the general hospitals. She explained that no stipulation was made for their being employed in such, and consequently no provision had been made for their pay.

It was a wide field for willing hearts, and no one needed to sit within the limits of that camp with idle hands. So, trusting that our generous Government would reimburse Miss Dix, I accepted an appointment at Camp Stoneman, received my papers, and, on the following day the Superintendent sent her housekeeper thither, with me and my effects.

The location was beautiful; a hill-side sloping down to the bright Potomac—a part of the wards under the overarching boughs of a peach orchard —in summer it must have been a lovely spot. Now, in the drear November, the winds moaned through the boughs, and they apparently stretched up their brown warty hands imploringly to the pitiless sky.

The tents were the most comfortable I ever saw; good board floors were laid down, and stoves threw out their genial heat, subduing the biting frost which had settled thickly everywhere without.

A room in an old brown house, a- short distance from these tents, served as our quarters, and the linen room was located on the same floor. A rebel family occupied the lower part of the house by sufferance—having a wild, frouzy-headed girl who went about with every soldier who would speak a soft word in her ear; and sons, drunken rough fellows, who did cobbling in a room directly at the foot of my bed.

The cook-house was the open ground on which Mrs. Alexander and I met, after parting our quarters in the old house, when the bugle call sounded in the early morning. She was an old French woman, whose home was in New York, where she had a son and daughter then living. I had been warned that I could not live in the same hospital with her; that although a kind nurse, to all of her sex she was a tigress in her jealous fear of usurpation.

She was old, past sixty, and fast verging upon her second childhood. A woman ranging the cook-house as she did was not to be tolerated in her pretentions, and I sought no favor from her She appropriated every stew-pan and kettle in the kitchen, and stuffed her patients with extra diet, while mine went without. She met me with angry looks of defiance and disdain, as I passed her to and fro in my rounds.

After a little studying I went to the dispensary, and procured long tin cans which had once been filled with medicines, cleaned them, and sent them over to St. Elizabeth Hospital, where a tinner put on balls and handles, and cut them down to a proper size—in these I cooked beef tea, chicken soup, rice, mush, oysters, eggs and scalded milk. I was constrained, through the operation, either to remain there myself, to see that they were not removed from the stove, or to detail a watch from among the cooks favorable to my cause—as at several times, on being called away by some little circumstance, I found them sitting on the bare ground uncooked, and the stove filled with utensils holding food for Mrs. Alexander's patients.

It was difficult for me to understand why she persisted in this annoyance of me, and the consequent discomfort of my men. I could hardly believe she carried a sound mind in the frame which seemed to have so little effeminacy about its immense proportions.

Sometimes, when the day was ended, and we were in our quarters together—for we both occupied the room in the old brown house— she would condescend to overstep her feelings of scorn, and converse on various topics. Her powers of endurance were astonishing. She said she had walked ten miles many an evening, and then danced all night. At times she would give, in her moments of relaxation, impromptu exhibitions of her lightness and gracefulness in a few changing steps on the floor, which shook beneath her unwieldy frame

In her jealous fear that her rights might be invaded by me, she resorted to a weak woman's revenge. I was endeavoring to serve the country's heroes, however, and I studiously avoided all causes for unpleasantness. I was not allowed to come into open conflict with her, even had I dared, and was constrained to suffer annoyance by the assurance of the surgeon that I should have a kitchen all to myself in the new wooden wards which were building, and would soon be in readiness for us.

The patients were divided between us for general supervision — each having seven tented wards assigned us. Shortly afterwards a small tent, in which the hopelessly ill were carried, was also given into my charge. Typhoid fever was the prevalent disease in my tents when I first entered them, and a hundred men lay tossing and burning in the coils of the insidious malady.

Our accommodations for cooking were insufficient at first, having only one stove and caldron by which to furnish food for five hundred men; but the new cook-house was in process of erection, and we waited anxiously for its completion. We had, in all, nine cooks. The raw material for our supplies, including milk and oysters, was brought daily from the Washington markets in very generous quantities. There was no lack of good things by which to tempt the flagging appetites.

It was a privilege to me to prepare this extra diet myself, and the cooks were equally glad to have part of their task taken from their hands. Sometimes, however, I grew disheartened under the difficulties that had to be contended with, and, but for the knowledge that so many waited for the daintily prepared bits of food, I should have given over the task at once.

The wintry winds whistled sharply through the bare orchard and about our hospital, but we were only prompted to greater effort to render our sick and wounded comfortable. We had patients who were very nigh to death, while some had already passed from us over the chilling tide.

Our duties began before daylight streaked the East, and continued till long after the sun had gone to rest behind the cloud-capped hills of the West. We washed the faces of those fever-tortured men, combed out the dry, tangled hair, administered the cooling drinks, and distributed the extra diet amongst them. No sights of distressing wounds and agonized faces unnerved us with their sudden presence; but it was sad to witness the delirium of fever, and hear the sick one call moaningly for mother, wife, or sister. At times they looked up with their bright, glassy- eyes, and fancied they saw the loved one standing beside them to comfort them in the hour of trial.

I had been there nearly a month, when, on entering the ward one morning, I was accosted by a sick soldier with the pleading words, "Oh, Mary, stay with me to-day; you can care for me so much better, than these men—do stay, Mary!" and he looked so earnestly and pitifully up into my face, I could not refuse him outright. I said, "I have a hundred men as sick as you are to look after today."

"I will not trouble you long," he continued; "you can care for them when I am gone."

I promised to pass all the time I possibly could by his bedside, and did so through the entire day. As night came darkly on, he said, "Will you stay through the night with me?"

I replied that it was against the orders of the surgeons for women nurses to remain in the wards after half-past eight in the evening. The ward master, however, obtained consent for me to remain if I choose to do so, and all through the gloomy hours I sat by the death-stricken man, my body chilled to the marrow, while the steady tramp of the sentinel around the camp sounded fearfully distinct over the frozen ground.

He was so fearful I should leave him when he dropped asleep, that he laid his arms across my lap, and clutched my dress with his thin, weak hands. Once only I left him, to warm my numbed feet and hands, when the intense cold became insupportable, and had barely seated myself by the stove, when he called out, wildly, "Mary! oh, Mary! where are you?" Quickly returning, he met me with the reproachful words, "How could you leave me all alone, Mary!? replacing his arms across my lap, where they remained almost motionless until morning. As daylight appeared, he said, "Now, Mary, go to your quarters and sleep awhile, for I want you to return to me to watch for the worst."

His lieutenant soon came in, and after conversing with him awhile, left the tent never more to look into his conscious eyes. Very often he would say, as the gray morning dawned, "I shall sleep good to-night, Mary, and then you can rest also."

His disease was in his heart, and he rested comparatively easy all day, only at times was he troubled for breath. As the day drew to a close he grew restless, and complained that his bed was hard. We changed him to another, and made his own up soft and comfortable again. One of his gasping fits came upon him immediately after, and in broken words he said, "I want to see my lieu- tenant—it is almost over with me now."

An orderly was dispatched to the camp, a mile and a half away, but when he returned, accompanied by the officer, he was unable to recognize him. I said to him, "Your lieutenant is here."

"I cannot hear you," was the faint reply, and as I spoke still louder, he answered, "I cannot see him."

"You had better tell him what you have to say now," I continued, "you may have another attack soon."

"It is too late—I cannot tell him," was the agonized reply, and he fell into a spasm which lasted about five minutes, and then, with a quick convulsive shudder through all his frame, his spirit was released, and his poor worn out body rested in the good sound sleep of which he had so often spoken.

While yet conscious, he had shown me a lady's ring on his little finger, and requested that it should be given to his lieutenant, who would know what to do with it even if he arrived too late. When the last spasm came on, he held up his hands motioning with the finger on which shone the little plain circlet, and after he was dead I removed it, and gave it to the officer, in accordance with his last wish.

Taking a shirt, drawers and stockings from the box of stores which the women of Cazenovia had forwarded to me through the Rev. Wm. Ready, pastor of the Methodist Episcopal Church in that place, the body was soon made in readiness for burial. His lieutenant, however, accompanied the remains to Washington, where an elegant shroud and coffin was procured, and he was forwarded to his parents in Syracuse for interment.

CHAPTER XVIII.

I WENT from this LAST scene to my quarters with a sad and heavy heart, to meet there a stricken woman just widowed by the death of her husband in the same ward. She had come on from Philadelphia to see him. She found him very low when she arrived, yet he seemed to realize the fact of her presence, and a more restful feeling took possession of him. He had been suffering many weeks from chronic diarrhoea.

She told me of her circumstances—of the four little children she had to leave at home; how she had taken in washing, and gone out to labor to obtain the money to enable her to make the journey to see her dying husband. She quartered with me in the old brown house, and I had the deepest sympathy for her in her forlorn condition. All night, while I attended the dying man in our ward, she sat by the bedside of her husband, agonized by the thought of the death which even then was stealing away his senses.

He died, and her case was laid before the surgeon in charge of the hospital, Dr. Higgins, and the story wrought for itself a considerate hearing. He gave her transportation for herself and the body home. A good coffin was procured, the body well laid out, his descriptive list found, and everything arranged to enable her to draw his back pay, which was for more than a year, on her reaching Philadelphia. We also made up a purse of forty-seven dollars for her, and I then felt that the cold weather, which was already set in, need not be passed by herself or children in want of any of the comforts and necessaries of life.

I was for a time more than ordinarily depressed by these scenes, and with the constant thought of sorrows with which each successive death was accompanied added to these, I found myself growing nervous and ill. On the following morning I awoke so hoarse that I could not speak aloud. I at first supposed I had taken cold in the long dreary night's watch. Soon, however, I found myself unable to perform my accustomed duties, and was necessitated to take my bed, where I tossed with pain, while I suffered considerable anxiety concerning my unfinished work.

The doctor soon pronounced my disease to be the measles, and I was left to the tender mercies of whoever could be spared to me.

Old Aunty Alexander, being sent up one morning with a drink and toast, brought me sage tea boiled in an ancient coffee-pot, to which the old grounds still adhered. The mixture was of an unbearable character. The toast was a tough blackened crust—so hard I could not have eaten it had I tried. Both were set so far from my bedside that I could only reach them by making the greatest exertion. They lay untouched when Dr. Higgins entered, who, after drawing the chair toward him, and scanning the contents, gave vent to the rough exclamation, "My God, what is this stuff?"

"Some toast and tea old aunty brought me," I replied. After an interchange of a few additional sentences he went into the linen room, which lay near, and where I overheard him say to private Harmon, who superintended there, "I w ant you to see to her—don't you let that fire go down night or day—anything she wants, that her disease will admit of, you see that she has it."

And so I had an attendant who watched over me like a brother. Through those long days and nights in which my restless fancy tortured me with images of every shape, my hands grew so tired of idly resting on the coarse blanket, and my eyes so weary of scanning the blank walls, that I thought I should lose my senses in the dull dreary place.

Soon, however, a soldier's wife came to Camp

Stoneman and made her quarters in my room. I was glad to see the face of a woman once more, and to hear a soothing female voice. Yet, all had been very kind to me. The great, rough, bearlike surgeon in charge opened some of the hidden recesses of his heart, and I was convinced that some genuine kindness lay buried deep under the rubbish of worldly ambition. Soon the tide of strength began to rise over the sluggish stream of life; and I assayed to step upon my feet and walk, clinging to the walls with my weak hands.

My recovery was rapid after the disease had left me. But I regarded my escape as fortunate in view of the many cases of the measles that were lost, after the patient had recovered sufficiently to go about the ward. Pneumonia usually attacked them, and death ensued speedily.

I took up my old work when I could little more than stagger over the simplest duty. I was so eager to escape the confinement and gloominess of the sick room that my tasks seemed like pleasant pastime if I could only perform them. I even felt that I was sustained by a strength not entirely my own, through those trying hours. I worked in the kitchen long before I was able to venture out into the mud, which, at times was ankle deep, through the streets of the hospital; but as soon as I dared, I went amongst my old patients, ascertaining by personal inspection how they hired—what each one needed.

I was met with the frequent complaint that the attendants had appropriated the extra diet for their own use since I had been ill. Although I could now remedy this matter, I felt somewhat indignant at the men who in their own daily rations had the best and most substantial of food. In my usual health I took the round of the wards with the doctor every morning, when each day's extra rations were served without delay.

In the bare kitchen—which consisted of a few rough boards on the sides, with a fly for the roof, and the bare ground for the floor, having a few unpainted hoards in one corner for a cupboard—I worked through hours of suffering and inconvenience. But I hoped soon to get into the new cookhouse, where I should be exempt from the annoyance which chafed my weak soul and perplexed me in the work of my still trembling hands.

"We prepared the food on the same rough table on which we ate, and ofttimes, with the nine cooks busy about the little tent calculating for the stomachs of five hundred men, we presented a scene of extraordinary confusion. I was many times compelled to take certain articles of food to my quarters to prepare them, for in my condition I grew almost wild in this seeming babel of tongues.

Often after my convalescence, while sitting on my bed, with the light on a little stand which the carpenter had made for us, and a fire warming the atmosphere through the musty little room, I devised plans for the relief of those whom home and its joys could alone really comfort in the despondency of their souls. Day after day passed with the steady changes which death wrought, and which were made by reason of new patients coming in.

At times when the air was calm, and the bright sun shone beautifully from the blue heavens, I pervaded upon Mrs. Alexander to walk out to the river with me, and down to the graves which lay in sight. We visited St. Elizabeth Hospital, used as an asylum for insane soldiers—used before the war as a hospital for insane persons.

Here artificial limbs were manufactured to a great extent, and it was quite curious to see the many intricate appliances harmoniously at work in this locality.

Not often, however, could we escape the sight of our suffering fever patients. Not often did we feel an inclination to have the opportunity to go out over the frozen roads during the cold days, or over the muddy pathways during the warm days. When an opportunity was afforded and we went out, the thought of the sick and their claim upon ' us brought us hurriedly back again into my small tent, called the "Mortality Tent," another soldier was carried to die, his distressing cries and groans resounding through the ward, and startling the fevered fancies of those over whom the same delirium was hanging. He had been a fast liver—had drank deeply of intoxicating beverages, and, upon receiving a bad wound in his side, his enfeebled constitution had not sufficient strength to resist it. He sunk into a rapid consumption, and died a wretched death.

Another man, the father of a large family, whose wife was giving all her energies to the proper care of the large dairy farm which he left behind to take up arms for his country, had been ill with fever, but was thought to be recovering. The danger was so evidently passed that, upon the arrival of every mail, he expected to receive his furlough to go home on a visit.

He was stricken down suddenly again, and I was sent for to administer to his wants. Doing what I could for him at the time, I promised to see him again early in the morning. When morning came I found his bed standing outside the ward, and his body was lying in the dead-house awaiting burial.

There were some distressing cases of erysipelas in camp. One soldier, who had been transferred from the Fifth New York Cavalry, was enduring terrible agony from it. The attendant wished me to give special attention to his case, and conducted me to his bedside. His eyes were shut with the swollen lids, and every feature swollen to immense proportions, whilst a bad wound on his shin bone was constantly irritated by the eruptive fever.

As I spoke to him of his sickness, the big tears rolled down his face, and he said, "I have two sisters, who would be only too glad to come and care for me, if they were made aware of my condition." I learned afterward that he was an only son, and a man of more than ordinary intellect.

I replied, "Let me be your sister for the time— I will do all that can be done for you here. Remember this is not their home, with nice rooms, kind friends and downy pillows to make them comfortable. You would not wish them here to endure camp life, when they are unused and unsuited to its hardships.

After some more conversation he seemed to grow quite reconciled to his situation, and when I went to his bedside the next morning he seemed overjoyed at recognizing my voice, and said, "How I longed for the morning; I wanted to hear a woman's voice; I can sometimes dream I am at home."

I bathed his scaled face in a cooling preparation, combed out his hair, and cleaned his finger nails, removed the dead scales from his cheek and forehead, and laid over the whole a wet cloth. What a glow of gratitude. I felt that I had been given strength to stand in a sister's place, when he sighed out softly, "How much better I feel; my sisters could not do more for me."

We had quite a number of these cases. One of the attendants was down with the same loathsome disease, and lying in the tier of beds directly opposite this soldier. There were then three tiers of beds standing lengthwise through the ward. Two more men were soon added to the number, one of whom died, after his head had swollen

128

to the size of a water pail, and the eruption had spread all through his system. He suffered intensely, and died in a delirium.

My strength was inadequate to the demand made upon it. I could not go through the wards as often as I had done, and finally arranged to see each man once a day, and the worst cases twice. The remainder of the time I passed in the kitchen preparing drinks and cooking extra diet. In this way I labored till my strength returned in part, when we were moved into the new wards which had been building the notice was given me in the morning by my ward surgeon, Dr. Christman, and, before noon, one hundred of the sickest was comfortable in his bed, and the cooked dinner was spread in the dining-hall for convalescents.

The ward had been thoroughly cleaned and dried, and everything was in order. The stoves were not up when I went over to begin the work of assorting the great heaps of new dishes just unpacked; but there were many hands, and the work was speedily accomplished.

It was a sad sight to see the stretchers borne quickly along the paths by the hands of the attendants. They looked still and death-like, reminding us of corpses being borne to the dead- house. They were, however, more comfortable in a short time in their new quarters. The new kitchen was a fine one indeed although open at the north and south, having no door by which to shut off the draught of cold air.

My quarters were located at the extreme end of the ward, and, with the exception of the dispensary, it was the only one partitioned from the wards. I was moved there, bed and baggage, leaving old aunty in undisputed possession of the room in the old brown house, and the stove in the old kitchen.

Everything passed off smoothly, and the full diet was cooked on our new stoves. A commissary sergeant was detailed to work for me, and for that purpose the kitchen was divided. I was fortunate in gaining the favor of the hospital steward, and the tables and trays were loaded each day with luxurious food, such as was seldom to be had in Hospital.

Soon the measles ward, containing thirty cases, was added to mine. A little later another, and still later the erysipelas ward, then the small pox ward—swelling the list of our patients to three hundred men, and severely taxing our strength to supply their numerous wants.

In the midst of all these labors, and at a time when I could illy afford to be sick, I caught a terrible cold which settled in my throat, with all the symptoms of diphtheria—still I worked with increased energy, feeling that each day would end the scene for a time at least.

My throat was burned with caustic and bathed with hartshorn each day, whilst in the intervals of the treatment I shook over the red hot stove like one in an ague fit. I kept at my post, loth to leave it till my throat was so nearly closed, that I could neither speak, nor swallow my food. The taking of water was attended with severe pain.

Then began an excruciating pain in my side and back, which I sought to relieve by trying new positions. But all was in vain, and at last I took a seat close by the stove, whilst my attendant brought me the material with which I worked as I motioned for it for three days.

On the following Sabbath, which only differed from other days in its being set apart for the regular weekly inspection, I summoned up all my courage, and went from ward to ward, bearing with all the fortitude I could muster the pains in my side and back. On my return I was taken with a severe chill, and, after issuing the rations for supper, heart and strength gave out together. I went to my room with a raging fever, threw myself across my bed of straw, and was unable to leave it for five long weeks.

CHAPTER XIX.

MY symptoms were so much like an attack of small-pox, that the surgeon in charge, who visited me in the morning to ascertain the cause of my non-appearance in the kitchen, pronounced it that awful disease.

The thought of the dreadful place to which they took those stricken down with this loathsome pest alarmed me to no small degree. I began to think that if I was taken there I would surely die. My already tortured fancy conjured up visions of a death-bed, where I would be left unattended, where the horror-s of the place would alone witness my last struggling breath, and from whence my putrid body would be hurried into a shallow grave, to moulder beneath the turf of a strange soil.

In my excited condition I reasoned with myself, as best I could, upon what should be done, and upon the various contingencies that might arise in my particular case. I remembered how I had braved disease and death among others—how strong my hands were, and how capable of endurance my constitution had seemed—and I gradually relapsed into a somewhat composed mood.

I lay with my clothing still on, revolving in my mind the possibility of being allowed to remain where I was; at least, I determined to risk being denied the privilege. When the surgeon returned, I said, "Doctor, can't I stay in this room—do you think any of the patients would take the disease from me?" He no doubt saw the anxiety portrayed in my countenance; was moved by the pleading tone of an invalid nurse for the right to live; beheld a woman far from home, and friends, and the comforts of civilization, and, although so coarse in his nature, he manifested some generosity of heart, and replied, "You shall stay here, and you shall be taken care of too, if the d 1 stands at the door."

He went out immediately to make arrangements for my care, sending in the ward surgeon, who, while he stood regarding my fever-flushed face, remarked, "We sometimes send small-pox patients to the pest-house."

The thought flashed over me that they had held a council upon my case in the outer room, and had decided that it would be exposing the whole ward to the dreadful disease if I was allowed to remain, and in my despair I cried out, "Oh! don't send me away—let me stay here in my own room P

I thought if I must die, death would be less terrible near those to whom I had ministered in their hours of pain, until they had at least passed out from the shadows of sickness into the light of health. "You shall stay," he said, adding that proper persons were to be detailed to take care of me, and I should make my mind as easy as possible.

Soon after an old gentleman from the First Rhode Island Cavalry came to stay in the room and wait upon me. Others were selected to give me medicine regularly, prepare food, chop wood, build fires, and keep my room in order. Amongst these attendants, to whom, under God's mercy, I owe my life, was the commissary sergeant who had been my kitchen assistant.

As my disease gradually developed itself, it was discovered that, instead of the dreaded small-pox,

I had a malignant attack of typhoid fever. Nevertheless I had the best of nursing, and could not have been better cared for had I been surrounded with all the comforts of home. For weeks I lay too ill to realize my situation. Had I in those days gone down into the dark valley I would have been unconscious of the final struggle. I was a helpless being, and with senses overcome I drifted along upon the swift current to the very brink of the stream from the waters of which no mortal ever returns.

A council of the hospital surgeons said I would die 5 no hope remained for me. They little comprehended the amount of endurance my constitution was capable of, and how, in a close contest, the love of life had its hidden advantages over death.

Only once was I honored with a call from old aunty, and that at a time when I was almost bewildered with pain. She never came again, urging, repeatedly, in extenuation of her neglect, that I did not treat her well when she did -call. I was fortunate, indeed, in not having been left to her tender mercies. Her morbid fear of losing her position of queen regnant might have tempted her to let the fever do its work.

When I began to convalesce, the patients would watch for my nurse, and beautiful cakes, and cans of fruit, and bottles of wine were proffered for my use. My heart ran over with gratitude at these kind expressions of respect, and I was almost thankful that even by this weary illness I had been taught how much kindness was in the stout brave hearts of our soldiers.

As no provision existed in this hospital in regard to our washing, each nurse was under the necessity of doing her own. My clothes had been wet several days previous to my illness, and it was by dint of great exertion that I got them dry in time to take my bed. These clean garments were all I had for changes until able to wash again.

Soon after my fever was broken I was able to sit up in my bed by supporting myself at the iron bar that crossed the head. Here I sat for hours, mending the stockings which had accumulated in huge forbidding piles—plying my needle, slowly and uncertainly at first, till faint with fatigue, then relieving my eyes by looking out upon the flowing river, on which the swift boats were gliding. Some were going to hospitals with sick men on their decks, others were bearing supplies, and still others were carrying untried soldiers to recruit up the old regiments to their standard proportions.

At times the cavalry would dash down to the flat, near the hospital, to drill, and I watched the graceful evolutions of the noble animals while training for the charge of death. It was always a fascinating sight to me to see the intelligent creatures learning to wheel, and charge, and I felt considerable regret that they, with no knowledge of the causes and effects of war, were also subject to the death which soldiers die, without a chance of life if wounded or disabled.

The corrals were also in full view of my window, the long, low wooden sheds seeming to stretch away over half a mile in length. The drill ground was trampled daily by the iron hoofs of three thousand horses.

I remember, when a stampede occurred, the noise of their scampering feet, which, swift-winged with fright, seemed like the sound of a hurricane's blast. Oar tented wards were then in operation, and by a providential interposition the inmates of one of the tents had been moved from the centre to an extreme end. As the horses swept up from the Potomac, their coarse lay directly through the hospital, and they dashed straight over the board floor of this tent, tearing down the guy ropes, and rushing on, leaving some thankful hearts that they had providentially been saved from the awful death of being trampled and torn by the iron hoofs of the frantic animals.

In crossing the river bridge, which lay in their path, numbers were crowded in the water, and their dead bodies were found days after. Some kept on their whirlwind course, and were not stopped until they neared Baltimore.

A slide was built on the river brink, near the camp ground^ and down its steep the dead and worn out horses were shoved into boats, and taken to Washington, there to be worked up. No one of these animals was in any way wasted, if he perished away from the battle field.

I think the most pitiful sight I ever beheld was that of one of these skeleton creatures lying in the stagnant water of a little brook, whither he had doubtless gone to drink, and falling in was too exhausted to rise. As we neared him the instinct of human presence seemed to nerve him with some little vigor, for he raised his head and neighed imploringly—the glassy eyes even then glaring with death. We could not help the dying creature, and for days the scene haunted my mind.

A house also stood' within sight of my window, and, as I lay with wandering fancy, catching at every floating thread with which to arrange the warp of a romance, I thought of the condition of the inmates of that dwelling. They were surrounded by Union soldiers; their own sons and brothers were in the gray ranks of the rebels; they were compelled to assume a peaceful demeanor, when their very hearts were agonized within them. They well knew that their idols were marching with a half-clad, half-starved army, and that

134

those, who would probably take their lives, surrounded them with all the pomp and circumstance of war. How could any one, endowed with ordinary human instinct, fail to pity them.

All eyes were now turned toward the giant army which centred in Virginia, and toward the iron man, whose taciturn and stolid features planned, and kept his planning to himself. Soldiers were eager for the fray. One, who had been wounded eleven times, told me each hit from the "rebs" only made him the more anxious to get a chance at them.

How I longed for the full strength which was coming to my sluggish veins gradually. Friends at the North, to whom my illness had been reported, wrote to me, urging my speedy return. But home and all its attractions paled in the light of my duty to my country, and my devotion to her braves. I could endure sickness, pain, and privation to be allowed to assist, in the humblest way, the cause of universal liberty. It was for that that many precious ones had been slaughtered in conflict, and even tortured in the noisome prisons of the "chivalric" and "magnanimous" rebels. It must therefore be maintained. No rest was evidently in store for us till victory crowned our arms, and the cause of the conflict was wiped out forever. I felt myself honored in being permitted to bandage the wounds of the meanest private in the ranks. Though an humble nurse in the hospital service of the Government, I had just patriotism enough to feel myself as proud in my position as a queen could be on a throne. There may be those who do not regard a feeling of this kind in a woman as proper, in view of her relation to man and the requirements of modesty (?); but there are also those who have an abundance of it, and are strong enough to lead a correct life in the full enjoyment of it.

Go home! Not while strength lasted; not while cannon-smoke darkened the air, and the hail of death rained over a trodden battle field; not while the wounds of our brave fathers, husbands, and sons demanded attention! Others might sit at home, regardless of our soldiers; or even scrape the lint, sew at hospital garments, and prepare luxuries for us to dispense—it was a noble work, but not for me. My hands were used to rougher toil; they had ceased to tremble

135

when hundreds of worms feasted upon the rank battle- wounds; they were no more timid when the death-damp bathed the soldier's face with its cold moisture. I had learned to look upon every dead man as a part of the inevitable sacrifice which was not yet finished.

Soon I was able to move slowly about. Some changes had transpired during my illness; the old dead-house—by which I had so often passed in the darkness of morning and evening hours, when the wild night wind blew aside the canvass, and corpses lay with exposed head or feet—had passed away, and a new one, further on among new wards, held its quota of stiffening forms.

Some faces were missed, but they had fought the good fight, and had taken their places on "fame's eternal camping ground." One little fellow, who was very ill with typhoid fever when I left the ward, had been treated for insects on his head. He v as given a compound intended to kill them, which proved so poisonous that he lost his senses in a little while, and did not recover from his idiotic condition.

He had been a bright boy before his sickness, and this total wreck of reason was a sad subject for contemplation. Some one mourned for him, though it might have been a little comfort to them to be able to care for the poor body after the soul within was a wreck. These cases always produced far more sorrowful feelings among us than the sorest wounded ones around us. It seemed as if carelessness and malpractice had a hold upon army life that no effort of the Government could throw off. Unskillfulness, at times, among army surgeons seemed among the

"Things that are not to be remedied."

136

CHAPTER XX.

I WAS sitting one day musing upon current events, and anxiously glancing, at times, into the future, when Miss Dix abruptly entered my room, and, in surprise, exclaimed, "Why, Miss Bucklin, have you been sick, and not had it reported to me? I have hunted the whole hospital over for you; don't you need something—a dressing-gown, wine, or some other food for your comfort?" adding a reprimand that she had not been notified, so that she might have sent a woman nurse to my assistance.

I replied, by way of excuse, that my disease had been at first pronounced small-pox, that I felt unwilling to subject any one to the danger of the contagion, and that I so soon after became unconscious that it mattered little who took care of me.

As she left me, she said, "I will send my carriage for you as soon as you are able to be moved, and you can go to the Sanitary Home to recruit." I had previously received an invitation from Dr. Caldwell and his amiable wife to come to them as soon as able to travel.

One cold raw April day Miss Dix's carriage was sent over, with her housekeeper in charge, to assist me in making preparations for the journey, and with two nurses to take charge of my ward; but the surgeon thought the day unfavorable for me to go out, and would not allow me to undertake the journey, promising, however, that as soon as the weather became pleasant and I was able, he would send me over himself.

A few days later, I went—enjoying to the fullest extent the hospitality of that luxurious home—blessing in my heart the noble movers in the great Sanitary scheme which provided such-a retreat for sick and worn out nurses. I shall forever hold Dr. Caldwell and his lovely wife in kindly remembrance for the hospitality extended to me during that brief but pleasant week.

At the end of this time, they sent for me from the hospital, with the word that I was not so much needed for work, but they missed me, and if I was willing I had better return.

I found the stocking-basket- full to overflowing again—three hundred pairs, with gaping heels and open toes. A woman had been sent to the hospital some time previous, and been directed to me for employment, but as I had nothing for her to do except mending, I proposed that to her, when she silenced my interest in her, with the petulant, "I didn't come to the hospital to mend stockings." Of course, I left her to walk in her own path. And this she did by taking nominal charge of the linen room—the clothes of which returned to the wards in the same condition in which they were sent out. But as a certain official was exceedingly friendly to her cause, we drew our own conclusions in regard to her, and kept aloof from her society.

Several of the wives of hospital surgeons were here, and, soon after my return from Washington, the wife of Dr. George and I became fast friends.

Her husband had been prostrated with an attack of erysipelas, and had sent for her to come on and take care of him through his sufferings.

Mrs. George assisted me materially in diminishing the contents of the stocking-basket.

Soon, in the sunny weather, when dainty fringes of grass began to peep up along the untrampled nooks, and delicate flowers lifted their tiny forms over the water's edge, I began to venture about, and into the wards once more. But the kitchen was barred against me. I had overtasked myself in it, the doctor said, and I should not go into it again. I was more willing to forego the labor, because I knew the men were well cared for in every article of food and luxury of which their progress in convalescence would enable them to partake.

A young man was transferred to my ward, about this time, who had passed a surgical examination, and entered the service, with one leg several inches shorter than the other, and a fever- sore which reached from his knee to his ankle. He had passed the entire winter and spring in the hospital—homesick and despondent—sighing for friends, and the far away home. While he was anticipating a furlough, and the arrival of his brother to accompany him North, he took the measles, and was prostrated upon his bed.

I sought to comfort, him with every conceivable word of encouragement. I told him the measles was not a dangerous disease—I had lately passed through it, and doubtless he would be able to go home when his furlough and his brother arrived. But no such comfort could reach his sad soul. Homesickness became seated, and he died, moaning for his home and his mother.

Another bright boy, of only sixteen summers, lay very ill in the ward, calling in piteous tones for his mother—repeating the dear name louder, and louder, ofttimes shrieking out, "Oh! mother, my mother, why don't you come," till the lamp of life went out in wild and feverish flickering. They buried him under Virginia sod, and the mother, doubtless, never learned how her boy agonized for her presence—how his fond heart pictured her image before him at moments, and then, almost broken at the recollection of her absence, gave vent to its despair in shrieks of her loved name.

Another, a massive framed man, was brought in suffering from an attack of pneumonia. He said to me, "I have served Uncle Sam now almost three years, and by the time I am well again my term will be out. I have written to my wife—she will be expecting me—and the three little babies, how I long to see them."

Two days later be lay in the dead-house, his stomach having been taken out, examined, and replaced, and his body gotten in readiness for burial.

Another, with the same almost fatal disease, lay near him, and for three successive mornings I expected to find his empty bed-standing outside the ward—but I was happily disappointed each time. I stepped to his side one morning after, and he looked up with such a bright expression, that I said, involuntarily,

"You are much better this morning."

"I guess not." he replied

"I think you are." I insisted.

"'It is no fault of mine, if I am," he answered. He was soon able to walk about the ward, and rapidly recovered.

A case, calling forth the greatest commiseration, existed in our hospital in the person of a blind soldier. His eyes had been injured by the explosion of powder, and he had lain for months without the treatment so necessary to restore his vision. At last, in his wretched condition, he was brought under our care, and when we asked for remedies with which to attempt relief, the attendant was told by the surgeon in charge that they provided no medicine for eyes. He therefore lingered along till confirmed blindness settled upon him— till the earth became a darkened place to him in which to grope along until the light of the eternal world should open up to his new sight.

He was poor, and no one saw fit to interest themselves in his case. A furlough had been promised, but it never came; but, worse still, by and by letters were received with a tale of wretchedness on their pages that made stout men brush the tears from their eyes. His wife, and her eight little ones had been turned out of their poor shelter, because unable to pay the small pittance extorted for their mean dwelling; and, with the helpless brood on her hands, the mother was unable to earn her own livelihood, much less the food for so many hungry mouths.

For eight months his pay had been withheld, for want of his descriptive list, while those, having the authority to find and present it, neglected the duty, and the helpless family was thrown upon the cold charities of a selfish community. It was hard to tell him these things, lying prostrate and helpless on his iron bedstead; but the letter from home must be read, and the truth, hard as it was, must be revealed.

The steward came to me one day, saying, "No. — was rapidly declining, and he thought he could hardly last six hours! He wished I would go to him, and see what could be done to comfort him.

I went immediately, finding a youth of about eighteen years, lying with a pained look upon his fair young face, and an uneasy wandering of the restless eyes. I talked with him of his future prospects, and asked him if he had any hope beyond this life.

"Oh! I fear it will not be all right with me in the future," he said. "I have been a hard boy since I left the home of my parents; my mother gave me good advice when I left her, and gave ' her wayward boy ' the last kiss. I was brought up under religious influences, my father and mother being both professed Christians—but I slighted the offers of mercy, and grew reckless and hardened in sin."

I told him there was yet hope; that the Saviour died for the worst of sinners, and if he repented and believed, he would yet be saved lie said, "Will you send for the chaplain?"

This I did, and when he came he talked and prayed with him earnestly. I sat by his bedside long after, as he lay in silent thought, until he said to me,

"I like to see you sitting there; it seems so much as if I was home again."

He lay, for a little while after that, repeating a prayer—the calm expression on his face indicating that his petition was answered, and that a genuine hope was newly born in his soul. While saying faintly the words, "Thine is the glory!" the last sigh fluttered forth, and another spirit had entered upon a new life.

One pleasant moonlight Sabbath evening we were enjoying religious services in the steward's office, when a man was brought in, who was reported to have been hurt by his horse falling upon him, and to all appearance he was in great agony. He groaned at every moment, and the whole ward was in excitement over his apparent distress. The surgeon was sent for, and an examination made, which revealed neither bruise nor wound lie was left till the second day, with the possibility of his injuries being internal, when another examination was ordered, and the man pronounced an impostor, and ordered to be sent to his regiment. His bundle was brought—for, on the entrance of a sick or wounded man into a hospital, his uniform is taken off, and nicely made up into a bundle, with his haversack, canteen, and blanket, and whatever effects he may have, and given in charge of a man whose especial business it is to receive and give out these bundles—lie was dressed in his own uniform, and amidst the groans of all the convalescents able to follow him out into comp, he was guarded to his regiment.

It appeared that they had been ordered to the front, and the anticipation of the thunder of the cannon, the deadly charges upon the enemy, and the onslaught of cavalry amid the storms of shot and shell, so worked upon his weak nerves, that he was willing to feign any distress to remain safely within the walls of a hospital.

Another, who complained bitterly each morning as the doctor came to his side, was told that he was a well, able-bodied man, fit for any duty, and not suffering from a single complaint he had urged. "If you had the disease you speak of, I could discover the fact across the ward' the doctor said, and added, "this hospital is for sick and wounded, and not for well men. No man would assist the soldier quicker than I, but I will not help you to shirk your duty. I shall assign you to the night watch."

He was a kind, faithful fellow in his new position, but his heart shrunk from the horrors of the coming campaign. Cowards seemed to have a thousand deaths to die, and the utmost contempt existed for them. No doubt pride kept many a quaking heart in the front ranks, when the natural impulse was to turn, and flee from the deadly peril.

Men were shot for desertion whose minds had become half-crazed with cowardice, until they looked with feelings of horror on the possibility of being drawn into battle, and risked all, and lost, in an attempt to evade the duty for which they had volunteered. Men, who were kindly of heart and generous of soul, were tempted in their weak moments, and their names forever after were stamped with disgrace. Though it seemed a hard necessity, the death penalty was essential to the establishment of proper discipline. If war must be waged, life must be sacrificed at times during the hush between conflicts. Had the first deserters met with their fate, hundreds might have been deterred from following their example; but, with a lenient Executive, loth to take life, pardon followed pardon until the cowards who slunk away, in hope of like reprieve, were retaken and shot upon their open coffins.

One of our night guards at the hospital showed even greater fear of apparitions than of living enemies. He was detailed at the dead-house, in the front and rear of which the wards ranged, and whence, a man coming out one night, dressed only in shirt and drawers, in the reflection of the light shining through the canvas, seemed to stalk out of the dead-house.

The man saw the white, ghostly dress—his limbs shook with terror—the blood seemed to freeze in his veins, and throwing down his gun, he ran away, screaming at every step. No persuasion could ever after prevail on him to do guard duty at the hospital dead-house lie was willing to go to the front, where, no doubt, he grew hardened to scenes of battle in the coming campaign; but the sight of dead men had no terror so effectual as the sight of the fancied ghost.

Experience usually hardens us to scenes of this kind. I myself have passed in the darkness so near the dead-house, as I walked to and from the wards to the quarters, that I have stumbled over the protruding feet with little, or no fear. Our situation even begot a remarkable recklessness, among some, to such accidents. Once, I would have been shocked almost beyond recovery over our occasional mishaps; now, they were almost forgotten after the moment of their Occurrence.

CHAPTER XXI

SPRING, with its soft skies and dropping showers, and with golden sunlight warming the distant hills into verdure, had not yet opened the blossoms in the peach orchard, where our hospital had been located for long and weary months. As if worms had gnawed at the roots, and sapped their substance, the trees died from the steady tramp of feet about them—except, in a few isolated instances, where sickly-looking boughs peeped forth in a few tufts of straggling leaves, ere giving up in despair. Even the delicate tints, which hung low like mists along the rivers brink, to which the dead roots of the trees still clung, did not make their appearance. Evidently the blight of war had overtaken that lovely hill-side, and I could but turn, with a sigh, from a contemplation of the scene in the direction of my duties.

During my illness, a soldier, from Syracuse, New York, named George Bolier, was brought in, slowly dying of consumption. His wife was sent for, at his request, when it was made known to him that lie had but few more days to live. She came, leaving two sick children at home, hoping by her presence to cheer her dying husband as lie entered the dark valley, and with her heart nigh broken by this accumulation of sorrows. She saw him, and remained by his side for days, comforting and soothing him, when a fiendish spirit tempted the surgeon in charge to insult her with infamous proposals.

She turned upon him with the most scornful indignation, as he told her that her husband should be sent home on furlough, and herself allowed the freedom of the hospital, and nobly said, "If my husband dies, he shall go knowing that I am true to him."

She was forbidden to enter the ward; every annoyance was put within her pathway, and the poor creature, torn with suspense for her children, and distracted with sorrow for her dying husband, had no resort but to return home and suffer on. Unaccustomed to journeying alone, she had employed a neighbor to come to Washington with her, but the man having an opportunity to get

Government employment, had concluded to do so, and she became quite nervous with fear.

I took the stage for Washington with her—bought her a ticket, cheeked her baggage through, and saw her comfortably on her way home. By some chance the surgeon learned that I had been absent, whereupon he questioned me in regard to alleged disobedience of orders. "If you were a man I would put you in the guard-house," he said, in a suppressed passion. I replied that he could do so as it was, if he saw fit, but I rather thought he would stand in some danger of losing his other eye (he had lost one), for I had some friends at Camp Stoneman yet—friends, who were well aware of the disgraceful proceedings which had lately been enacted, and who were eager for the opportunity this would afford.

The tiger was roused in the man—the brute passions were in the ascendant, and, although he had hitherto been kind and considerate to me, I feared him almost as much as an enraged beast. No opening for escape remained only to see Miss Dix without delay, report the case to her, and obtain my relief.

I took the stage again, which ran to Washington hourly, and was soon with the superintendent, to whom I related the whole story. I remembered her friendly caution to me on being assigned to Camp Stoneman; I remembered the suspicious woman, who had no duties to perform in the hospital, and then everything was revealed to me in true colors. The monster had been enraged at me for aiding Mrs. Bolier in her escape from the hospital—there would be no safety for me, either, only in hurried flight.

Miss Dix said, "Go back immediately; do not let him know you have been absent again, and I will arrange the matter to your satisfaction." I effected my entrance into camp without his knowledge, and resumed my labors as usual on the following morning.

Miss Dix had sent a woman nurse to this hospital at the time of my partial recovery from the fever, who still remained, and quartered with me. She was with Mrs. George while I was absent. Soon the usual mail came along, and brought orders to us from Miss Dix,

145

directing the Misses Bucklin and Ballard to report to her for duty elsewhere; also, a circular, stating that no woman nurse would be paid in that hospital after the first day of June. It was then the thirtieth of May. A storm of excitement swept through the wards, as it was whispered about from patient to patient. Soon a note came, inviting us to the old brown house for a farewell visit. We found the room occupied by a few fast friends, and an elegant repast of cake and fruit, which had been ordered from Washington for the occasion, was served.

We passed the swiftly-flying hours in social converse, speaking lightly of past sorrows, and hopefully of the days in the future. The uncertainty of a soldier's fate lumg over our parting with some of these noble men; we knew the battle and the chance of rebel prisons lay before them, and we took the proffered hands with considerable sadness. No other meeting remained for us on earth with some of those brave fellows.

George Bolier was failing rapidly, and a dispatch was sent to his wife, praying for her immediate return. He plead with me to remain until she should arrive, but my orders were positive; I could only promise to obtain the consent of Mrs. George to remain by him until she came.

But the worn-out body gave up the spirit while she was speeding on her way to the hospital hoping to stand beside him when the last struggle should come. The surgeon was beside him when he died, and when no sign of life remained, said, heartlessly, "She can have him now."

Was there no compunction in his narrow soul for the terrible offence he had committed? for the sorrow he had heaped upon the stricken widow, who journeyed twice over the long route, only to take home, at the last, the emaciated clay, without even one parting word to reconcile her to the almost insupportable loss? Her grief was heartrending, and every one experienced a sense of mortification at the conduct of the brute, whose beastliness sought to stand between her and the death-bed of him she loved. She returned brokenhearted to the little ones who, still weak with their illness, waited for her coming. It was a little satisfaction, afterwards, to learn that the surgeon was safe in the old Capital Prison, with several charges preferred against him. He was court-martialed, his pay withheld, and himself disgraced and dismissed from the service.

On the last day of May we were called for by Miss Dix, and left Camp Stoneman for duty elsewhere. Our trunks were conveyed up to Washington in an ambulance belonging to the hospital, after the contents had been overhauled, by the surgeon in charge, to see that we took nothing away that did not belong to us.

We arrived in Washington about ten o'clock, and, as Miss Dix kindly offered to provide each of us with a shaker, Miss Ballard and myself, accompanied by a Miss Vance, who was also going to the front on the following morning, took a pleasant stroll down the avenue, and made the purchase, paying the uniform price of one dollar apiece for cape and shakers. Then Miss Ballard and myself returned to Miss Dix's to select two changes from our trunks, and pack them into satchels, no other baggage being allowed us—Miss Vance going to the hospital, where her trunk had been left.

Our passes, transportation and orders having been, received, I took the street cars for Georgetown, where I was to remain at the Seminary Hospital for the night, and report to the superintendent very early in the morning. I was still weak, and the day's fatigue had so debilitated me that I was unfit to remain, for any time, even in a sitting posture—but, my shaker remaining to be trimmed, I sat up a part of the night to accomplish that extraordinary feat of millinery.

Upon finishing my task, I laid down upon the hard floor for a few of the hours intervening till dawn—after which I took my way through the streets long before the sun shone over the Capital. Being too early for the cars, I was obliged to wend my way on foot for the distance of two miles. Without food, and still unrefreshed since yesterday's fatigue, I arrived at the house, and found, my fellow-travellers partaking of a hurried breakfast. They were just on the point of starting for Sixth Street wharf, whither I accompanied them to take the boat for White House Landing.

We sat in the broiling sun till about ten o'clock, when the boat started, and again delayed at Alexandria, where we sat in a coal office till I thought I should perish with hunger. I was not allowed to touch the lunch which had been put up for our use on board the boat. Finally, feeling the sickness of an empty stomach coming upon me, and my head throbbing with pain, I besought Miss Ballard to go to a hotel with me and call for dinner. We waited in extreme distress till it was cooked, fearing the boat -would leave us, and still unwilling to go on without something to sustain nature in the tedious journey before us.

We succeeded in getting on board just as the boat pushed out into the river, where it again lay until morning, crowded to its fullest capacity. Upper and lower decks were packed with soldiers going to the front to fill the ranks which had been decimated by the late battles. The cabin was filled with officers, several of whom vacated sofas—one of which each of us occupied during the night after rolling them closely together.

Two other women—one a State agent and the other in the employ of the Sanitary Commission, the latter from Williamsburg, New York—made them each a bed close together on the floor, while the officers lay around like sheep in a packed fold. Many persons were ill, and the suffocating atmosphere increased the distress until the suffering was general.

Mrs. Lyon, the New York State agent, devised a method of relief, having the assistance of a gentleman from one of the Eastern States, who, leaving his pressing business cares, had volunteered to spend a few weeks in helping the work of mercy. And we cannot but remark that it was pressing enough, even here, among the dense numbers who were lounging and moving slowly around us. Hot water was brought from the cabin kitchen in a wash-bowl pitcher, and Mrs. Lyons dropped dry tea into it, which, after standing a sufficient length of time, gave out its aroma to the no little relief of the suffering crew.

By the time this relief came, it was too late for me, as my sickness had reached its culminating point, and no medicine but sleep could restore me. I could not sit up, as every available space on the floor was literally covered with men in the army blue.

On the afternoon of the third day we reached the White House, on the Pamunky river. It had been the home of Gen. Fitz Hugh Lee, son of the rebel commander, and under its roof Gen. Washington was married—therefore much interest was associated with it in my mind. All that remained of it now were two stacks of blackened chimneys, and a row of negro huts made of hewn logs, standing on the brink of the river. The narrow river, with its ragged banks, was somewhat like a city harbor, being filled with boats of every description. It was necessary in making a landing to lay planks from one boat to another—and over these we walked, to the extent of half the width of the river, to the thronged shore.

CHAPTER XXII.

THE sight which presented itself baffles every effort at correct description. On the ground men and mules lay together asleep—the mules still in the harness, lying forward on their knees—the soldiers with their trusty guns beside them. They had been walked over, till the dust half- covered them; some so deeply that their heads only were visible, and they crawled up upon the legs of the animals to keep from being earthed alive.

The huge army wagons, still attached to the creatures, were loaded with all manner of supplies, and underneath and about them many lay sleeping amid the noise and confusion—so weary that their repose was unbroken.

Between five and six hundred contrabands—old, young, male and female—the halt, the lame, the blind—cannon, cattle, prisoners of war, and squads of soldiers added to the strangeness of the scene. Some were running with tents, others with the pole; some with a box of crackers, others with a piece of pork; some gathering sticks for a fire, others boiling their coffee—and each intent on his own peculiar errand.

The miserable contrabands were huddled in heaps, yet, grinning with looks of astonishment— now and then, as we passed, giving utterance to expressions like this, "Laws, missus, we never 'spected to see white wimmen from de Norf!"— "Bress de Lord, we is free!"

Mr. Shafer, the gentleman who had come on from Washington in our company, tried vainly for two hours to procure a conveyance to take us nurses up to the hospital ground, which lay a mile and a half away. Each one was for himself, and cared little for those less fortunate. Everything was strongly guarded, in fear of lurking rebels, as White House was in the rear of Coal Harbor, where a battle had been fought only a day or two previous.

Mr. Shafer eventually succeeded in obtaining conveyance for our baggage in Mrs. Fogg's ambulance, which followed the army with hospital supplies, whenever it was possible, and she was here before us. We were thus relieved of the satchels, which seemed to grow

150

heavier every moment. We walked on in rear of the ambulance, reaching the ground to find only one small tent put lip, and that occupied by Dr. Burmeister, the surgeon in charge of the Second Corps' hospital. It was a wide, grassy plain—not a tree or fence to break the monotony, and, as yet, not a wounded man in sight.

We reported to the surgeon for duty, and he said, if possible, a tent should be put up for us—so we sat down on the grass till the sun was sinking low in the West, and the chill of evening upon us. A night in the open air, without even a blanket to cover us, seemed inevitable. When I had settled it thus in my mind, and nerved myself to endure it with all the fortitude in my soul, I saw the welcome face' of one of our stewards, whom I had known at Camp Stoneman. Never was a faithful friend greeted with greater joy. After learning of our forlorn condition, he said, "I am going down to the landing, and, if I can get them by any means, I will bring each of you a blanket."

Before the sun's last rays streaked up into the darkening sky we had a tent erected, and, shivering with cold, although in the month of June, we were glad to crawl under its white wings, and try to sleep. Presently we heard a scratch on the canvas (which answers to a rap on a civilized house-door), and, following it, came a blanket for each of us, from generous hands.

We were without supper—the supplies not having arrived yet—and tired, cold, and hungry, (my sick stomach for several days refusing any nourishment save a cup of tea,) we rolled ourselves up in our new, clean blankets, and, with our satchels under our heads, lay down to rest on the bare ground. I had lain on the uncovered slats of a Government bedstead, on straw, on husks, on shavings, and on the bare floor, but never before on the ground, which was chilly with the heavy fall of dew.

Rebels were on every hand; we knew not at what moment they might dash down through our pickets, on whom we distinctly heard them firing at intervals. Sleep refused to refresh us, only now and then a drowsy unconsciousness would steal over our senses, to be startled by the rapid shots again. At length the morning rolled away the misty curtain that hung around us, and I looked out to see the trodden grass glittering in the first^ rays of sunlight. {

Chilled to the vitals, we gathered together for consultation in regard to some means of obtaining provisions, with which to break our long fast. Mrs. Jenkins, of the Sanitary Commission said she would go to their supplies, which had arrived during the night, and procure something for us to eat. They had a huge caldron of coffee already made, and she asked for coffee and crackers for five. The agent in charge said "Not one mouthful shall a woman nurse have from this Commission." She returned indignant at the heartless treatment, and we sat down on ground, faint with the hunger which gnawed us, trying to consider what we should do, as we felt ourselves to be almost in a starving condition.

We knew we must have -relief soon, or we should be rendered unfit for the duty which had brought us hither, and it was uncertain how long we must wait for government supplies. Presently, in the stillness of the bright morning, I heard the sound of a hammer, and looking out across a little creek, which ran babbling through the tall, dewy grass, I saw another tent going up, and the familiar face of one of God's noble women, Mrs. Brainard, Michigan State agent, appeared very close by it. I had known her at Gettysburg, and knew that we would not apply to her for relief in vain. She had been followed everywhere by the blessings of thousands, who had appreciated the kindness of her heart, as- she dispensed, with a generous discretion, the comforts and luxuries which had been entrusted to her care, acting in concert with the Christian Commission.

I called upon her and stated our failure to obtain food from the Sanitary Commission. She said, "Our table is spread, and the delegates are now breakfasting—come in, and partake of what we have." And it seemed a feast as she named over good soft bread and butter, raw ham, and plenty of tea and coffee. You are welcome to eat here until your supplies come," she added, as I departed with the glad tidings to my tent-mates.

Our morning meal was somewhat moistened with the briny tear-drops, which would fall silently in spite of our efforts to repress them. Our hearts were brimming with gratitude to the noble-hearted woman, who went busily about the tent, unconscious how

152

royal she appeared to us in her soul. "We were supplied with our meals from Mrs. Brainard's tent until our supplies came in—which was not for two or three days. We- were then entitled to back rations, and I drew mine—taking, the bread to the generous State agent. I found! them at the dinner-table" about twenty of the- soldiers messing with therm. As I entered, my arms loaded with the staff of life, Mrs. Brainard exclaimed, "The Lord bless you for this— we haven't bread enough to finish our dinners— nothing could come more opportunely "

We were waiting for our work bright and warm June days during those bright and warm June days, when during those shone tenderly upon the tall grass, the little roots of which seemed to be affording ample nourishment to the graceful leaves. The days were warm—at times, quite so—while the nights, were cold and raw. The transition from sultry afternoons to nights of November chilliness was so rapid that we could, scarcely, realize, it. We suffered from the, heat and cold alternately through, the twenty-four hours.

A Government kitchen was going up; a dispensary was being erected, and the medicines arranged in their proper places; the commissary was getting the hospital supplies ready for use; boxes of bandages were opened, and the hurry of preparation was on every hand. Tents were being spread, and the ambulances came upon the field with their ghastly, bloody freight—unloading them, dying and groaning under the sun—the small number of tents being entirely insufficient to shelter the constantly arriving throngs.

I came across Surgeon Welch, whom I had known at Gettysburg, and he was quite anxious to obtain my services amongst the wounded under his charge; but I had reported, and was ordered elsewhere, and, as it was all in the line of duty, it was a small matter to me whether the boys in blue, over whom I bent, wore the clover leaf, the shield, or the cross. All were my country's soldiers, and I had no choice amongst the brave fellows.

Equipped for labor, with a box of bandages, a box of lint, adhesive plaster, sponge, shears, and chloroform, we went out to begin our labor of mercy, and found them lying in every imaginable position on the bare ground. Men were in attendance to bring us the water, with which to wash the gore from the lacerated bodies. We worked under the scorching sun from early morn till late at night, the ambulances still bringing them in steadily. '

I never beheld any worse sights than here met my gaze on every hand. I had seen as distressing wounds, but the awful circumstances which heightened the distress of the wretched, dying men, had never been more glaringly presented to my sight before.

Men lay all around me, who had been left for days on the battle ground, wet with the dews of night, disfigured with powder and dirt, with blood oozing from their torn flesh, and worms literally covering the festering wounds—dying with thirst, starving for food, unable to attend to nature's wants, groaning in delirious fever, praying to die, to be rid of the intense pain which racked the poor body.

Such dreadful suffering I hope never to witness again. The field was one vast plain of intense mortal agony, tortured by the sun, and chilled by the night dews, which fell upon them, causing more terror than death itself. Everywhere were groans and cries for help; everywhere were the pleading and glassy eyes of dying men who were speechless in the delirium of death. It was a scene to appall the stoutest hearts, but the excitement nerved us to shut our senses to everything but the task of relieving them as fast as possible. The dead lay by the living; the dying groaned by the dead, and still one hundred ambulances poured the awful tide in upon us.

We had four soldiers brought up, and laid under the guy ropes of our tent, spreading blankets over them to afford the necessary protection from sun and dew, and all through the night we heard their groaning, and arose, at intervals, to minister to their wants. But it was little that any human hand could do for them, and by the dawn of the chilly and misty morning two were sleeping calmly, never more to awaken to trial and suffering—never more to smile upon the distant, anxious loved ones. The remaining two were also dying. I lifted a corner of the blanket, and looked in upon them, standing aside for a moment to allow an officer, under whose command they had been, to speak to them. The glassy glare of death was in the fixed eyes of one, who gasped but a few moments longer.

The last one died ere the shadow of the tent had fallen toward the east —and the nook was empty.

CHAPTER XXIII.

WE soon had our quarters arranged quite comfortably. A stove, bedsteads, straw-ticks, with one blanket, and a table made by driving sticks into the ground and laying boards upon them, completed the inventory of our tent furniture. We also bad a boy detailed to cook for us, the moments being too precious to be wasted by us in preparing food for ourselves—and we forgot even to partake of it for hours together, so intently were we engaged in the work of alleviating the terrible misery.

We dreaded the nights, for we lay, through the dark hours, insufficiently protected from the cold, 17 yet knowing there were hundreds of wounded in the open air who had far less covering than we.

The Sanitary and Christian Commissions were on the ground at work, as were also Mrs. Brainard, and a New York State agent, by the name of Mrs. Spencer—a noble woman, who did her work of mercy well. She occupied one of the log houses, vacated by the negroes, on the brink of the river. Her stores had been brought on the medical purveyor's boat, the stoves erected, cooks detailed, and the food sent wherever a scanty supply existed.

I was constantly meeting with men whom I had known in former hospitals; dirty, ragged, starved, and wounded they would beg of me for the merest morsel of food—their hollow eyes pleading as the parched lips framed the request, "Oh! Miss Bucklin, you used to get us nice things to eat, can't you find us something now?"

The cry for food was the standing one in the hastily constructed field hospitals. The men had been stricken down in full health, and the drain caused by the constant discharges of wounds seemed to make a greater supply necessary than was really needed before. "Something to eat— something to eat," was the cry everywhere. Things that had been common fare at home were luxuries now, and in the feverish moments of sleep many were tormented with dreams of loaded tables, to aggravate their distress. Those thirsting for water, could hear the little rill dropping into a cool basin, not a stone's throw from their side, but heavy swollen limbs refused to drag them hither, and certainly there were not hands enough to attend' to the wants of the many thousand sufferers.

One of my former patients, learning that I was on the field, came a mile and a half on crutches to beg of me for something to eat. It was while we were living on charity ourselves, and I could neither deny him, nor promise him food with any degree of certainty. Seating him in our tent, I ran over to Mrs. Spencer's, where I procured baked pork and beans, and a dried apple pie— the last one she had. Hastening back, I sat it on a corner of the table, and bade him eat.

I saw tears trickle down his cheeks, as he partook of the fare which he could not but regard as generous. On leaving, he requested me to obtain food from the Sanitary Commission for him on the morrow, promising to return if able to walk so far. He complained of great weariness as he left the tent, and, although I procured several articles, I never saw or heard of him more.

Another one called in behalf of himself and comrades, and I collected quite a quantity of nice things as they termed them— amongst other things, a can of condensed milk for their coffee, and some canned fruit.

The cook, who had charge of the kitchen at Wolf-street Hospital, during my stay, and whose extravagant fondness for biscuit had so suddenly ended my duties in that model institution, came to me here one day, and asked, as the greatest favor I could confer on him, the making of a pan of biscuit, provided he would furnish the material.

I promised to do my best for him, and away he hurried, soon returning with flour, lard, tartaric acid, soda, salt and water. I am sure I never achieved a greater success in the cooking line than was exhibited in those same biscuits. They were tender as puff-balls, and as I took them from the stove, which stood in the open air, the old gentleman who had attended me through my illness with typhoid fever, at Camp Stoneman, came up and exclaimed, holding out his hand, "These look like home—do give me some!" Of course I gave him some, and also was informed as he ate them that he had been home since I saw him at the post hospital, and had returned in time to participate in the late battles.

The remainder of the biscuits were taken away by the soldier for whom they were made, to share them with his tent-mates. At this time, also, a one-armed soldier, whom I had known at Gettysburg, came up. He had come out as a wagoner, eager still to do for his country, while she needed men. He had lain by the side of a companion who had lost an arm also—one having lost his right arm, and the other his left—thus making one pair still left between the two. I remembered him all the more distinctly, from the circumstance of a theft having been perpetrated on the poor fellow a few nights previous to leaving Camp Letterman. ' A roll of greenbacks, amounting to one hundred and eighty dollars, was taken from his pocket, as he lay sleeping on the outside of his bed. Every one felt that the wretch who could rob a disabled soldier was too vile to live. The t;wain always spoke of themselves as one flesh, and when I gave them food often remarked that it mattered little which had it—what I gave to one I gave to both.

After our stores arrived, and our immediate wants were less pressing, we often procured orders for lemons, oranges, nutmegs, eggs, milk, sugar and soda, upon the promise to divide the cooked food between the officials and the patients.

The transports were soon in waiting to convey the wounded men to Washington, and they were often taken on board in a dying condition. The hard necessity for immediate removal proved the death of many a noble fellow, who else might have been restored to those who loved him. They were packed on decks and in cabins so closely that there was scarcely room to turn when tired of any one posture, had the nature of their wounds rendered motion possible. To those who lived the journey proved a horrible torment, on which they will, no doubt, reflect with a shudder.

One evening, when assembled for supper, we saw full ranks of able-bodied soldiers marching steadily by. They gazed wonderingly on the little group of women, who had never before seen so many fit for duty together, although thousands of their wounded comrades had lain close at our hands. "Them's good for sore eyes, boys," remarked one. "I haven't seen one before in six months," said another. "Nor I in eight," said a third, while many similar expressions fell from the lips of the men, as they passed on. They were dirty and ragged—some shoeless, some hatless, some with scarcely clothes enough upon their bodies to cover their nakedness, and with long unkempt hair, and grizzled visages—and were loaded down with cartridge-box, rifle, haversack, canteen, blanket, and tent-cover. They were marching to join the grand army, which was swinging round to the front of Petersburg, and to-day many a poor fellow of that ragged throng lies in the trenches which were there dug for the bodies of the slain.

The day following we watched another crowd, which, coming on, revealed in the centre the gray uniforms of rebels. I was told they numbered six hundred, and had been captured a few days previous. They were under colored guard, and the ebony escorts walked proudly along with fixed bayonets, ready to hurry on those who had been their former masters, if the ranks were not kept well closed up.

It was ludicrous to see the air of conscious superiority which they assumed at times toward the former chivalry. A gaping throng of contrabands followed at a respectful distance, old men and women, wrinkled and bent, hobbling along, eager to watch the progress of the crest-fallen foe. Some of these professed to have been the property of George Washington—one old woman, who gave her age at one hundred and eight years, was an object of much curiosity.

I will never forget the look of her black eyes, which lay far back in their hollow sockets, while the wrinkled skin of her black face and hands, seemed to have been dried down upon the bones and muscles, and the great full veins which seamed them stood up like round cords raised on the surface.

The former owner of the plantation, Gen. Fitz Hugh Lee, was said to be amongst the prisoners, and was being marched over his own grounds, a spectacle to the knot of negroes who once called him "master."

I was called, while looking at the prisoners, to an ambulance, within which I found a former patient of mine, who gave me an account of his wound and of his narrow escape from being taken prisoner by the same men who had fallen into our hands a little later. He said, "My companions here are our Southern brethren." I remarked that I had taken care of a great many of them. One whimpered out, "We won't shoot Yankees any more" "You'll not have an opportunity for some time to come," I replied, giving him all the consolation in my power at the moment.

In another ambulance lay a boy, who, by his looks, I should judge to have been scarcely fourteen—a torn and bloody shirt, and ragged pants, the only clothing upon his body—his right arm thrown over head, and his white lips moaning, "Mother! mother!" I mounted on the steps of the vehicle, and tried to talk with him, to find out the nature and severity of his wound, but he was too far gone to make any reply. Only the one last dream of home, and the mother on whose fond breast his dying head should have been pillowed, was present in his mind. His condition was dreadful in the extreme. Filth covered him from head to foot, but his young face, framed by the bloody sleeved arm, was fast taking on the livid hue of death, and I saw that he was past human ministration. In sadness I left him to die that others might be saved.

Often the look of that boyish face haunts my recollection, and I wonder if the mother, on whom he called in the last extremity, ever knew how her boy suffered before death released him. No sight of manhood's agony ever moved me like these scenes of youthful distress. It seemed like the tearing up of a plant which was just putting out its buds with the promise of a fair summer nestling deep in its heart. When strong men were stricken down, it was the grain,—the yellow heads of which lay low upon the field, and the harvest seeming more naturally to succeed its ripeness.

A most magnificent specimen of physical perfection lay on the ground in my ward, with nothing visible to denote where his wound had been made. He lay very quietly—a heavenly serenity seeming to light up his splendid features with a beauty that almost dazzled my eyes when they fell upon them. The full round bearded face was as white as a girl's, and the large blue eyes were like the sky when deepest summer twilight crosses its azure depths.

I could hardly turn my fascinated eyes from this feast of beauty, but he seemed to be so quiet and easy that I gave my attention to those whose wants were more pressing. At length it came his turn, and I bent over the prostrate figure, which lay with the noble head resting on a little knoll, and said,

"How are you wounded?"

"Unto death," was the sad reply.

"I hope not, sir," I responded. "We will do all we can to raise you."

I questioned him about his family, when he said, sorrowfully, but calmly,

"I have a wife and child—but they will never hear from me again."

"I will write for you," I said, and he replied,

"You may, if you please."

I took out a little scrap of paper on which to note the address, but ere I had obtained it a convulsive shiver passed over the great, noble frame, and his breath had gone forever. I could not but weep over him as though he had been a kindred of mine, and I looked upon the dead face with sorrow such as fills us at the death of those all admire, reproaching myself that I did not forego all other themes of conversation, until I learned the address of those who would mourn for him with no knowledge of his fate. I made every inquiry, hut no one knew him, or to what regiment he belonged, and reluctantly I left the beautiful dead, regretting that he so suddenly passed to the better land.

To the wife who would, doubtless, never know how he died, my soul went out in bitter agony. I upbraided myself for a neglect in regard to which my reason told me I was in no manner culpable. Others demanded their share of attention, and I could only push forward in the work of saving the dear ones to those who loved them, as that wife loved him, with the strength of an idolatrous affection.

Amidst all the suffering which those brave boys in blue endured, through those awful days, ft was truly wonderful to behold the amount of patience they uniformly exhibited. Their very nearness to death seemed at times to rid them of all selfishness, and in utter disregard of self, each one seemed remarkably mindful of the claims of his comrade. Often I was told, as I carried little delicacies to them, "Give it to , he needs it more than I do."

So long as reason held its throne, so long they generally endured in silence. Only when delirium

preceded the agony of dissolution, then the groans and shrieks were heard that baffle all attempt at description. Day and night they were dying during each lagging hour. The bloody stretchers bore them away beyond the companionship of comrades, and forever hid the loved forms from the anxious sight of the distant waiting ones.

CHAPTER XXIV.

About the amputating tent lay large piles of human flesh—legs, arms, feet and hands. They were strewn promiscuously about—often a single one lying under our very feet, white and bloody —the stiffened members seeming to be clutching ofttimes at our clothing.

A few tents were up, for shelter, and, as fast as they were vacated by transportation to Washington, they' were filled up from the numbers who were lying upon the ground, waiting to have their wounds dressed. A general and hurried care was exercised for their many and pressing wants —it was all we could under the circumstances afford them.

I was passing to the ward one day when, outside of its limits, I saw a man lying carelessly across a stretcher, and, going to his side, saw that he was dying. Only one word could be distinguished and that was the one peculiar to the human soul as its first and last cry—the fond name of "MOTHER!" The spirit was nearly set free, and, as it fluttered in its efforts to leave the body, I felt that nothing could be done for him. I passed on—not however without regarding it as seeming heartlessness to let him die there and meet the King of Terrors while unattended. But scores of men were waiting for me, my morning duties were elsewhere, and hard as it was, I could not remain away from those with whom there was a hope of recovery. When I again returned, I paused to look upon this man and found that he was dead.

Death met us on every hand. His cold bony fingers grasped at the heart of private and officer alike, and they lay on the blood-stained stretchers, side by side. It was a time of intense excitement, when we could scarcely wait for the night-shadows to pass away, before we began the new day's duties. Scenes of fresh horror rose up before us each day. Tales of suffering were told, which elsewhere would have well- nigh frozen the blood with horror. We grew callous to the sight of blood, and great gashed lips opened under our untrembling hands, while from there ruggedness slowly dripped the life of the victim.

163

A soldier came to me one day, when I was on the field, requesting me to dress his wound, which was in his side. He had been struck by a piece of shell, and the cavity was deep and wide enough to insert a pint bowl. This cavity was absolutely filled with worms; not the little slender maggots from which a woman's hand is wont to shrink in nervous terror, but great black-headed worms, which had grown on the living flesh, and surfeiting of the banquet some of them crawled into his hair, and over his torn clothing.

While I was endeavoring to clear them from the wound, one of the surgeons' came around, and paused to watch me at the work. "That is too hard for you; I will assist you some," he said, and taking the can of chloroform—which always accompanied us on our rounds, the contents serving our purpose instead of fire in causing the strips of adhesive plaster to remain over the wounds—he poured the entire contents of the can into the mass of creeping life, which for a moment fought the contest with the fiery fluid and then straightened out.

Turning to an attendant, the surgeon ordered the wounded man to be stripped of his torn and bloody uniform, and a clean shirt and drawers to be put on him instead. "Then," said he to me, "you can dress the wound as you see fit."

I took a full pint of the dead worms from his side, thoroughly washed out the wound, and filled it with soft lint, wet in cold water, then bandaged him about the waist. I never saw him again— the transport being about to leave, all who had been attended to were put on board, and this soldier among the rest.

A squad of men under a fly were the next 'claimants for merciful attention. They lay packed closely together, with knapsacks for pillows—two rows of them, with feet in direction of the centre. As I asked, "What can I do for you, to-day?" they lifted up their heads, and gazed at me, as though an unfamiliar sight had greeted their visions.

"Everything—everything," was the reply on every hand, and I had a full task.

164

As our general cook-house was not in good working order some of the patients were being fed by Sanitary, and, as we women nurses were absent the greater part of the day on the field dressing wounds, the rations were distributed with great irregularity. One day my men reported that they had been fed ten times—the day following not once. I went to Mrs. Spencer for help at near noon on the third day, when no breakfast had been sent in for the men, who, after feasting one day, were fasting now for a day and a half, and immediately two men were called, and they, with Mrs. Spencer and myself, repaired' to the famishing soldiers with all the food we could carry in our arms.

After that they were regularly fed by this- noble-hearted woman, until I was released to take charge of their diet myself.

One man said, when asked if I could do anything for him, "If you will get me a pie, I will give you five dollars." "I will get the pie for you if I can," I replied, "but I will not be guilty of taking a soldier's money." I obtained the desired article of Mrs. Spencer, and, as I came in sight with the coveted prize, exclamations of God bless you!" Oh! thank you!" "Did anything ever look so good as that!" "I haven't seen such a thing for months!" "We were not grateful enough when we had such things at home—we thought we couldn't eat anything like that—we would starve first!" were poured out from the score, who each hoped to taste of the pie.

Often they would long for a drink of clear, cold water, and lie on the hard ground, straining the filthy river water through closely set teeth, while they were evidently annoyed by thoughts of clear springs and deep, cool wells, with the mossy stones sprinkled at each swing of the full iron-bound bucket.

So tortured were we all, in fact, by this thirst, which could not be allayed, that even now, when I lift to my lips a drink of pure, cold water, I cannot swallow it without thanking God for the priceless gift.

In the midst of our labors Miss Ballard was taken ill—the toils and hardships, the food and drink, the excitement of attending to such terrible wounds brought her down upon her bed. Her ward was composed of the worst cases in the hospital, the greatest number of severely wounded I ever saw together—most of them amputations—and their groans night and day were almost past endurance, for many of them were fighting the fever in their delirium. The ward fell to my care after she was taken ill.

One little fellow, wounded in the bowels, lay amongst them, and I obtained a stretcher on which to place him, for I thought he could not live the night out; but he was soon taken upon the transport with the whole ward, and I never knew whether or not he survived the voyage.

The time for our departure came on in the course of military events. "We were startled by the division surgeon, one evening, as we had retired to our quarters, with the information that we might hold ourselves in readiness to leave at any hour during the night. We sat up, shaking with the cold, not daring to go to bed, until the surgeon again appeared and bade us retire, as he would call us early enough to arise and dress ourselves.

We sought our beds, and had scarcely got warm under the blankets, when the steward called out to us, "Get up—you must get up—we are going to take the tent down."

We arose and dressed, and the next piece of intelligence had a tendency to materially increase our hurry, as the CRY was, "PACK YOUR THINGS AS SOON AS POSSIBLE—THE REBS ARE COMING!" Our small possessions were collected with considerable despatch, and our satchels were soon pretty well filled. Wen about to he turned into the darkness of the chilly night, the order was countermanded, and we sat waiting for the morning twilight, being' unwilling to attempt to court sleep again.

The remainder of the wounded were taken from the tents on the following day, and we had no work for our hands to do. Surgeons, nurses, stewards, and cooks alone remained. Mrs. Husband had gone across the country in a wagon to City Point, a distance of sixty miles—the infantry having previously marched over the same road.

The Christian and Sanitary Commissions and State agents had already gone to the landing, and we were in momentary expectation of an attack from the rebels. We were obliged, however, to wait for the boat, and I sat about preparing some rations for myself, remembering my journey hither, only a little more than two weeks before, and the circumstance of the guarded basket.

I had part of a boiled ham, some pork and beans, pie, coffee, tea and sugar. We had each a tin cup and a blanket which we resolved to cling to closely at all hazards. For four days we waited in anxious expectation, living upon our ready lunch, boiling our coffee in our tin cups, as soldiers do when making the hurried bivouac. The last tent was taken down on the third day, and we sat in the hot sun, our eager eyes watching steadily in the direction from which our deliverance should come; our hearts growing sick with deferred hope, as night came on and darkness came trailingly down from the cold, pitiless sky. Two tents were again spread, under which we crawled and stretched out our weary limbs.

Morning came, and, no lunch remaining, we were preparing ourselves to submit, as cheerfully as circumstances would allow, to a fast, the duration of which we could not determine, when Dr. Garslin kindly gave us two loaves of bread and some dried beef. Boiling some coffee, in addition to this timely supply, we got up a refreshing breakfast, wondering, meanwhile, whence Providence would send the coming meals, as rations were getting scarce everywhere around us. If the boats were delayed much longer there was certainly some suffering in store for us. A new nurse, Mrs. Stretch, had been sent down just as we were on the eve of breaking up, and her box of supplies was left on board the boat Lizzie Baker, which brought hen. 'While she had been looking for the hospital" the boat" which carried the mail" left for Washington, again, taking her stores along. About ten o'clock on the last day we saw a boat coming down the river, which Mrs. Stretch recognized as the one on which her goods remained, when she asked me to go to the landing with her and ascertain what had become of them.

On our return we found the order had arrived for our departure and we immediately took our way to the landing again. The guards, and few attendants who were left, met the anticipated attack soon after we were safely off the ground. As we left, we looked wistfully back over the wide field, on which the early June sunlight had smiled in its fresh beauty, when first we trod the tall grass which waved over it.

All had been transformed in the short time, since we first stepped upon the shore at the ragged landing. The soft green was trampled into the earth, and beaten squares, planned in diamond shape, showed where the tented wards had been spread. Everywhere there was evidence of the great work that had been crowded into those two weeks of the hospital's existence.

The souls which had gone up thence!—who could number them, or who could measure the extent of agony which made that field henceforth a place of sorrow! I at times imagined, as I looked upon these grounds, that the spirits of brave men would ever move among the tall grass, and whisperingly commune over the little knolls of earth on which they breathed out their lives; that, with the small mounds for their pillows and the sod for their beds, they would yet wear their heaviness of soul, and, with the wailing of the wind, sigh for the loved mother, or wife, or sister whose presence they longed for when their eyes closed to earth.

CHAPTER XXV.

AT the landing a new and commodious wharf had been built, alongside of which steamers had been quietly lying awaiting our arrival. Soon the eagerness of every one to be the first on board produced, a scene of the wildest confusion, accompanied by a general scramble to reach the decks of the vessels.

Whether by mistake or premeditated purpose, we were put on board the mail boat Lizzie Baker, and, as she shoved out into the stream; Dr. Burmeister called out to us, "Have you any. Rations?" "Not a mouthful," was the reply; whereupon, with an injunction to the captain to take good care of the Government nurses, the doctor got aboard the right boat, to which four barges were attached, containing our stores and rations. Thus we were again in possession of our accustomed luck. The rations on the boat were scanty for the crew of themselves, and, long before the scorching sun had gone down into the west, hunger gnawed at us, and everything and every one seemed unconcerned as to our fate.

Mrs. Stretch found her box of stores, but it had been broken into, and the most of the eatables abstracted. Seven eggs, a pound of crackers, a little tea, and some lemons made up the sum total of food which was to sustain four grown persons through a journey of not less than two long summer days;-

We passed down the Pamunky without interruption; and did not find much to admire on the low, scrubby banks. As night drew on we anchored at the mouth of the York River—for night travel was dangerous, several captains having been shot by sharpshooters who lurked along the banks and who aimed the deadly rifles at the pilot houses with fatal effect.

The morning sun rose cloudless over the scene. No sense of personal danger or discomfort could shut our eyes to the beauty which lay spread along, to' an unusual degree, on either shore. The deep, narrow channel was full of sharp windings, and, as we looked back into the distance at the boats following our course, they seemed ploughing through beautiful meadows—their black hulls crushing

169

through the soft grasses, and tearing rapidly through great beds adorned with myriads of white daisies.

We had entirely lost sight of the hospital boat and barges—our eggs and crackers had disappeared—and as the second night came on, we rolled ourselves in blankets, and lay down to ease hunger with warmth and think of the meals for which we had not felt sufficiently thankful— vainly suggesting to our minds that if only manna would drop upon us, or a storm of sea-birds be dashed upon deck, how happy we would be.

Our passage was resumed on the following morning,-which was as glorious as the preceding one. At ten o'clock we came to a stand before pontoon bridges at Charles City, which had just been swung across the river for the Grand Army of the Potomac to make the passage over. We watched the solid columns in long, apparently unending, lines constantly crossing, which, however, were eventually followed by wagons, cannon, cattle and all the immense paraphernalia of the safe-guard of the Republic.

The long steadily moving lines- occupied a day and night in crossing over. In the morning the supply wagons had just begun the passage of the river and, it was said, the train was fully twelve miles long.

In the night our barges came alongside, when some of the soldiers let down the life-boat and went to them bringing back a piece of pork, with some hard crackers and coffee, setting up the remainder of the night to cook it.

In the morning—the fourth after leaving White House landing— each of us was served with a cup of steaming coffee, a slice of fat boiled pork, and two hard crackers. The meal looked inviting, indeed, but the first attempt to swallow a piece of the fat pork resulted disastrously, in the face of stomachs made weak by long, fasting; therefore we could but indulge in a little coffee, with a moderate taste of the cracker after it was thoroughly soaked.

The Lizzie Baker was now ordered back to Washington, and we were given the choice of returning or being landed on the shore, upon & narrow ledge, whence an almost perpendicular ascent of many feet led to a fort which was being built. Mules and men looked like mites in their high-up position, and I did not fancy the idea of attempting to crawl on my hands and feet up that shelving and yellow steep. I preferred a few days more of suffering to being left exposed to the sun and night without hope of immediate relief.

But the captain was anxious to get rid of his somewhat unwelcome crew, during their scarcity of provisions, and, after a time, we were put on board another boat and taken to our own barges. These were crowded to suffocation, and there was scarcely a spot on which we could set down our feet. The Sanitary and Christian Commissions, and all the agencies, with their supplies, were on board, and we, the employees of the Government, who had a right to transportation had been shut out. By and by a place was cleared on top of the barge, a tent was put up, some bedsteads were put in, and we were shown to our new and comfortable quarters.

The Massachusetts agency spread a nice table for us, but the difficulty of reaching the vessel from the flat top of the barge made it necessary to decline the attempt to clamber up, and we obtained our own rations, and ate them, having our hunger for the sauce. We slept soundly that night on the bare slats of our bedsteads, having been completely worn out with the tediousness of the yet unended journey. After passing one night and the most of two days in our tent, exposed to the sun and cold alternately, we landed at City Point in the afternoon, scrambling up the steep bank to mingle in the confusion which greeted us on every hand.

Here again were cannon, cattle, contrabands, rebels, and the boys in blue. The army supplies, heavily guarded, were also there, and while the women of the commissions and agencies went to seek Gen. Grant's headquarters, we gathered in a little knot, apart from all others—keeping ourselves aloof, as much as possible, according to the instructions of Miss Dix.

Seeing a soldier, and not knowing whether he could make a cup of coffee, or boil a potato, I asked him if he would be our cook. He assented, and went to work, making a handful of fire, digging some potatoes which had grown wild in one of the deserted gardens in the ruined town, and boiling them in a quart cup.

An old coffee pot, rusty, and black with age, which had doubtless lain there since McClelland's [*sic* General George Brinton McClellan] peninsula campaign, was pressed into service, and in that he cooked our coffee, which we drank with nothing else to make it palatable and without so much as a murmur. Standing around the steps of an old dilapidated building, we ate what seemed to us one of the most savory meals of our lives— although we had only potatoes without salt, raw' coffee, and "hard tack"—using for butter the slice of boiled pork which I saved from my breakfast on the boat.

Our repast over, we sat down to wait. Herein consists one of the great secrets of soldierly discipline: to wait for orders without a murmur—to sit patiently under the sun's fervid heat, or the chill of night-fall—do make the hasty bivouac, or take up the toilsome march. To waft—with faith in something, or somebody, while the heart, and soul are travelling back along the highways of the irreclaimable past, and roaming across old fields where lie buried many dead hopes, withered joys, and extinguished affections.

The first colored wounded I had ever seen filled these old buildings. We could see them as we stood around our extemporized table, and the sight, under any other circumstances, would have sickened me at once. Some of them had gashed lips, turning out over a glossy black skin which was stained with blood. Others had faces and bodies more or less covered with gore, and- they presented an awful sight to me. These poor fellows were evidently suffering acutely.

A group of sullen prisoners, surrounded by a guard, were also near by. At a little before sundown we received orders to march, not knowing where or how, for the land was well broken, and the sand a foot deep. In our way we found a deep and wide gully, with rough and ragged edges, over which it was impossible for us to pass, and we had to walk around it a distance of two miles before either rest or sleep could be obtained. In this the men carried our satchels, thus relieving us as much as possible.

I have often, since those days, thought how strange it was that no feeling of home-sickness ever came over me whilst in the midst of these trying circumstances. I scarcely ever even stopped to think that if I had remained at home I should have been spared these privations. I seemed to be sustained by an almost unnatural courage, and strengthened to a remarkable degree.

The welcome word "halt!" was passed along. We were in the midst of a large field covered with rye stubbles, an extensive corn field lying on one hand, and a wide spreading meadow on the other. In the midst of the growing com a log house lifted up its clumsy roof and uneven sides, whilst behind it was a piece of woodland. A large house once stood near at hand, hut the blackened chimneys alone remained, leaning over the half destroyed foundations.

We sat on the ground until late—choosing rather to keep each other company than to sleep without a shelter on the stubbly ground. There were fourteen of us nurses in this little anxious and weary group.

Tents finally arrived, and were put up in two pairs with a fly in the centre—one of which was assigned to us and the other to the officers. As our blankets had been our travelling companions we were not altogether without comfort. We spread one on the ground, and three of us lay down upon it, using our satchels for pillows, and spreading the remaining two blankets over us.

It was the night of the 19th of June, and we were occupying a ground which was destined to be one of the most extensive hospitals which had ever been organized under the authority of the military government of the Union—but as yet not a wounded man was to be seen. The radiant morning broke our slumbers, and we looked out, from under our white shelter, to see the bright dew drops everywhere, and their promise of a bright day. Even the dry stubbles over which many little knots of grass had crept, seemed thoroughly sprinkled with dew, while a refreshed earth looked up through the myriad tiny tears as if anxiously awaiting the smiles of the summer's sun.

The green corn-field glistened in the sunlight, and the rustling of the winds among the long leaves made a music that would have fallen dolefully upon our ears on a less beautiful day. Birds flew in and out of the wood, busily chirping their thankfulness in the delightful morning air, and occasionally seeming annoyed at our proximity to their present abode. They were soon frightened away however by the screams of shells and the whiz of bullets.

The horses had been turned into the corn-field, and were busily feeding upon and trampling down the promising crop. There was no regard for the rights of humanity in war, and the claims of nature were even more readily disregarded by wastefulness. Our own need of food soon became a subject of concern, and we began to wonder whence succor would come to us, when Dr. Garslin came along, and made inquiry concerning our rations. We told him we had nothing to eat, when he said, "Come with me, I believe I have found a barrel of pork."

I followed, him, and soon returned with a piece of pork, and three loaves of mouldy bread. Giving these in charge of our cook, we were very soon supplied with a breakfast. We used for a table an old stretcher which was dirty and bloodstained. No one could tell how many dead and dying had been home upon it, as it gave evidences of having done considerable service. We received our pork on a tin plate, which had been used as the frying-pan, while the dingy bread was cut in slices and laid around. Our cook had unearthed an old iron tea-kettle from some quarter, and our coffee was boiled in the rusty and uninviting utensil. With our bread equally divided, and using our fingers in lieu of forks in taking the meat from the questionable-looking dish, we passed our tin cup around the group, each sipping at the coffee, and all surrounding the stretcher alluded to.

When breakfast was over I took my pen with the purpose of informing the dear ones at home that through all the dangers and hardships of the past few weeks I yet survived. I had only commenced my letter, when the cry, "The WOUNDED ARE COMING!"- was heard on every hand, when active search was at once instituted for lint, bandages, sponges, and shears. The wounded soon arrived having the badges of the Ninth Corps upon their caps, and as no nurses belonging to that corps had as yet arrived, and a boat was in waiting to convey them to Washington, as soon as their wounds were dressed, we went to work.

Our tent was given up to as many as could be laid under it—straw having first been carefully spread upon the ground. As rapidly as other tents could be brought up from the boats they were spread, and the wounded put under the welcome shelter. The first boat load was sent away on the afternoon of that lovely Sabbath.

We thought of chiming church-bells, and well- dressed crowds of people who were hurrying to divine service at the call; of the many who were breathing fervent prayers for their dear soldiers, who were even now the suffering subjects of the surgeon's knife and saw, and were struggling against death with the little life that remained. It was well that their vision could not penetrate the intervening distance, and witness the terrible agony, or look upon the death-struggle and the fearfully pallid brow.

That night hundreds of men lay upon the cold ground, without shelter, the heavy dews falling upon them and producing considerable chilliness. We worked over them till darkness set in, and were then relieved to go to our second meal for the day. The same quantity of mouldy bread, coffee, and bacon, was served on the old stretcher out in the open air. When we sat wearily about it our thoughts and remarks were of the cheerful tea-tables, covered with snow-white linen, and clean plates, and furnished with the choicest provisions. We were perhaps too ready to ponder upon these things—but the remarkable contrast was so apparent frequently, that it was a relief to imagine we were surrounded with the indulgences of a bountiful home. We were soon interrupted, however, by two officers whose wounds we had that day dressed and who, issuing from the tent which we had vacated for their accommodation, came forward, begging permission to sit and eat at our table, and of our fare.

Room was made for them on the ground beside us, and they drank from our cups, and sopped out of our bacon dish, seeming to enjoy themselves amazingly. It had been so long since they had seen a woman, or heard her voice, they said, they greatly enjoyed the meal and hoped to be pardoned for this intrusion.

It was ten o'clock before we had a tent erected under which to creep for a little rest, and we were chilled through and through, our clothing thoroughly wet with the heavy dew. We passed more than a week in this way, vacating a tent in the morning for the wounded, and at night waiting for another to be spread, or having only the blue sky for our tent-roof and canvas, and no place which we could really call our quarters. Our wounded officers went to Washington the next day, after breakfasting with us, and I never saw their faces again. Their wounds were not serious—one having been struck in the neck, and the other in the arm.

CHAPTER XXVI.

The Second Corps fought for forty days and nights in front of Petersburg, and all that time the field was covered with wounded, and our work went on without cessation. Dead and dying lay amongst them, and they were carried under tents and rolled together like the logs on a corduroy road. The condition of those for whom shelter could not be obtained was pitiable in the extreme.

Worms soon bred in the fresh wounds; the sun burned their faces till the skin pealed away, and in the agony of thirst and fever it seemed like a merciful relief when their spirits rid themselves of the mortal and mutilated bodies.

Soon I had charge of three hundred wounded under tents, with men detailed to dress their wounds, while I looked after their diet and the stimulants, dressing wounds the remainder of the time in the field till the Second Corps was relieved and the Ninth took its place. At that time, beds and bedsteads began to be brought in both for patients and ourselves, and a tent was assigned to four of us. We had a man to cook our food—which he did, in true soldierly style, on the ground.

We could have nothing that was not boiled; yet we did not complain, for the stove, which had been ours at White House, was doing duty in another division, cooking for wounded men. We had a full diet kitchen, but it was insufficient to furnish all the hospital, and at times some of the soldiers were in a starving condition, or reduced to wormy, mouldy "hard tack." It was resolved to remedy this defect by starting an extra diet kitchen, and in this corn-starch was boiled, often burned, then thrown into an old tub, and allowed to stand until it had a green mould over the surface. Tea was cooked in an iron kettle and poured into another tub where hot or cold water, whichever seemed most convenient, was turned in to reduce it. These, with an occasional soup of the poorest quality, and deficient in quantity, and with bits of dry bread, were often and again served to the sick and dying men, whose appetites had been sharpened by the drain upon their systems of wound discharges. It was dreadful to have to take such food to men whose anxious eyes were evidently watching for something which looked inviting. I asked the surgeon in charge if there was no remedy. He promised to make an endeavor to obtain relief; but, whether from neglect or want of executive ability, matters grew worse, if that was possible, and confusion and suffering reigned everywhere.

I grew sick of the mould, which rose like dust when boxes were opened, and of seeing fat worms drop out of broken biscuits which, even poor as they were, could not be obtained for some days. These things were calculated to make any one grow wretchedly nervous. Sleep almost forsook my eyelids, while I vainly strove to devise some method with which to afford relief. Even if T could obtain raw material from the commissions and agencies, I had no stove to cook them upon and was thus utterly helpless. The Sanitary Commission was forbidden to deal out anything except by the expressed will of the officials. By dint of long pleading, however, and setting forth the case in its true colors, I sometimes obtained a pail full of crackers— which was an allowance of about two apiece to my men—after which they waited again and said things which dared not be uttered in the hearing of the officials.

Occasionally they would break forth and declare that the country might have gone to the devil, if they had known that they had to endure such treatment as this. They had expected hardships on the march, and in the chances of battle, but when wounded, and in the hospital, they had a right to expect enough to eat, so long as Government provided it abundantly—and they were only deprived of it through the most culpable neglect of duty on the part of the officers who had charge of the stores.

I was not enlightened in these things until matters developed themselves naturally, when I found that some one, somewhere, was to blame, and the crime—for it was nothing else—could be readily fastened on the right one.

Our division surgeon, Dr. Garslin, soon after the organization of the hospital, was sent to the front, and Dr. Hammond assigned to his post. When first introduced to the stern-visaged surgeon, he said, "I am an ugly man when things don't go right with me," for which reason, for some time, I stood in awe of him in his presence.

His tent was near ours and had to be passed as we went to and from our quarters. I usually hurried past it as though an unchained bear was within, and I never harbored the thought of going to him for an order. This state of things went on for days, when one night, as I was passing down the walk which ran in front of the wards to his tent, and then, by a right angle, led straight to mine, I saw him sitting under the fly in his quarters, as if in deep meditation.

As I came in front, he said, "My Christian friend, are your labors done for the day?" I replied, "I believe they are." "Then," said he, "come here and sit down, I want to talk with you." I tried every way to excuse myself, but in vain. The authoritative, "I say sit down here," was not to be evaded, and I reluctantly took a seat. As I did so he remarked that the women all seemed afraid of him. I replied that, according to his own account, he was an ugly man, and we had reason to shun all dangerous persons, for we had seen and were annoyed very considerably by persons of that description.

I told him frankly that the boys said their rations were all they could possibly eat when they drew them themselves; now, with a full diet, and an extra diet kitchen, and all we could beg from the Commissions, the men were actually starving. I told him, also, that if I had a stove I could do something toward relieving them; but, as it was, I had nothing to work with, and could only see them suffer, without any prospect of relief.

The doctor promised to procure a stove and cooking utensils, if possible, remarking that the most the men needed was something decent to eat, with clean beds to lie in.

About this time I was detailed to go to Washington with a boat load of wounded. I was the only woman Government nurse on board, and the boat was literally packed—the men lying together, nearly all on the bare boards, many of them with no clothing only a cotton shirt, some so thin that the bones protruded through the skin. My heart grew sick with pity for those emaciated creatures, who lay so patiently enduring their sufferings. Not a murmur or complaint escaped them, although they were exposed to the sun by day, and the chill winds by night, while the steamer ploughed on through river and bay.

In the silent watches of the night the angel of death came to many of them, and the morning light revealed how peacefully they had braved, amid suffering and discomfort of a formidable character, the terrible struggle with the King of Terrors. Many of the stiffened dead lay by the living who lifted up their languid eyes to greet the dawn of the last rosy day which should ever open its gates to their sight.

During the night a heavy thunder-storm broke over us, and, while the waves w ere rolling and tossing our boat dreadfully, the cry of "A MAN OVERBOARD!" startled us all to our feet. The boat was under full headway, and, in the dense darkness, it was impossible to save him, therefore he perished in the waters of the Chesapeake Bay.

It was said that his mind was unsettled, and he had availed himself of the opportunity for self- destruction, when he knew no efforts could save him after he had made the fatal leap.

When morning came, as soon as the stoves could be cleaned for our use, we set about preparing the food which was to be distributed to every class of patients, according to their needs. While passing over the deck, I saw a man lying near to the wheel-house on a little loose hay, without any clothing upon his body, which was partially concealed by the coarse bedding. His eyes were fixed upon the likeness of a beautiful woman, which he held clutched fast in his death-cold fingers. With the last struggle he pressed it to-his heart, and I hurried away to return with the surgeon after all was over and the spirit was free.

After breakfast wound-dressing was the first thing in order, and in that duty I was assisted by Mrs. Anna Larnard, a regimental nurse, who belonged to a Michigan regiment, and had done excellent service on the battle-field among the soldiers of her State. She had carried water to them when the bullets were falling fast about them, had bandaged their wounds while kneeling on the blood-wet grass above which they fell, and had pillowed the heads of dying men till their lives went out. She was rapid in her movements, and while I took the men on one deck, she volunteered to take those on the other. We had our work nearly completed when we reached the wharf, at which the stretcher-bearers were already in attendance.

The most severely wounded were borne away first on these, while ambulances were in waiting for those who could endure the ride in them. The most of the men were taken to the Armory Square Hospital. While they were being removed, Mr. Stacy, of the Sanitary Commission, one of the faithful men who did his duty to the country's heroes in a noble manner, brought lemonade, crackers, and pocket handkerchiefs wet with cologne, distributing them amongst the weary and wounded crew.

He expressed some desire to know the previous condition of many of the men and how they had been cared for. We could but recount many of the wrongs that our eyes had witnessed, and although we dared not breathe the wrong-doer's name, we left him to imagine it without any great stretch of his fancy. Nurses and soldiers were supposed, by many of the officers" to be mere machines, incapable of thought, and unworthy of any attention beyond requiring them to be obedient, without questioning whenever their rights were infringed upon. To men and women accustomed to untrammeled thought and speech, who neither suffered from nor knew an oppressor, this was a difficult thing at times.

Mr. Stacy invited Mrs. Larnard and myself to come to the Commission and take a cup often, remarking that we looked worn and tired. We accepted the invitation, and after the meal was over, I took the street cars and reported to Miss Dix. She sent me to the Seminary Hospital, as on several occasions, for quarters during the night. I found there two nurses who had been at Point Lookout with me, and also one from Gettysburg.

We passed the hours together in relating our experiences since parting, and all expressed a wish to go to the front. Wilmington had just fallen into our possession, and there was need of efficient nurses. Miss. Dix afterwards sent them there, together with a number of surgeons. One of these nurses, Miss Kimbal, from Boston, died of fever while doing her duty in the hospital—a martyr to her country's cause.

She was an excellent, faithful woman—a self- sacrificing energetic nurse, and willingly laid down her life in trying to save heroes. Miss Goodrich, her companion, also from Boston, was spared to accompany the remains of her lamented sister-nurse hack to the city whence she came, nearly two years before, as her companion among the trials and dangers and sacrifices of war.

CHAPTER XXVII

The morning sun beamed forth beautifully over the many cheerful-looking marble buildings and spires of the Capital, and the dome of its chief building shone brilliantly in the soft sunlight, as we moved' down the river toward Alexandria, where a number of passengers were awaiting us. We were soon loaded with human freight and on our way to scenes of blood and death.

Summer seemed to lay on every hand in perfection. Golden grain fields awaited the reaper; tall shocks of corn stood upon hill sides, and from many bent boughs the fruit hung near to the grass-covered ground. Beautiful country seats, lovely farms, and deep quiet woods, at times, lay on every hand along the slopes near to the water edge. I not only became for a time enchanted with the beauty of the scenery, but I felt proud of the fact that it was but a part of the vast grandeur to be found along the many bright rivers of our loved land. How my mind grieved at the thought that war with its desolating influences should visit such a country and threaten its existence.

While crossing the bay, a boy, who was standing on the upper deck, and leaning against the railing, seemed to be intently watching the waters as they parted in white foam at either' side of the boat while it ploughed through them. Suddenly his support gave way, and, in an instant, he was struggling in the deep water.

The boat was stopped as quickly as possible, the life boat was lowered, and sent, well-manned, after the sinking boy. As he came over the- wildly leaping waves, we could hear his anguished cry for help, and see his hands spread out imploringly towards us. The water fortunately bore him hearer and nearer, and he was soon caught up, the happiest mortal living—rejoicing over his salvation from a watery grave.

We entered the James River, stopped at Harrison's Landing, thence took our way to Bermuda Hundred, where Gen. Butler's headquarters were located. His army wagons were in straight rows on the banks of the river. We could hear the heavy cannonading every few days, and the word went round that, "Gen. Butler was after the rebs again." From my ward I could see the smoke arise in dense clouds, while every now and then, at long intervals, a stray shell fell somewhere in our hospital ground. One of the soldiers here made me a ring from the fuse of a shell which came seven miles from the rebel fortifications in front of Petersburg.

On landing from the boat I found that Dr. Hammond had succeeded in obtaining a stove from the Christian Commission for our use. I had not seen him since Dr. Burmeister, who was a regimental surgeon, had been ordered with the Second Corps to Deep Bottom, when he was put in= charge of the hospital, Dr. Omar taking his place as division surgeon. He queried,

"How do you like your stove?"

I said, "Very much indeed, but I am afraid I shall hereafter have to trouble you for a great many orders."

"You can have them for anything you need to make the soldiers comfortable," he replied, and desiring me to accompany him to the full diet cook house, he said to the attendants, "Give Miss Bucklin anything she calls for from this cookhouse, and consider this a standing order till countermanded" Turning to me, he said, "The other nurses can have the same if they will only ask for it."

Immediately a change came over the face of things in our camp. The walks between the tents, which stood in two rows on either side, were straightened, and ditches dug to drain them dry. Pine trees were set all through the centre of the ground, and in the front and rear of the wards; arbors were built, making a beautiful shade over the walks, and, over the door-way of the tents, arches were formed with evergreens" having corps badges suspended from the centre. Paper lanterns were made of variegated material and hung out at night to guide us on our way— their cheerful appearance reminding us of a village illumination in which Chinese lanterns were universally used.

A wash squad was organized, and contrabands were employed to do the work, after thousands of white linen sheets had absolutely rotted to the ground for want of some one with authority to attend to the matter of cleansing.

An oven was made to bake our bread and a second extra diet kitchen erected, and in full force; the tents were made very tidy, with little stands at the head of each bed, covered with a white cloth; cupboards were put in each ward for the dishes used by the patients, and the dish-washing was nicely done in each section.

Everything moved along like -clock-work. While the former surgeon wished to have a large hospital fund on hand in the event of the men being reduced to starvation, Dr. Hammond declared that the money belonged to the patients, and they should have its value; if not able to eat it in full diet, they should have it in extras.

The gun boats lay thickly along the river, to protect us from the rebels, and we felt secure. Every one seemed, delighted with the change of those in authority.

I had rice, corn-starch, sugar, nutmegs, lemons, condensed meats, eggs, condensed milk, flavorings, and ice from the dispensary, and made ice-creams, custards, corn-starch puddings, and an excellent cream of condensed milk. I also frequently baked cakes, pies, and warm biscuits, and had butter for them most of the time.

Apples, peaches, and nearly everything which any one could want, were in abundance, mostly from Government supplies, while but a few days before the men were struggling along with wormy - crackers and mouldy corn starch.

The Commissions, no longer under the control of the despotic surgeon, responded to our calls for dried fruit and other delicacies, and the New York, New Hampshire, Ohio, and Indiana agencies gave of their substance without stint. I frequently gave pie to all of them—a large old- fashioned piece, on which they seemed to look lovingly for a moment, and which soon quickly disappeared down throats unused to such civilized fare. Every day I also got a pail full of applesauce from the Christian Commission, which was served at tea—a large spoonful to each man in my ward.

Miss Dix visited us while we were enjoying this new regime. She brought us green corn for ourselves and the wounded, a barrel of potatoes, and a tub of butter, and kindly tented with us. She spoke of the hospital in the highest terms of praise, and referred to our labors in words of gratitude in behalf of our beloved country.

We had the satisfaction of seeing men recover rapidly under the current generous diet, and hoped Gen. Grant would see fit to keep the Second Corps, with Dr. Burmeister attached, at Deep Bottom for some time to come.

New lots of wounded were brought in nearly every day and night, and yet we had plenty for them to eat. The surgeon more than once scratched on our tent and said, "A lot of men have just come in, and they must, have refreshments, or many will die before morning" Many a cold night have we turned out of a warm bed, and gone upon the field, to make milk punch, and to help distribute tea, coffee, bread, crackers, and stimulants, till all were fed, and as many sheltered as possible.

The Christian Commission had a little cart, with all the necessary appliances, in which they could make tea or coffee in fifteen minutes, and run it where the soldiers were lying, which facilitated operations very much.

One of our women nurses—whose patients were in the habit of saying, as I passed along with my hands full of prepared food, "I wish our nurse would do that for us,"—made daily complaints of me to Dr. Hammond, telling him, among other things, that I drew their rations. She manifested a very unkind feeling toward me,- when I could conscientiously disavow having anything but the best good of those suffering men in view. I went into the service with other than vindictive feelings toward those laboring as I did, and certainly, as a hospital nurse, I could have no thought of personal aggrandizement.

I heard of these attacks daily, and the generous- hearted surgeon said, "Cook as much as you like, but don't talk to those women—talking always makes trouble—you can work just the same—the boys are doing splendidly, and those nurses can have the same privilege I give you for extra diet, if they will only take it."

Therefore I labored on in silence while about the tent, busying myself with thoughts as to my most difficult cases, and with such new plans as suggested themselves to me. In attending to the wants

186

of the men around me, I found no difficulty in keeping my tongue to myself.

A woman, who came out at the instigation of Mrs. Edson, who spoke publicly in New York for the purpose of obtaining volunteer nurses, we took into, our tent about this time. Many had come out, like her, without the least means of subsistence or transportation. Some were sent to one place, and some to another, while this one, from motives of pity, we took into our tent, and gave into her charge some wounded men. I found her quite a charge upon me during the many severe attacks of a sickness to which she was subject.

After one of these attacks she took occasion to report me to Dr. Hammond—saying I had obtained stimulants of her surgeon. This would have been w ell enough if correct, but, as I was amply provided with stimulants, I was no little annoyed at her ungratefulness. Dr. Hammond soon perceived the disposition to make trouble, and even tell falsehoods, and said to the woman, "If you come here again with another complaint against Miss Bucklin, I will send you away immediately."

Miss Ballard, who was taken ill at White House Landing, had' never fully recovered, and was still under medical attendance. As she had been put in my charge by Miss Dix, on being sent to Camp Stoneman, I felt an interest in her welfare which soon became deep and abiding. I took every possible care of her, until her recovery for further duty seemed doubtful. Dr. Hammond thought it best for her to go home, and he gave me a furlough to attend her to Washington.

She was carried to the ambulance in the arms of the surgeon, and, on arriving at Washington, I procured a conveyance from the Sanitary Commission to take her to the superintendent's house, where she remained several days. She was again taken to a hospital, where the Sisters of Charity were the angels of mercy to the languishing suf- 20 ferer, until, eventually, her father came for her, and took her to his home.

Upon returning to the hospital, I took several bottles of wine and medicines for myself, given me by Miss Dix, who seemed fearful that my strength would not hold out under the wearying nature of my work.

Mrs. Lee, who had charge of the extra diet kitchen when I left, had resigned to go home, and the surgeon desired me to fill her place. I could not think of leaving my men, while they needed me, but the surgeon insisting that I should have supervision over that and retain my ward also, I consented.

I had just got into the new position, everything moving off to my heart's content, when I was ordered to report at Washington to Miss Dix. Learning this, a petition was sent up, by my ward and division surgeons, asking my retention at the hospital, and another, at the same time, by the ward master and male nurses, without my knowledge.

On receiving no answer I decide^ to go and report, when, on my arrival, I was met by a suppressed, ' "Why have you come, Miss Bucklin?" She said she had written to me, giving me permission to remain. She sent me back without delay.

We had divine service after we were established in this hospital. The Christian Commission erecting a chapel, and in it services were held evenings and Sundays.

Many a soul was here aroused to a sense of its danger, and embraced the promise held out of everlasting life. Converts were made—many were baptized, and joined this church as a temporary refuge—uniting, no doubt, with the people of their choice, in the homes to which they went after the war was over. Some went from this baptism of the spirit to the baptism of blood, laying down their lives for the perpetuation of our civil and religious liberties throughout the land.

The generous men and women, who kept alive the work of mercy in the commissions and agencies, strove to reach beyond the temporal wants of the boys in blue, and books were distributed, schools established, and much good seed sown, which shall blossom and ripen into fruitage as sure as the bud, which, unblighted, hangs on the bough in the spring time, shall at last glow in the golden mist of the autumn, perfect as Heaven's agencies can fashion it.

CHAPTER XXVIII.

I was the unintentional means of putting a man in the guard-house while in the hospital at City Point. A soldier, a loyal Southern man, seemed strangely affected by a lethargy which kept him almost constantly sleeping. I made inquiry, but no one seemed to know anything of his case, and time went on smoothly until one evening, while making my last round, I was followed out of the ward by this man, who said, "Good lady, what can I buy for five dollars, that you will accept of?"

I replied, "I never take presents from gentlemen." He persisted in urging me to mention something that I would like, and seeing that he was intoxicated, and thinking there was nothing that he could buy in the hospital, I said, "Buy anything you choose."

"If you will accept of the nicest silk dress you ever had, I will send to Nashville and get one," he said, quickly adding, "I have an uncle there who don't care how much money I spend; if you don't take it, I'll use it for something worse."

I made no reply, fearing to cross him, and passed on through the ward. On my return he met me with something tied up carefully in a handkerchief, which I took with the purpose of returning it in the morning, in case he was sober, and without having the remotest idea what the strangely shaped package could be. I soon ascertained it to be canned fruit. As I neared my quarters Dr. Hammond hailed me with the query, "My Christian friend, what have you there?" "A present from one of my Southern brethren," I answered, adding, "I took it intending to return it on the morrow, provided lie is sober" "What 1 you don't pretend to say he is intoxicated, do you? Where did he get his liquor?" queried the doctor, quickly. "I cannot tell," I answered, when he exclaimed, "Show me the man—I will have him in the guard-house 1" "Oh! don't, doctor," I plead, "don't compel me to be his informer, when, but ten minutes ago, he handed this to me." But he was inexorable; I was compelled to give the desired information, and he was marched off to the guard-house.

A few days later two wounded rebels were brought into the ward, when this soldier, fearing they would recognize him, desired to be transferred to Washington. While packing his effects he thanked me again and again, saying, were it not for fear of being recognized, and the consequences thereof, he would prefer remaining; still, he had no regrets, in leaving men who had the disposition to inform against him and put him in the guard-house.

I told him that no one among the men reported him.

"Yes, they certainly did," he answered.

"No, it was myself."

"Oh! it could not have been you, good lady; you could not do so with any one of your patients!"

I related the circumstance, whereupon he expressed himself as satisfied that it was all right— although I felt as if he questioned the correctness of my statement, and as if he would always censure the men for it. I never heard from him again, and, of course, was not the recipient of a silk dress.

The two rebels, who were brought in, were badly wounded while on picket in front of Petersburg. One was a Georgian and one a-Kentuckian. As the stretcher bearers bore them along, Dr. Hammond inquired if I had any more empty beds. "I think I have," I replied, at the same time I urged him to place them in another ward—relating the circumstance of the fatality at Gettysburg amongst the rebels put under my care, having somewhat of a superstitious feeling in regard to taking charge of the ghastly-featured sufferers. But they were placed in my empty beds, and one died the same night; the other on the following morning. Both were Christian men and died peacefully.

I had still another Southern man, a Virginian, loyal to his country, who had been compelled to enlist, or be shot down. Thinking he might avoid killing any one in action, by lifting his gun out of range, he went into the ranks, and in the first battle was taken prisoner and paroled. He remained home for fourteen months, when he was driven out again, being hit by a minnie ball on the bottom of his foot before he had fired his gun.

190

A willing prisoner of war, he was brought to our hospital. He was suffering greatly, his appetite was very poor, and I took especial pains to bring him delicacies. I never made any distinction between the grey and the blue, except where there was a small quantity of anything to be given, when the loyal boys got it of course. But, when all could be served, no partial feeling was ever entertained.

I went to the extra diet kitchen one day to prepare this man some food, when the woman in charge said, "I have some tomatoes some one might have." I spoke up immediately, "Give them to me for my rebel." "No, not if he dies for the want of them," she said, and I could not prevail on her to give me anything after the obnoxious words "my rebel" had been spoken.

He had asked for tomatoes more than anything else, and they were to be had from no other source at that time. I searched about, and found a few other things he wanted. While he was eating his dinner that, day he remarked, "If I ever get well, I am going to try to get me a Yankee wife—they prepare food so nicely, and they seem to know how to make everything." He also added that no one could ever have made him believe they were so kind, if he had not witnessed it himself. After a little while he expressed some doubt as to the propriety of seeking among Yankee girls for a companion, as they looked with considerable disfavor upon those who maintained the cause of the slaveholder.

Some soldiers were brought in terribly mutilated. One had his head partly blown off by a piece of shell—one ear, one eye and part of his forehead being gone, while the brain seemed to be oozing out of the horrid gap continually. He lay with a squad of men, on the ground, so close that they could scarcely be placed straight, and with their feet toward the centre of the tent. As I passed him he caught at my dress with his hands, and made a noise, vainly endeavoring to articulate a single word. He lived for several days in this terrible situation, without taking a particle of nourishment.

Another had been sun-struck, and lost his mind. He continually asked for things which he could not have, and cried like a child when he was refused.

One man had his hair turned white in spots of about the size of a quarter of a dollar—presenting a curious appearance. Some were subject to distressing fits, some to chronic diseases, and others to other diseases. The greater proportion were, of course, wounded men, and squads" of these were constantly coming, and going again as soon as able to be transferred to Washington. Squads were also made up to go to the front as the convalescents became able to do duty.

One morning, as they were falling into line, ready to march, I stood in my tent, watching them getting to their places, when a man from ward D came out equipped with overcoat, cap, haversack, canteen, cartridge-box, and gun, and placing the latter on the ground, he put his foot on the trigger, leaned over it, and, as it discharged, he fell dead.

A note was found in his pocket showing that the act was premeditated. It stated, also, that he had never been noticed by the surgeon, was yet unfit to endure the fatigue of marches, and battle, and he preferred to die outright rather than to linger through miserable months of torture, and then perish at last. He was carried by my tent door to the dead-house with all his equipments on, the warm blood saturating the blue uniform, his half open eyes growing glassy under the hand of death.

The thought of the despair which had actuated him to die by his own hand was dreadful. It was from no lack of courage to meet the tortures of ' life that he did it; but the prospect of a certain death, at the end of his sufferings, made up the horror that tempted him, and he chose instant death.

The picture of a fair mother and child was found in the knapsack of a soldier, who was brought into the hospital, too weak to speak his name, or to tell to what regiment he belonged. They laid him under the sod in the hospital graveyard, while, in our sadness, we sighed for those who should always mourn the uncertainty of his fate, and who would never know where he slept. The word "UNKNOWN," was the only inscription on the white board at his head.

One morning, while passing up to my ward, I was attracted by the appearance of an old stretcher standing near the path, having on it a man's body which was hanging carelessly over one side of it.

I went up to it, with a curiosity to know if the man was alive, and if so, what could, be done for him. I started back at the ghastly sight which presented itself. Death had seized upon his victim days before, for the bluish flesh was putrifying, the limbs were stiff, and the hollow eye- sockets were filled with worms.

I turned away shudderingly, and inquired at the ward if any one knew aught of his haying been placed there. Every one seemed as ignorant as myself, and we could only conjecture that he had fallen by a bullet, or by disease, in some unknown spot, had been discovered by accident, and was brought in for burial by some persons who were unmindful of hospital interests.

Dutch Gap was being dug at this time, and men were daily slaughtered. Hundreds of lives were sacrificed at this place, until my fancy could but regard it as an immense hollow monument, lying upon its side—its inscription, the bones of the men whose precious lives were there crushed out. It is not for a woman to question the ability, or inquire into the motives of a military general, but I am confident that the sufferings and the fearful slaughter of the men should have been sufficient to cause the abandonment of the work.

Had it proved a success, the lives lost would have been counted well-spent. In the exposed position, however, no way of protection could be afforded the men, while clearing the channel of obstructions, and it was eventually blown open, to lie a gigantic failure. The dull rumbling of the explosion was plainly heard, and the vibrations it caused were felt for the space of fifteen minutes within our hospital grounds.

We had been invited to attend and witness the explosion, but had seen too much of the horror of its progress to want to behold the end of the farce. Many a night had I gone out of my tent, from a snug bed, into the damp, misty air to give food and drink to these hungry, thirsty fellows, and bind up their dreadful wounds. I was not rested by the longest night of sleep during those months of hospital service, and my feet and fingers were always stiff and lame, until warmed up with my work in the morning—yet I complained not, while so many noble examples of patience and endurance were continually set by the brave sufferers around me.

We were startled one day by a near explosion, the sudden shock of which sent one of my attendants from the bed on which he was lying, straight to the door of the ward. For several seconds report followed report, during which a grape-shot raked across my tent corner, marking the canvas, and ploughing over the ground till its force was spent and it lay buried a little distance under the surface. I dug it out of its hiding-place, and it lies to-day amongst my relics of battle-fields.

Some prisoners had been retained at the Point —so many arriving that it was difficult to obtain immediate transportation for them— and it was supposed to be the work of their hands. An opening had been made into the magazine, and an attempt to blow up the valuable stores was the result. An acquaintance of mine at the Point hearing the first sound jumped under the heavy timbers of the bridge, which alone saved him from destruction.

Mrs. Spencer, New York State agent, was on her horse upon the elevation above, and the balls flew quite thickly about her, and even upon her; and, although her stay springs were broken, and herself bruised from head to foot, no portion of the skin was rent. Looking up, at the sound, she said she saw a clear path in the sky, and reined her horse toward the opening.

CHAPTER XXIX.

THE days began to shorten, the green leaves became tinged with yellow, the mists grew heavier, the nights grew longer, and the dew began to freeze upon the dying grass blades. Cold weather was coming upon us with its chilling winds and dark, lonesome days—and no rays of sunlight came through the deep mists.

Our canvas dwellings, in which we had passed weeks, seemed insufficient for the coming winter j yet we drew a great amount of comfort from the fact that a season of plenty had fallen on the hospital since Dr. Hammond took charge.

In the midst of our congratulations that all was going on very well Dr. Burmeister returned, Dr. Hammond being relieved, and things relapsed into confusion and disorder. He asserted that the hospital had run down in his absence, although all concerned knew better, and succeeded in having Dr. Hammond court-martialed—from which trial he came out bright and shining, and was sent to the colored portion of the Ninth Corps as surgeon in charge.

Our men were brought down in one week to wormy crackers again, while the best fare we had was bread, without butter, and tea. Under this diet every one complained bitterly..

For the purpose of keeping the men employed Dr. Burmeister commenced building stockades for winter-quarters. Squads of men were detailed to chop an d draw the logs—for the new wards were to be built of these.

My extra diet kitchen was merged into that of the ordinary diet, and I prepared such extras as I could beg of the Commissions over the stove which Dr. Hammond had procured for me. But under the new restrictions I was unable to procure the usual quantities, and my men were suffering.

Some soldiers were brought in one day starving and dying. I went to them with my pail full of milk punch, giving each a glass full before getting their breakfast. Their coffee was made at the general cook house, but being out of bread I went to the Sanitary Commission for crackers. Through dint of persuasion, and the frequent assurance that it was for a fresh lot, I obtained a pail full for a hundred men. Although I felt rather indignant, yet

I could not blame the Commission for withholding that which it was the business of Government to provide.

The return of Dr. Burmeister was ^he beginning of a series of trials for me, as there were nurses among us who were ever ready to harass those who tried to do their whole duty.

Miss Dix sent a box of grapes to me by Mrs. Lyon, requesting me to -divide them with the nurses tenting with me, for the benefit of the patients. I did so, but soon discovered that the grapes were left untouched for days, and were not appropriated to the purpose for which they were intended. Because ready to fault these things I was daily reported to ears quite ready to take in slanderous tales.

Miss Dix appeared in the hospital one day, when affairs were near their consummation, accompanied by a woman in search of her son. We were going through my ward, vainly seeking him from section to section, until the mother's heart began to sink, when she said, "I fear I shall pot find him alive, even if I get a trace of him." As we were passing into the last section, the lost son came face to face with the desponding mother. The meeting was a truly joyous One. The woman remained with her son, while Miss Dix accompanied me to our quarters.

As the evening drew on, and we were all together in our tent, Miss Di^ began a conversation which enlightened me somewhat in regard to some things that had transpired. She asked one of the nurses, who manifested no little enmity toward me, "Will you state the reason why you cannot tent with Miss Bucklin?" She remained silent, and Miss Dix continued, "If Miss Bucklin does cook for her men, the process cannot discommode you—for the stove is under the fly and out of your way, while she has a box and cupboard to keep her materials in. Surgeon Hammond is highly pleased with her labors. You are both good nurses, but I would not be justified in sending Miss Bucklin away because you do not wish to tent with her."

Then turning to me, she said, "Why don't you talk to your tent-mates?" I replied, "Because I was told by Dr. Hammond to keep silence, as I was reported to him every day." I then rehearsed the story of my trials since Mrs. Stretch and Miss Ballard left, and the hitherto silent woman cried in her rage.

The nurse's face grew scarlet with passion, and she broke forth, "I never was sent away from three hospitals" "Stop!" interrupted Miss Dix, "you shall not talk in that way. Miss Bucklin was relieved from two hospitals for simply doing her duty, as she seems to be doing now. I understand all of that."

Miss Dix could get no specific accusation against me, and she left me to the mercy of my tormentors, apparently in the full conviction that I was strong enough to take care of myself.

I had been advised by a few friends to resign, but I choose rather to remain, under all the unpleasant circumstances, than to risk being sent home while the end of the war seemed yet far off. I had little terror of being relieved now. I understood that men and women could be easily annoyed for simply attending to their duties, and I was sufficiently hardened for such contingencies.

I saw the enraged nurse go to the quarters of the surgeon in charge, and in a short time thereafter he came over, and abruptly asked, "Where the devil did you get this stove?"

"Dr. Hammond procured it for me of the Sanitary Commission," I replied. "Well," he continued "I want another stove, and I'll send for this." I protested—but, in vain, the stove was taken.

I went immediately to the Christian Commission, and obtained a larger and better one, and prepared food as before, when able to obtain it. I was now reported as cooking for other wards than my own. The woman who had charge of the extra diet kitchen, and with whom the surgeon in charge boarded, came in one day and asked what I was going to have for my boys, adding, that she would keep back the Government supplies, if I thought I could beg enough to feed them.

I only replied, "My boys are entitled to their rations, and you must not withhold them."

Soon I received another call from the surgeon in charge, and he interrogated me in regard to extra cooking again. I replied, as before, that I only prepared food for my own patients. Any way," he said, "I will take this stove, and that will stop the devilish work."

An order soon came for it, and I was left without the means of cooking for the wounded. One of the nurses went to the extra diet kitchen to board, another went to the Christian Commission, our cook was sent to his regiment, and I was left alone. In this dilemma I decided to go to Washington and purchase a stove and furniture, and see what virtue there would be in actual possession, and to go without Dr. Burmeister's knowledge.

I went over to Mrs. Spencer's for consultation. The commissions and agencies were all, with her exception, located on the one side of the hospital grounds, quite a little journey from our quarters.

Mrs. Spencer was located on the opposite side, directly on the bank of the river, where the wounded passed daily in being brought from the front. She fed hundreds each day and was allowed to draw Government supplies in addition to what was furnished her by her own State. She had eight men detailed to cook and distribute, and the noble woman seemed unwearied in her extensive work of mercy.

She often went to the rifle-pits to distribute supplies of tobacco whilst the bullets of the enemy were dropping around her. She asked me to accompany her and Mrs. Lyon—another -of the noblest of women, whose name soldiers delight to honor—on one of these trips, Mrs. Lyon purposed going up to Washington in a day or so, and I accepted the invitation, with the prospect of having company to the Capital on the day after.

We went up to what was called the Yellow House, beyond the Weldon Railroad, and dined with Capt. Ames, of Battery B, and then pursued our journey to the front, taking tea with Quartermaster Beadle.

The rebels were cannonading briskly that day. We passed from company to company, and it was a real pleasure to see the bearded and bronzed faces light up as we handed them the little papers of tobacco. We were constantly surrounded by officers and privates. Death was in the air, the noise of the cannon was about us, and the expectant faces of those who soon might lie in the mud of the trenches, cold and bloody, were before us—thus the scene was truly exciting.

One officer told us that he came out with his regiment thirteen hundred strong, had seen it reduced to five hundred, again filled up, and again reduced until he was disheartened. He thought he was., kept for a target. He had been lying on his bed in his tent not long before, -where he was struck with a piece of shell, which tore through his coat and overcoat, leaving a dark line across his back. His time had long expired, but he could not obtain his muster out, having accepted a commission. Mentioning, the fact that we were going to Washington on the next day, he begged of us to intercede for him with, the Secretary of War. (We had the pleasure of seeing his name on the list, for muster out, two days later, while waiting at the Secretary's office whither we had gone to advocate his cause.)

It was quite dusk when we prepared to return from our day at the rifle-pits, and we were fourteen miles from City Point Capt. Ames had sent his orderly with us in the morning, and he was with us now, a welcome escort. Mrs. Spencer and Mrs. Lyon took turns in riding on horseback, while I kept to the ambulance. It was eight o'clock when we reached Capt. Ames' quarters, where we warmed ourselves and fed our horses.

The captain accompanied us a goodly part of the distance—as we were in the very haunts of the rebels, and obliged to pass a locality frequented by their sharpshooters—and we arrived at our hospital near midnight.

CHAPTER XXX.

DESIRING to go to "Washington without the knowledge of Dr. Burmeister I went to Gen. Grant's headquarters for a pass. I found the hero sitting in his tent and obtained the requisite paper without delay. I stood in awe before the gentlemanly little man on whom the fate of the nation seemed to hang. I had often seen him sitting under a fly, in our hospital, smoking at his cigar; at times going amongst the wounded men, talking cheerily of the prospects of speedy peace; shaking hands with dirty, ragged fellows as heartily as though they were the highest dignitaries in the land—but I- never stood before him till now with a personal matter to urge upon his attention, and certainly felt no little embarrassment. Mrs. Lyon accompanied me on board the boat, and our journey was a very pleasant one.

I visited Camp Stoneman Hospital during this trip. Several women had been there since Dr. Higgins was locked up in Old Capital Prison, and, amongst the number, I found Dr. George's wife. The doctor was on a visit to City Point at the same time. A large proportion of my old acquaintances yet remained, and I met them in the old brown house, where they assembled to have an entertainment and compare notes with me. The following morning I was aroused from my slumbers by the familiar notes of the bugle, and I breakfasted for the last time with those who had been my patients and companions at that place.

After purchasing my stove and packing some winter clothing I returned to City Point, the familiar sound of cannonading greeting our ears while yet far away.

Two nurses returned with me, whom Miss Dix had sent down with the request that I should obtain comfortable quarters for them, if possible. As all nurses were obliged to report to the surgeon in charge for duty I accompanied these to his quarters on our arrival. He said he was about to consolidate the wards, and did not need all the nurses he had, but finally assigned one of them to duty, ordering the other to report to Dr. Mitchell, of the Cavalry Hospital, sending her over in an ambulance, with myself as her company.

Dr. Mitchell had all the women nurses he needed, and there was no other resort but to take her back with me. In the afternoon I was relieved, and Mrs. Smith also, although she had never been assigned to duty.

We were under the necessity of washing our own clothes in this hospital, having a small butter tub and cold river water for our convenience, with the ropes of our tents for clothes lines.

No smoothing irons were to be had, and ironing under such circumstances became rather a doubtful employment. With mud, and dews, and rain about us, it was impossible to keep our clothing neat. Some of my clothes were in the butter tub when my relief came, and it was raining in torrents. The weather was extremely cold, and I had no means of drying my clothes, yet I was ordered to Washington without delay.

Seeing the surgeon in charge passing bj, I laid the case before him, asking permission to remain until the weather would admit of drying my clothes. He referred me to the medical director, Dr. Dalton, and to him I hastened in the rain, receiving the ungracious reply that "he wished I wouldn't trouble him with such questions."

The day following was still rainy, and I went to Mrs. Spencer for advice. She told me to remain, and if it was pleasant the next day, I should go up to Point of Rocks with her to distribute a lot of tobacco, as she had a right to detail an assistant. On the appointed day we set out, in company with Mrs. Smith, the other "relieved" nurse.

The day was a bright one and it had its effect on my spirits. I enjoyed the October sunshine exceedingly and watched with interest the flood of light which swept over the landscape. The hand of war had not lain as heavily on this route as on that which we took on our journey along the Weldon Railroad. There, the fields had been stripped of fences, and the tree boughs lopped off by shot and shell, fires had burned through the woods, and white ashen heaps and charred trunks marked the track of the destructive element. Here, the trees were yet unbroken, some fine fences yet remained, and the houses stood with the doors and windows entire.

We were received with courtesy by the officials at Point of Rocks, and mention being made of the expected battles, by Mr. Dow, clerk of the surgeon in charge, and of their need of more nurses and intention of asking for them, Mrs. Spencer remarked, "Here is one Miss Dix has just sent down, and as Miss Bucklin is not needed at City Point, perhaps both will remain with you."

Dr. Storrs, temporary surgeon in charge, was called, when he sent me to look at the quarters we could have, saying if we thought we could quarter together till better arrangements could be made, they would be glad to have our services immediately. We replied that we had no idea of escaping hardships, and that any little nook into which we could crawl, with blankets wrapped around us, would be sufficient. We decided to return on the following day—trusting that I could make this step satisfactory to Miss Dix when next I should see her.

It was late at night when we returned from Point of Rocks, and we were met, on our arrival, by friends who urged me to remain with Mrs. Spencer until morning. In some way Dr. Burmeister had learned of my journey to Washington without his permission, and, by his order, the corporal and guard had been out all day in search of me.

I did not fear the guard-house. Brave soldiers had been innocently thrust into it, and I decided to go to my quarters, and remain there as long as I chose, if not arrested in the meantime. Others urged me to keep away from the tent; but declared that they would shed their last drop of blood before I should be taken to the guardhouse.

I went up to my quarters, however, accompanied by a soldier, packed my effects, together with the bundle of dried clothing, and gave them into his charge till morning. I then made up a bed with the blankets which were yet scattered around in the tent, and, weary with the day's adventure, I slept soundly, and without disturbance till morning broke mistily over my little white tent.

It was the 20th of October. My stove had not yet arrived, having been sent on another boat when I returned from Washington, and, I left City

Point, purposing to come over for it when I should learn of its arrival.

I soon afterwards learned that Messrs. Burmeister and Dalton had been relieved from their positions, and that the hospital was then in charge of men whose executive powers, or their wills, were more favorable to the condition of the wounded.

CHAPTER XXXI.

POINT OF ROCKS HOSPITAL was located on a large plantation belonging to the Rev. Jack Strong who was formerly a Baptist minister. It overlooked the Appomattox River, and had been deserted by its owner as he beheld the first long lines of glistening guns and bayonets advancing from the pontoon bridges, just crossed, and steadily nearing his residence.

The negroes said that the affrighted clergyman, on seeing the blue uniforms of our soldiers, had ordered up the mules, helped his family into the wagon, and driven off at full speed toward Petersburg.

The buildings were all guarded, and 'log stockades had been erected for the receiving 'wards.

My first appointment was to the charge of two of these enclosures, perhaps a hundred feet long, with canvas for the roof, and neither floors nor doors. A large fire built of heavy wood sent out its streams of flames and smoke—the latter escaping wherever it found egress.

In these all soldiers, black and white, were brought to be divested of their torn, bloody uniforms, and to have their swarms of graybacks and their wounds attended to. The Tenth and Eighteenth Corps were consolidated and designated the Twenty-fourth Corps, or the Army of the James, and they furnished the material for the work we had to do.

The log stockades were principally filled with colored men, wounded on picket, or in the charge on the enemy's works.

There were nine Government nurses here, and we soon had three tents assigned to us, one to each three. Miss Dame, New Hampshire State agent, and superintendent of the general kitchen, quartering alone.

We had a very large cook-house, in which each cook had his own stove, and certain articles of food to prepare. We had large quantities of canned fruit, canned meats, milk, eggs, white sugar, butter, oysters, fresh and salt fish, fresh and salt beef, sweet and

Irish potatoes, vegetables of all kinds and poultry. Lemons and oranges were brought in by the box and daily distributed.

We had a little drove of cows, affording milk for the patients, and a bake-house which turned out hot rolls for breakfast and tea. Apples we had, by the barrel, which were given daily to those able to eat them. As the days were short, the surgeon in charge decided that it was not best to get the men up very early in the morning, and two meals only were served through the day—giving the nurses however the privilege of feeding the sickest at her option.

To Dr. Fowler, surgeon in charge, was due the credit of obtaining this abundance, which the men enjoyed irrespective of color or of State. Our own table was bounteously spread also, and, from the contrast with my late abode, the opinion that something was wrong somewhere seemed confirmed.

Soon after my arrival at the Point of Rocks Mr. Stacy and Mr. Sperry, of the Sanitary Commission, came on to distribute their supplies. These noble men dealt them out unsparingly. From Mr. Stacy I received a tea-kettle and coffee-pot—each nurse being expected to provide her own dishes for cooking and take care of them also.

Ginger tea was made twice a day, thick as syrup, almost, with white sugar, and carried to the poor chilled negroes, who were constantly coming in, hungry, ragged, covered with filth, and crowded into these uncomfortable stockades, on which the cold rain fell heavily and froze as it fell.

It was a terrible task to cleanse these wretched creatures; and when fresh clothing was needed, as it was daily, I knew of no other place to ask for it, except at the commission. I wanted so many changes I dared not ask for them, but requested a dozen each of shirts, stockings, and drawers, adding, timidly, that I needed a hundred. Mr. Sperry said, "I will send them over," and I retired, expecting to receive the dozen for which I had asked, when to my joy and astonishment the hundred sets of underclothing arrived, together with Mr. Sperry to help distribute them.

As fast as the men were cleansed up they were put into the wards, and each woman nurse had white and colored patients. For a long time my ward surgeon was changed almost daily, till I had fourteen in the space of a few weeks; at last Dr. Fox remained permanently in charge. He was a kind and considerate surgeon, and the soldiers were carefully looked after day by day.

The dreary November skies were drawn over the scene; the leaves had fallen dead from the tree tops, and all the world seemed shorn of bloom and beauty. My clothing grew insufficient for the inclement weather, and I turned toward City Point where my winter clothing was stored amongst the belongings to my as yet unclaimed stove. Taking an ambulance one day, I went over to procure them.

I found that the stove had arrived, but by the blundering of a half-drunken clerk, it had been directed to Miss Dix, and the surgeon said it could not be delivered only to her order. I stated the fact of my clothing being stored in the boiler of the stove, but he would listen to no reasoning of the case—the stove could only be delivered to Miss Dix or to her order.

I said if I wrote to her for an order, as she knew nothing of my purchase, she would not be likely to give me one. Several standing by said that the stove was undoubtedly mine and they would not hesitate a moment to deliver it up, if the case lay with them. Seeing the surgeon so determined to withhold it, I finally said I would turn it over to the provost marshal, and was about to execute my purpose, when the surgeon said, "If you will write to Miss Dix I will let you take the stove."

I assented, confident, however, that she would take no notice of the matter—nor did she, for I never had a line or a word from her on the subject. I returned to Point of Rocks with the long coveted stove in my possession.

The hospital was on high land, and the winter severe in the extreme. Rain fell in torrents and froze till the tents were one sheet of ice, whilst the one fire on the bare floor could not Warm the atmosphere.

White and black were treated alike—both occupying the tents and wooden wards. The cold was intense at times. Many of my men had their feet frozen to their ankles; others lost their toes in bed during those terrible days and nights of storm and cold.

Our first duty was to look after the breakfast, after which the ginger-tea was in order. Having but few white men to look after, and the plenteous fare obviating any necessity for cooking, I passed the most of my time with the colored soldiers, teaching them to read from books furnished by the Christian Commission.

That Commission established a church, near to the hospital in which service was held every evening and on the Sabbath.

Plenty of reading matter was always to be obtained from the Commission, and I read papers and books to the colored men by the hour. Some became so deeply interested that they purchased papers of the news-boy on his morning round, and, on entering the ward, I was often greeted with a chorus of voices, asking, "Please, missus— won't you read to us if there's anything about the war, or what the prospects are?"

I was exceedingly interested in these men— many of whom had just been liberated from bondage, and were fighting to retain for themselves and children the newly acquired boon of liberty. They were universally polite and deferential to me, again and again expressing their gratitude, for the good care which Northern women gave them, by the remark, "Jest as if we had white faces, missus."

I often heard singing and praying, as I came into the ward, but could not see a single face. Putting my ear down to the beds, I found the voices were those of the occupants, who, with their heads entirely enveloped in the blankets, were performing their devotions in bed.

Everything seemed as favorable to nurses and patients at Point of Rocks as it was possible for them to be in a field hospital, and, in point of civilization, it went far beyond any other in which I had ever labored. We could tell the days of the week, especially the Sabbaths and Thursdays, and remember when meal time came, whereas, in other camps, the rising and setting of the Sun often denoted the time for the serving of our rations.

On Christmas and New-Year's day we had turkeys, chickens, and oysters, and an extra meal was provided for all. The convalescents dined around a beautiful table, in the great dining-room, which accommodated nine hundred persons, while the patients were served in their wards.

CHAPTER XXXIX.

SOME deaths occurred amongst my colored men, one of which, amongst others, was of a very affecting character. His wound was a severe one between the wrist and elbow, and seemed, for a time, to be doing well, but suddenly changed for the worse.

He said to me, "Don't you think the doctor talks as though I would die?" "I hope not," I replied. "He talks just as I should if I thought so," he said, speaking again. His pain was so intense that the perspiration stood in great drops on his face, and the five blankets on his bed were wet to the topmost one.

It was too late to have an amputation performed and he was sinking very fast. When I was about leaving the ward, to go to tea, he said, "How I would like to have the ladies come and sing in the ward to-night." I promised to ask them to do so.

They cheerfully complied, and the scene presenting itself was quite an affecting one. He exhorted all to follow the Christ who was able to save the chief of sinners. As we neared his bedside, he turned to us and said, "Don't you see the angels all around my bed, waiting for my soul? My sufferings will soon be over—I can see Jesus waiting for me across the river—he will take me by the hand."

Taking a silver ring from his finger, he gave it to me, requesting me to send it with a lock of his hair to his mother, giving, at the same time, her address. When contemplating the great change, he asked, "HOW do they bury the dead here?" I replied, "You shall be buried as well as any of them,"—not liking to tell him they were each rolled in his blanket and laid coffinless in the grave, some one receiving the eight dollars which was allowed for the burial of every soldier who died in hospital.

I gave the attendants a shirt, drawers and stockings after his death, and, with these and his usual clothing upon him, he was rolled in his blanket and laid in his last resting-place.

Another, who had his feet frozen in the extreme cold weather, when about to leave the hospital in the spring, came to bid me good-by. He said he was sure the Lord would take care of him—he had

209

always tried to do right, ever since he left his home in the South to fight for his liberty, and he thought God would still prosper him.

One boisterous day, as I was passing into my ward, one of the men accosted me with the information that he had just received a letter from his wife, who was at Fortress Monroe, adding, "How much I want to see her. I don't expect a colored man could get a furlough, though—do you think he could?"

I said I had never known a colored man to have one, but I would see if I could obtain one for him. That evening I was in Miss Dame's quarters, and Dr. Fowler being present, I asked him if it was against orders for a colored man to have a furlough. "Why?" he queried, "does one of yours want one?"

I related the story to him, and he said, "Get Dr. Fox to recommend him for a furlough in the morning, and I will give him one."

He was recommended, and received his furlough, leaving for the Fortress within twenty-four hours from the time he so anxiously asked of me the information. A few days later I received a letter from him, thanking me for the interest which I had taken in his welfare, and confiding to me the fact that a little dusky daughter had been born to them, to add to their mutual happiness, and "IT HAD BEEN NAMED FOR HIS KIND HOSPITAL NURSE!"

Our convalescing colored men were sent to Fortress Monroe— squads being made up every few days to make room for the freshly wounded.

One man, in my white men's ward, was slowly wasting away with consumption. He had enlisted to avoid a draft, and was passed into the service by the examining surgeon from malicious motives. Soon after leaving home he contracted a heavy cold which prostrated him upon his bed.

One day he begged of me to assist him in obtaining either a discharge or a furlough. I interceded with Dr. Fowler, who assured me that if, on an examination, Dr. Werne thought him entitled to a discharge, he should have one. Dr. Wendell, the surgeon in charge of the ward to which this man had been moved, was present, and asserted that nothing but homesickness was the matter with him, that he was "playing off." A squad was sent to the front in a few days, at which time the consumptive disappeared.

The ward master assigned to my colored ward was a young Virginian only seventeen years of age. His father, a loyal man, had moved to Philadelphia at the breaking out of the rebellion, and the son entered the Union army. He became sick after seeing some service, was brought to the hospital, where he became convalescent, and was detailed as ward master. He obtained a furlough to go home, while I was working amongst the men, and a man by the name of Smith was assigned to his place during his absence. This soldier told me he had several times tried to obtain a furlough, but could not, and that thirteen months had elapsed since he had heard from his wife and children. He wished me to intercede for him on the return of the former ward master.

He had not been paid in eleven months, and it was easy to imagine the circumstances of his family, left without any means of subsistence this great length of time.

The young Virginian returned, and reported to me that he saw one of Smith's little girls begging in the streets of Philadelphia, and on inquiring of her where her mother lived, the child refused to tell him. This I revealed to the surgeon, who said if Smith went home he had no means with which to help his family. I said if he would give him the furlough I would get up a purse for his benefit. As it happened, after I had obtained quite a little sum, the paymaster made his appearance, and Smith received his eleven months' pay, and on the same day received his furlough, when he had plenty of money.

His family had been turned out of the house in which they had lived and were tenanting a miserable room, to pay the rent of which his wife took in washing when able, while the children begged in the streets for bread. Her health, never very good, had broken down under these trials. After his return, he seemed to be always brooding over their situation—but the fortunate closing of the war, in the spring, sent him back to his family with two strong hands to work for their comfort.

Boat loads of returned Union prisoners were brought to Point of Bocks. Wrecks of men they were, with ghastly countenances, with bones protruding through the sallow skin, and great hollow eyes—all telling of their starving condition.

The charity of the people had covered their nakedness before they reached us. Their condition would not admit of their taking milk without having it reduced. Many had become idiots in the horror and hopelessness of prison pens, and sat continually crying for something to eat. Great, bony men, the pride of honest hearts, and once in their health and strength, were helpless as infants.

I saw one poor, wasted creature holding on to a hard crust of bread, from which no sustenance could be drawn—yet he tugged at the morsel with all his' little strength. It was enough to draw tears from eyes unused to weep to look upon these unfortunate heroes with shattered minds and skeleton frames. Thin faces told of days and weeks and months of torture—of starvation—of exposure to the sun through almost intolerable heat—of nakedness while covered with the dews of night, and of every grade of suffering.

Better, far better the shock of battle—the rending of limb from limb, the shrieks, the groans, and the gory sod—than torture like theirs.

How small was the terror of the actual conflict of arms when contrasted with the infernal rebel prisons where men were shot daily for the crime of looking through the grated windows to the blue sky of heaven. I was told by a soldier, who assisted me in the extra diet kitchen at Camp Stone- man, of the scenes to which he was witness, and of the tortures which he had experienced; but I never imagined the dreadfulness of the Southern prison pens until I beheld these real wrecks of humanity.

My attendant had been a prisoner at Libby and Belle Isle, and, while cooking, he often told me of the awful food with which nature was expected to do her work at those places. Soups made of peas and beef bones, with red worms floating on the surface, and corn ground up with the cobs, and mixed with water, without salt, was their most generous fare.

212

These men were robbed of their clothing, shoes and money, and were compelled to submit to whatever indignities or cruelties were heaped upon them. They kept soul and body together by digging in the ground for worms, killing a stray rat or mouse for food, and devouring the disgusting morsel with avidity. At last, to some of them, the deliverance came, and they were sent to Annapolis, where they received the best of care and attention. Those on whom no disease was preying gradually recovered —my informant amongst the number. From Camp Stoneman he went to his regiment, and in a few days was taken prisoner at the battle of the Wilderness, and lay for eight months in Andersonville. He lived to see peace smile over the land once more, and all prisoners set free.

CHAPTER XXXIIL

IT WAS late when the wooden wards were commenced, and quite late when they were finished. Chill winds had been whirling over our tents, and ice had been congealing on the guy ropes and canvas. As each ward was completed, and the men were moved into it, we had dedicatory services. The surgeon in charge, executive officers, ward surgeons, nurses and all attendants, gathered into the building, which was lighted with two or three chandeliers, hung along the centre of the ward. The chaplain delivered a short sermon, after which the surgeons each made a speech, and the ladies concluded with singing.

Many evenings were spent in this way, and, with the lyceum twice a week, prayer-meetings on Tuesday evenings, and regular preaching on Sunday, we were enabled to keep up a flow of sociality, thus' preventing the lapse into barbarism which threatened a life in camp.

Many little incidents were enacted and laughed at. Amongst others was that of an earnest sober-minded convalescent named Fountain, who appeared in the doorway of the Church, as the officiating chaplain was reading the words of the hymn, "Come thou Fount of every blessing," when he stalked in and distinctly said, "Yes, I'm coming."

Our hospital cares and labors made fast friends of many of us, and we met in our quarters during many evenings and narrated interesting personal adventures. The steward of our ward told us how he had stood three times with death confronting him from the shining barrels of the guns, held by the firing party, and once led by the cook who was present, who had been corporal of the guard.

He was a West Virginian, and like many other loyal men, was thrust into the gray ranks of the rebels and compelled to fight. He fell into our hands in battle and was sent North. After a little while, eager to do something in the great work, he enlisted in a New Hampshire regiment and set out for the seat of war. While on the way to Norfolk, Va., two or three murders were committed on board the vessel, pockets were picked, and other depredations of so vile a character that he concluded he was among a band of murderers and robbers, and resolved to escape, and seek a transfer to another regiment.

He changed his clothing for that of a contraband, and started for the office of the provost marshal, was overtaken before he had travelled a quarter of a mile and was soon tried and sentenced to death for desertion. He told his story to a chaplain, who volunteered to obtain a pardon for him.

The fatal day came, but brought no pardon to the condemned man. He was taken out to be shot, walking behind the ambulance in which his coffin was home. As he stood by the open grave, while the preparations were being made, it suddenly caved in, and the shallow opening was half-filled with stones and clay.

He was returned to his quarters, and, on another day was taken out as before. Strange fatality! The second grave also caved in, and once more he saw the gloomy shadows of night draw around him in the desolate prison house. The chaplain redoubled his exertions, but, when the third day arrived, he made his way to him, and said, "Charley, I fear it's of no use—I am afraid you will have to die!"

"It is all right," was the reply, "I wanted to do something for the old flag; but if they think it is best to shoot me, don't mourn for me, chaplain. My peace is made with God; the future is bright."

The third time he marched out behind his coffin and stood by the open grave. The firing party held their guns at a rest. The order was given—"Make ready,—Aim." Six shining tubes were leveled at his breast—his soul was about to bid adieu to earth—and in a few seconds more the bullets would pierce his breast. Childhood, youth, manhood, home, mother, and the circle of dear ones—all passed before him in rapid, but distinct procession. He fancied he heard the crack of the deadly rifles, and his heart almost ceased its beating, when along the air was borne the hoarse shout, "YOU'RE FREE, CHARLEY! —YOU'RE FREE!"

This came to his ears at a time when he did not expect to hear the sound of human voice again. The chaplain rushed up to him, and, in the extravagance of his joy, laughed and wept in turn. He had

215

succeeded in obtaining a pardon from the merciful hand of Abraham Lincoln.

The corporal, now a cook, also narrated how he had been so badly wounded, at the battle of Malvern Hill, that they ticketed him with name and regiment, and laid him out on an old stretcher to die. And thus adventures were plentiful amongst those on duty at the hospital.

Spring already was breaking upon us ere the last ward of the hospital was finished, and my colored men were moved into it. My white men, being only a few, were distributed amongst the vacant beds in the other wards, and I was put in charge of the linen-room.

The room had been used for messes' quarters. It was long and low, and had a room partitioned off for my use at the extreme end. A great table stood in the centre, on which the ironing was performed, and, at the fire-place and on a large stove, forty irons could be heated at once.

Each night I sprinkled and folded the clothes for six or eight contraband girls to iron the next day, giving to each one hundred linen sheets. Through the day I mended shirts and drawers, and took care of such patients as did not belong in the wards.

Twenty-two men washed daily at the washhouse, which was located very near to the Appomattox, and the convalescent camp and hospital, numbering four thousand men, furnished the work in plenty. Each night, when the weather was favorable for drying, a great supply-wagon drove up to the door, full of clean clothes ready for the ironing.

The girls, who worked in the linen-room under my superintendence, were very quick at their tasks, and all were more intelligent than I had supposed it possible for them to be, having just emerged from a life bondage. All but one was very obedient, and she was one of the neatest and smartest of them, but fancied, as freedom had been given them, they were entitled to their support without work. She would remain at her quarters while the rest came up to work, Government paying them six dollars a month and rations. Sending for her by one of her companions had no effect whatever. The corporal and guard were obliged to bring her with fixed bayonets arrayed on each hand. By and by I heard her tell her companion that she was going to be married that evening. I called her into my room and questioned her about herself. She told me she was about to marry a colored corporal. I said, "As you seem to be in need of kind treatment, I will make a wedding for you, if you prefer it." She seemed delighted, and said if her lover was willing it would please her greatly. The event was agreed upon, and the linen-room was illuminated with chandeliers and some clusters of early wild flowers.

I procured two kinds of cake, some apples, and a pail full of lemonade, and invited, as guests, the surgeons and their wives, the ward masters, cooks, women nurses, and Chaplain Hager, who was to officiate. At the appointed time the bride appeared, dressed in a snowy muslin robe, a beautiful white head-dress, with little knots of flowers for ornaments. She was accompanied by Martha and Amelia—her bridesmaids. Presently the dusky lover came in, dressed in a glossy black suit, with a colored corporal and sergeant for groomsmen.

They came forward under the bright light, and Chaplain Hager soon pronounced them husband and wife. After partaking of the refreshments they retired to their quarters, and resumed work in the morning as usual.

A week later the colored men were ordered to Texas. Celia came in with the girls that morning, and said, "Good-by, Miss Bucklin." "But where are you going?" I asked. "The Lord only knows; I am going where the corporal does," she replied, and the girl left for Texas with her soldier-husband.

While in charge of the linen-room I occasionally had a leisure hour, when I strolled into the surrounding country. I walked at times to the signal station where I was taken up by a windlass, to the distance of one hundred and twenty feet. Through a spy-glass I could distinctly see over into Petersburg and Richmond.

There were a number of primitive bomb-proofs near the signal stations, made by sinking barrels half way into the ground, with small holes out of which sharp-shooters fired their unerring rifles.

Our pickets were stationed near, and the rebels about half a mile distant. They often tried to make a break through our lines, to enable them to get to City Point, where our supplies and ammunition were stored in immense quantities.

CHAPTER XXXIV.

As spring gradually warmed the earth into verdure the hospital officials planned an immense garden on the rebel plantation. One hundred acres were planted in vegetables, and soon the long straight rows of green appeared above the earth's brown surface.

Mr. Strong afterwards remarked that his place was worth much more than before the Yankee occupation, for his buildings had been preserved, and large quantities of valuable material were left on his grounds. The wine, cider, pork and other articles of food had disappeared, but he was left a beautiful garden which compensated him fully. An order, unfortunately for him, was soon issued, that all such crops should be appropriated to the use of the contrabands.

A small house belonging to the plantation had been fenced in, with about twenty acres of land, and was occupied by a colored couple, and a part of their family of eighteen children.

Some of these were Union soldiers—one of whom, named David, was orderly to our hospital steward, and was quite a pet in camp. His rendering of the popular negro melody, "The Day of Jubilee," was the most original and appropriate of anything I ever heard.

The mother, Aunt Adeline as she was called, was a woman of consequence on the plantation, and we all rejoiced to see her installed on the little farm, to which, by order, they were entitled, on fencing in the grounds.

The Rev. Jack Strong told this woman, after the death of the President, that Abraham Lincoln was dead, and her freedom died with him, and she was his property again. But, thank God, freedom lived and Rev. Jack Strong had no power to roll back its mighty tide.

One pious old contraband habitually came to our Government kitchen for his subsistence. He was lame, very aged, toothless, and worn out, yet could sing beautifully, and often, after the cooks had filled his basket with bits of meat and vegetables, they induced him to sing something in payment for the broken fragments. While, at times, they were laughing at his ridiculous appearance, he would break out in full sweet tones, as clear as the notes of the bugle, and

219

the words lingered in my memory for days. These lines were often sung by him, and, as he gave out the invitation, the lightness with which the kitchen attendants regarded them seemed terrible to me:

"Come sinners to the gospel feast,

Let every soul be Jesus' guest;

There need not one be left behind,

For God hath bidden all mankind.

Sent by my Lord on you I call,

The invitation is to all;—

Come all the world—come sinners thou,—

All things in Christ are ready now."

He could not read a word; all he knew was a few verses of similar import. He had been a slave all his life till set free by the proclamation of liberty. His whole life had been spent in toiling to give others ease, and now, at the night-fall of his day, he was turned out upon the selfish world.

Many of our convalescent soldiers here passed days with jack-knives and peach or cherry stones in fashioning tiny baskets— several of which lie in my treasure box to-day, together with bone rings and countless little articles, each of which has its history.

A regimental dog in our hospital became an object of no little interest to all. He was a noble-looking fellow, of the Newfoundland species, and was possessed of remarkable intelligence. His master had been detailed to work in the cook house, whence he would carry a basket of meat as faithfully as a man and with astonishing quickness and fidelity. He seemed to prefer the active service to a hospital life, and he again and again ran away to the front, and joined the regiment, in which he seemed to be as well drilled as any of the soldiers. He enjoyed the crack of the rifle, and the boom of the cannon, and had been thus far through the war without receiving injury.

I found some little time here in which to visit the different wards. I dropped into Mrs. Cahoon's ward one day to see a patient who was rapidly declining with consumption. He told me a sad story of a misspent life, which he ♦ concluded with these words, "I have two children, but they are well provided for, and I do not wish them to know how their father died. My course of life for years has been such that it would only cause them shame if they knew it. It is better for them to remain in ignorance of my fate. What I have here, I shall dispose of here. '

An elegant gold' watch he gave to his nurse, to be taken possession of after his death. When he died the effects of the soldier were turned over to a chaplain, and in two hours no trace of the gold watch could be obtained in the hospital. A slight investigation of the matter only served to show plainly in whose keeping it had been placed, and upon whose soul the guilt of the theft rested.

There were men in every hospital who shrank from the duty of a soldier and who feigned sickness and even acute diseases. One miserable fellow, of this stamp, often came to me, begging for underclothing and telling of his forlorn condition. It was not until I had given him two sets of shirts and drawers that I began to suspect he was dishonest.

I met him one day and asked him, "Why don't you wear the new shirts?" "I am saving them to take home," he replied. "Where are they?" I asked. "In my box, over to the quarters," he answered. I then saw a boy, who even at that moment was wearing one of the garments, and asked if he had not bought certain articles of underclothing from the accused, to which he assented, giving the price which he paid for them. At that moment the hospital steward also came up and demanded of the soldier to return the money to the boy. He said he had no money. "Take out your pocket-book, and let us see," was insisted. The pocket book was produced, and enough money found to repay the four dollars which he had received for the garments—giving the boy the money and the clothing.

When this soldier was about to leave for home, the surgeon found in his possession a box containing supplies, which he had stolen from the Government kitchen. He was allowed to go his way, but the contents of the box was retained.

CHAPTER XXXV.

The order was at last issued that all non-combatants from the Armies of the James and the Potomac should be sent to the rear. The ambulances and supply wagons had been thundering into our hospital camp for days, and stood in long lines, closely packed, ready to move at a moment's warning.

The clouds of war seemed to gather over us, as the signal guns were fired, and everything around us warmed into excitement. The report came into the hospital that an encampment of soldiers rested about two miles from us and would cross the river on Sunday afternoon. We knew that the second tier of pontoons had been laid and we waited eagerly to see the Union army drawn more closely around the rebel capital.

On the morning following the order the long lines of blue crossed the bridge in steady column. We had breakfasted, and were just leaving the dining room when we first saw them. They were cavalry, and, in my eagerness to see if any familiar faces were amongst them, I went down to the landing with several nurses.

The men were ordered to dismount and pass over on foot behind their horses. Some of them knew me, but I scarcely recognized any of the long haired, full bearded, dirty fellows before me. In the hospital they had been kept so trim and neat, even the buttons on their blowses were polished with care, their shoes nicely blacked, and their clothing clean and whole. But they had endured long marches; had lain for nights on the bare ground, and through days their watchfulness had been unceasing, and the battle ground was only a little way before them.

First came the straggling scouts, disguised in rebel uniforms, going out into the country across the river to pick out the way. Next came the cavalry seventeen thousand strong; then sixteen thousand artillery, with ponderous caissons, glittering cannon, and gaily decked horses. They were hours in passing, and when fairly over, the cavalry remounted, and taking the different roads, some wound around the hill, while others passed among the scattering trees.

The battle began that day, and lasted through six more. We distinctly heard the cannonading, and saw the bursting of the shells in the air. In feverish excitement we sought to know the progress of the struggle and awaited the end. At last Petersburg fell. The victorious army, without delay or rest, pushed on to the rebel capital. Hungry, worn down with incessant fighting, they eagerly marched onward. Through the long, dark night they moved on until the daylight revealed to them the beleaguered capital in flames: Ninety of its most magnificent buildings, including stores, were enveloped by the devouring element.

With magazines bursting, bricks falling, fire brands whirling through the air, and women and helpless children flying in terror, the boys in blue began to fight a new foe. The fires were quenched, and prisons were opened, whilst in the noisome dens the rebel prisoners of war took the places just vacated by our starved men, to whom deliverance had come.

Whilst the exchange in prison life was going on, one of our surgeons from Point of Rocks, Dr. Bresbine, was present. As a rebel lieutenant was passing in he asked the doctor if he would do a favor for him. "Certainly," replied the doctor, not waiting to listen to the request, "yonder in all that filth and gloom I lay for six long months, with only one blanket for my bed and covering— you can have my place now," and he passed the lieutenant in.

Through those days of conflict many terrible deeds were done. In one of the forts, the last to yield, a soldier of the Tenth Connecticut and a rebel met, while our men were at one side, and the greys at the other. Rushing upon each other, with almost unparalleled desperation, each touched the others heart with his fixed bayonet, and fell dead, rebel and loyal blood mingling.

I saw the body of a soldier in which seven minnie balls were lodged, and which had been pounded with the butts of guns till his eyeballs protruded from their sockets. He belonged to a scouting party of five men which had been sent out, just before the battle, and been surrounded and surprised—the other four surrendering to the demand of the rebels, and he being shot in his resistance.

223

Whilst the fiendish work of mutilation was going on over his murdered body the other four escaped and came to our hospital. A squad was sent out to find the dead body, and it was brought in, disfigured as described—his companions relating the horrible incident.

Soon the wounded began to pour in. Rebel and Union, side by side, were borne in on the stretchers, from the boats, and all cared for alike. Freshly wounded men lay in the beds from which former patients had convalesced, and death was a frequent visitor in the wards. Our supplies were ample, and we frequently distributed oranges and fine fruit at Point of Rocks.

Joyful faces were now on every hand, even in the midst of suffering. LEE HAD SURRENDERED. The rebellion was virtually dead and the Nation survived the struggle. Soldiers waved their hats and cheered with all the vigor of their lungs. One dying soldier, who had been brought in from the victorious field, and who heard the sound of the cheering, summoned all his energies, and lifting himself upon his elbow, cried out, Glory to God! Thank God I lived to see this day! I can die satisfied, now!"—and soon after breathed his last.

The rebel capital, for the possession of which we had struggled for years, had at last fallen into our hands, and Abraham Lincoln walked its streets without a body guard. Where Southern women spat upon our boys in blue, as they were marched to prison, he walked, followed by a people who from their hearts cheered their deliverer.

On his return from the last visit to Richmond, President Lincoln called at our hospital and passed through the wards. His plain, honest face lighted up with a winning smile as he talked to the boys of speedy release. Nor did he withhold the word of cheer from the rebels; they were assured they also should soon return to the bosom of their families. Little did we then think that in life we should never look upon his noble face again.

On Sunday morning we received the intelligence of his assassination on the Friday night previous, in one of the theatres in Washington. Suddenly, as though the sun had dropped out of heaven, darkness seemed to come upon our land. The chief had fallen, in the hour of triumph, brutally murdered. Truly, our joy was turned into mourning.

Men whose hearts had beat high with exultation, looked gloomily into the faces of their comrades, and took the proffered hand in silence. Would it prolong the struggle? Would the rebellion receive fresh impetus from this blow at the soul of the Republic?

Gradually again the clouds lifted, and, with the surrender of the last Confederate army to the victorious, swift-footed Sherman, our souls were lifted up out of the gloom and darkness and soldiers caught up visions of home, and friends as they yet sorrowed for him who had lived through all the din of the conflict, and borne the weight of the Nation's cares, to die when the dawn of peace was lighting up its horizon.

CHAPTER XXXVI.

I WENT UP to Washington on personal business during the search for the murderers of the President. Every free on the boat was closely scanned, and when it drew near a landing the little tugs swarmed around us like bees.

The Capital presented a scene long to be remembered. The streets everywhere were draped in mourning. The body of the assassinated President had just been taken from the Capitol. The gloom was universal, and no one dared to whisper an approval of the horrible deed by which the nation was robbed of a loved chief, and the name of Abraham Lincoln was made SYNONYMOUS with that of "THE NOBLE MARTYR." Miss Dix sent a nurse to Fortress Monroe under my care, when I returned, thus affording me a visit to the gigantic fortifications, and a look at those who had been for months, under my care at Point of Rocks. The hospital being two miles from the landing, we took the horse- car from the boat, and soon reached the surgeon's office, where the nurse was assigned to duty.

I procured a pass and visited my colored men. As I passed the bars, one of them recognized me and uttered a cry of pleasure, when I was soon surrounded by many black faces. Upon asking some of the unfamiliar ones, "Did you ever see me before?" they called my attention to circumstances that transpired when they were in my charge at the hospital.

Everywhere there was joy that the war was over. Black and white shared alike in the promises held forth to them in the surrender. I found only a few old friends in the white wards, who were now convalescent, and were about to be sent to their regiments, to be thence transferred home when the hour should come.

The morning on which I took the parting hand of some of the old nurses here, who had been my comrades at Gettysburg, and at Georgetown, was a beautiful one. I walked to the Soldiers' Cemetery to visit the grave of old Aunty Alexander. She had gone from Camp Stoneman on a brief visit to New York, and on her return was detailed for duty here. She had been a good nurse and had worked hard until sudden death overtook her. In compliance with her request she was buried with military honors amongst the soldiers who died in the hospital.

I had been for more than two years and a half in the military service of the United States and during that period had only seen three familiar faces. Learning that the regiment to which a friend of mine belonged was at the front, I asked for an ambulance one clay, and, accompanied by another nurse, set out to find him.

We jolted through mud almost knee-deep— through ravines where dismal shadows stretched along the frequent windings and reached the Ninth Corps' headquarters, where, upon making inquiries for the regiment, we learned that our destination was still two miles ahead, in the direction of the Jerusalem Plank Road.

Arriving at Gen. Meade's headquarters [George Gordon Meade, Union commander at Gettysburg] we were directed further onward toward Gen. [Winfield Scott] Hancock's division. It was getting late in the day, and -we were exceedingly weary of riding over the wretched roads, yet felt unwilling to return without finding a trace of the regiment of which we were in search. Reaching Hancock's division we were told that the regiment was not there, nor could any one inform us where it was.

The shadows of evening were already gathering about us, and we were twenty miles from the hospital, with a miserable road between us and certain rest. No way remained for us but to warm ourselves and brave the worst as soldiers do. We made our way into an old-fashioned house, having a wide hall running through, with rooms, on either hand, above and below.

The windows were out—the doors were unhinged, and everything bore the evidences of rude usage. In one room we found two women and four or five children gathered around a handful of coals on the hearth.

We remained here long enough to take the chill from our weary bodies and become disheartened at thinking about the rough, corduroy road which lay before us. We again entered the ambulance and turned our faces toward the hospital, where we arrived late.

Shortly after our return a half-dozen women came, one day, to see a man who had visited one of them. The steward, getting tired of them, brought them to my room, near to where the contrabands were ironing. Each race saw the other, and the working girls, feeling indignant and having a keen appreciation of their newly acquired independence, talked so loudly amongst themselves that we heard every word.

One said, "There isn't a decent woman in there, only Miss Bucklin," to which the others assented in strong terms. I paid no attention to their conversation, and was soon told by my callers, that they were as likely as myself—an assertion which I had not questioned—and if I did not stop the talk of the "black wenches" they would go out. They reported me to the steward who met me, shortly after, highly offended because I did not "Slap the wenches on their mouths."

I felt sure that my ironing girls appeared far superior to the snuff eating women—and that they best knew to what indignities they had been subjected under their hands. I felt no disposition to interfere in the matter. I will add that it was a warm May day, and these women were dressed in' muslins and furs, with ribbons of various colors on their heads.

Vie found it necessary to extend assistance to the confederate soldiers in the hospital. Their suits were ragged, and swarms of insects had eaten sores upon their bodies, half as large as a man's hand. Many of these men had lived in the country about us, and their wives and children frequently visited them.

The pleasant days went by, and the hearts of the war-worn veterans yearned for their homes, and the companionship of friends in the dear old North. Many of them bore honorable scars, and were eager to tell the wife, or child, or mother, how they had been snatched from the jaws of death.

CHAPTER XXXVII.

HAVING some curiosity to see the cities, before which so many of our gallant men had fallen, Mr. Soyer and wife, of the Sanitary Commission, and several nurses, myself included, took ambulances for Petersburg. We passed over a narrow road, made by our soldiers while on their way to the battle field, which had the Appomattox River on one side, and a pond on the other. It was made of logs and brush, and was a dangerous path over which to pass in any other way than on foot.

The rebel defences were ingeniously constructed. The four tiers of works and three rows of abattis seemed impregnable to any force which could be thrown against them. The sharpened stakes bristled up into the air, about three feet 24 from the ground, and so close that a man could not pass between them. Torpedoes lay just under the earth between each one, and if by chance our men should succeed in passing one, another and yet another lay beyond, ready to explode under their tread.

The evidences of hard contested battle lay on every hand as we entered the city. The streets on the outskirts were sadly damaged— every building had upon it the mark of a shot or shell. Bridges were broken, fences were burned to ashes, and trees with immense boughs were lopped OFF.

We stopped at the residence of a very agreeable Southern woman, who extended to us the hospitalities of her home. She expressed herself rejoiced that the war was ended, and that her sons, who had been in the Southern army, could return home. Her "niggers" were free she said, and, if every body was like her, there would be no more trouble on account of them. A lovely flower-garden was attached to this dwelling in which, on the orange and lemon trees, were quantities of fruit as beautiful and well developed as that from the tropics. Buds and blossoms and flowers were on every hand, and much taste was shown in their arrangement. Beautiful groves had once surrounded Petersburg, and some magnificent shade trees yet remained along the broken streets.

We saw the headquarters of Gen. Lee, and the last fort to which he was said to have retired hut half an hour before it was taken. With what emotions he must have witnessed the entrance of our soldiers into that city, so long regarded as secure against our arms. The Confederacy was built upon the sandy foundation of human bondage and could not stand. Blood could not cement it—valor and enthusiasm could not hold it up. Any other and more righteous cause, than that of the iniquitous rebellion, could not have failed of success, if sustained with equal courage, fortitude and endurance.

Near the last of May, when our hospital was on the eve of breaking up, Steward Browning came to me one day, and said, "If you wish to go to Richmond, before you go home, you may select some one to accompany you, and I will furnish the requisite pass." I was eager for the opportunity of seeing the rebel capital and I selected Charles Crompton, my ward steward, knowing that he was familiar with the city. When the morning arrived Miss Leonard, Mrs. Cahoon, Steward Crompton, and myself went together to the landing below our hospital and took the boat for Petersburg, en route for Richmond.

We moved very slowly down the river, from which the torpedoes, put there by the rebels, had not yet been removed. Our boat often touched the sides of the great upright posts, in passing between them, placed there to obstruct the channel, but we reached Petersburg in safety.

The cars in which we took passage for Richmond were box cars, without seats, or the ordinary travelling conveniences. A bench, which would hardly have borne our weight, was standing on the platform, and some of the boys proposed taking it, when a man stepped up and said we could have it by paying the sum of two dollars. We of course declined the moderate proposition.

As we were not in the line of duty just then, and at liberty to exercise our judgment in the premises, we preferred to sit on the four corners of a crockery crate which had been put in. Our unstable seat swung to and fro with the motion of the cars—which, fortunately for our equilibrium, did not move rapidly. Several gentlemen were also on board, bound for Richmond, each bringing in a stick of wood for a seat.

We went, for a- few miles, slowly through the lovely wooded country, and then switched off to allow a train of cars to pass. A short distance on, and another pause was made, in which the fireman and engineer went to a desolate-looking house, away up in a clearing, bringing us back a cup of water. It was evident that the demoralization of the country had even driven railroad companies and their employes into a disregard of systemization.

The road being exceedingly rough, and the train hands corresponding with the road, we did not enter Richmond until about five o'clock. The only vehicle which awaited the convenience of the passengers was a one-horse wagon driven by an Irishman—both considerably dilapidated.

We found a lodgment, and on the following day, while strolling through the city, we met some of the men from our hospital, who had just made the round of Libby Prison and Castle Thunder. They accompanied us to Castle Thunder, where we saw many of our men confined. Why they were there I had no means of ascertaining, but presumed they had perpetrated offences of some kind in the knowledge of the authorities in charge. The place, a dismal one, looked perhaps more hideous to us because of the enormities that had been practiced there. We even said to ourselves, looking back, as we left the place, "Could those walls but recount the barbarities they have witnessed!"

We next visited Libby Prison, which we found to be a gloomy brick building, standing at the foot of the road—its three stories seeming quite low as we descended to it. The rooms were long, low and narrow, having small grated windows, as indeed nearly every dwelling and barn in the Confederacy seemed to have.

On the cold floor—paved with round stones, which were hurtful to the feet at every step—our martyred men had lain till the bones wore through the flesh and they died from starvation. The lieutenant pointed out to us a hole in the cobble-stone floor, large enough for a man to pass through, and told us the story of the men who dug through fifteen rods of solid earth, with only their plates and spoons, scooping out the hard clay till they reached a point on the outside. My mind naturally recurred to the details of their long, patient toil; how they had managed to elude the vigilance of the guards, while crawling at a snail's pace with their puny tools; how near they had been to exposure, before the tunnel was finished, and how, in the hope of soon reaching the Union lines, even through swamps, and rivers, and deadly foes, one hundred and fifty men dropped themselves down, one by one, into the mouth of the den, and passed noiselessly out. Some of them were retaken, to suffer over again the horrors of the prison; others received the boon of liberty for the indescribable toil of weary days and nights.

It was dusk when we began our way from this- place, made infamous by the torture of hundreds of the nation's best men, and we soon after reached the hospital at which we were favored with accommodations during our brief visit.

In the morning we visited the cupola of the capital building and took a survey of the devastated city. Ewell had left the evidences of his destructiveness in the black ruins which lay around us. In the distance we distinctly saw Belle Isle, with the demolished bridge, over the James River, leading to it.

We next entered the office where the "ironclad" oath was being administered. We overheard one person remark, as he passed out, "Wall, now, that's about the tallest swearin' I ever done," while others seemed unconscious of the meaning of the act. Some came in unable to tell what they did want. Of one such, the officer asked, "What shall I do for you, sir?" "I want a parole," was the reply. "Are you a soldier V "No." "Have you been one at any time during the war?" "No." "Then YOU do not want a parole." "Don't I want a pass?" asked the rebel, the happy thought giving just a little ray of light across his stolid face. "Those are done away with now," replied the officer, and the anxious rebel stepped back. About one hundred or more took the oath, and all were, with one exception, ragged, dirty, barefooted and bareheaded.

The poverty apparent in these rooms gave rise to many reflections. The Senate Chamber was covered with a rag carpet very much worn.

In another room we found a common ingrain, while the stair carpet was so far gone that we were obliged to use care to avoid tripping in its rents.

Our curiosity finally led us in the direction of the buildings that had been temporarily occupied by Gen. Lee and Jefferson Davis.

CHAPTER XXXVIII

SATISFIED with our visit to Richmond, WE started for City Point. While on our way from the hotel, at which we obtained refreshments, to the boat, we visited the Sanitary Commission boat—which was thronged with rebels, begging for food. Here they told us that, the day after Richmond came into our possession, they issued from the Government supplies sixteen thousand rations, and, from the Sanitary and Christian Commissions and Union agencies, fifteen thousand more—thus giving a faint idea of the destitution which had prevailed in the capital. For months the poor were thus fed by the Government, on which they had heaped vile epithets, and by the very men whose lives they had sought. We were soon well provided for in the carpeted cabin of our boat, where we rolled ourselves in blankets, and slept comfortably until morning. We started from the Richmond landing at an early hour, and had a remarkably pleasant trip. The captain very kindly pointing out to us the different forts and hard-contested battle-fields. We passed Dutch Gap and arrived at City Point about noon, where we lay waiting for the arrival of the tug which was to take us up to Point of Rocks.

The river was full of boats laden for their final departure. Sutlers' boats, Sanitary and Christian Commission barges, and Government boats, having all manner of supplies, were awaiting orders to leave. We watched with deep interest all these signs of the breaking up of the Grand Army of the Republic—our own hearts beating anxiously as we thought of the rest which we too had won, and that no more brave soldiers would be brought, in shattered condition, to our white hospital tents, from bloody battle fields.

At three o'clock we went on board the tug, and in thirty minutes thereafter were ascending the flight of steps which led to our hospital home. We were tired and hungry—the rest of the nurses had gone, and our mess tent was taken down—and were obliged to "forage" for the time.

The steward told us to go to the Government kitchen and cook whatever we liked best, and, being entitled to our rations from

Government while in Government employ, and preferring to take what I liked, rather than to have it dealt out to me at the option of those who had no right to limit us, I gave little heed to her instructions.

Ve took our cooked food to our quarters, and ate it from the top of a dry goods box, relishing it exceedingly. For several days we lived in this way—Mrs. Cahoon attending to the only ward remaining, and I busy in finishing up the mending yet on hand. Miss Leonard had left us the day following our return from Richmond.

My shelter here was very faulty. A rain storm came on one night, and upon awaking in the morning, a stream of water was running down upon my face, and another upon my feet, from holes in the canvas roof. It rained without ceasing for two days and nights, leaving us without a dry article of clothing or bedding. Yet, drenched as they were, we were compelled to sleep under them, keeping a fire near at hand a portion of the time.

On the succeeding Sunday morning the bright sun broke cheerily upon us and we passed the day in drying our wet clothing.

On Monday morning we bade adieu to the few remaining attendants at Point of Rocks, and took the boat for Washington. We had a very pleasant journey, and were accompanied by rebel officers and women—many of whom had large amounts of baggage stored in long coffin-like boxes.

On reaching Washington I did not look for an abrupt breaking up of my military life, having left Point of Rocks under the impression that I would be assigned to duty in a hospital at Alexandria—but an order was issued, to take effect on the first day of June, that all hospitals kept open after that date should be at the expense of the surgeons in charge. So few patients remained to be nursed officials were suspected of a design to nurse the "good job" a little longer. The order had the desired effect, and the hospitals were broken up without delay.

Home was now the beautiful port in view. It was the first time that I felt a willingness to seek its shelter during three long years. While battles were to be fought, I was ready and truly anxious to endure suffering, to be near the scene of conflict and to help minister to the bleeding heroes. I have even thought that imprisonment alone would have kept me from my country's service after the way to enter into it had been opened up.

Among the sad memories of these years in hospital and camp, of some fast friendships formed when the dead lay around us, with the suffering and groaning on every hand, there remain some pleasant ones—the cherished of my life. In the silent watches of the night and the peaceful hours of the day they come to me as ministering angels to soothe my soul, when troubled with life's many little perplexities, and awaken in me a charitable view of earthly affairs.

I fully realized the truth of the parting words, "You will have some pleasant as well as sad remembrances of your military life!" spoken by Miss Dix, as I left her residence, for the depot, on my homeward way.

I arrived at Auburn, New York, just in time to meet with an old friend, and hear the salutation, "Well, I suppose you have fought, bled and died for your country," when, in the wildest excitement, several ladies rushed in and exclaimed, "They have come!" and without giving me time to effect a change of clothing, I was marched off to assist in welcoming the remnant of the war-worn One Hundred and Eleventh Regiment back to its native city.

Sick, weary with travel, dusty, and ragged, many were taken into the clean rooms of the hotel, and laid on the white counterpanes, while I, who was supposed to know how, went about at my old work of washing begrimed faces and combing tangled hair. THIS TIME THE HEROES

WERE NOT BLOOD-STAINED.

MISS BUCKLIN'S OFFICIAL PAPERS.

The following are exact copies of the official papers received by Miss Bucklin, at various times, and are properly attested and on record:

OFFICE OF WOMEN NURSES, UNITED STATES HOSPITAL SERVICE, WASHINGTON, D. C., May 30th, 1865.

To Whom it may Concern:—This certifies that Miss S. E. Bucklin has been employed in the United States Military Hospitals, in the capacity of nurse, *with credit,* and has now retired from the service *with credit,* and she always has my kind and friendly regards for her generous labors.

D. L. Dix,

Superintendent United States Hospital Nurses.

Seminary Hospital, Georgetown, D. C., July 16th, 1862. Miss S. E. Bucklin was on duty at Thirteenth Street Hospital, while I was connected with that institution, and I take much pleasure in recommending her as an attentive, faithful and industrious nurse, and deem her a valuable assistant.

T. W. MILLER,

A. Ass't. Surgeon, United States Army.

The above certificate seems to me just and correct. I readily testify to the good character of S. E. Bucklin.

D. L. Dix.

CAMP LETTERMAN, GENERAL HOSPITAL, GETTYSBURG, Pa., Oct. 9th, 1863.

This is to certify that Miss Bucklin has been acting lady nurse in ward B, Third Division, discharging her duties to the perfect satisfaction of patients and surgeons, being of untiring industry, energy and perseverance, and indefatigable in her efforts to alleviate the sufferings of our noble wounded patriots.

WM. B. JONES,

A. A. Surgeon, U. S. Army, in charge of Third Division.

GENERAL HOSPITAL, CAMP LETTERMAN, GETTYSBURG, Pa., Oct. 29th, 1863.

I have much pleasure in testifying to the kindness and attention of Miss Bucklin to the patients in Ward B, Third Division, of this hospital. I have no hesitation in recommending her as a most efficient and indefatigable nurse, whose equal I have seldom seen.

JAMES NEWCOMBE,

A. A. Surgeon, in charge Third Division.

CAMP LETTERMAN, GETTYSBURG, Pa., Nov. 8th, 1863.

This will certify that the bearer, Miss S. E. Bucklin, has been on duty in this hospital in the capacity of nurse; served a part of the time under my immediate notice. I recommend her as having performed her duties diligently and faithfully.

Very respectfully,

W. M. WELCH,

A. A. Surgeon, United States Army.

Camp Stoneman, D. C., April 22d, 1864.

It is with great pleasure that I can conscientiously state that Miss S. E. Bucklin, hospital nurse, who was connected with ward No. 1, of which I had charge, always discharged her duties faithfully and cheerfully. She never was called upon by those who were suffering for aid that she did not respond promptly. As regards moral character, it was, while connected with me, irreproachable.

H. G. CHRITZMAN,

A. Surgeon, Eighth Regiment, Pennsylvania Cavalry.

CAMP STONEMAN, POST HOSPITAL, CAVALRY DIVISION, DPT. WASHINGTON, D. C., May 30th, 1864.

This may certify that Miss S. E. Bucklin has been a faithful and attentive nurse in this hospital for the last three months. I can with pleasure recommend her as being of good character and worthy of the confidence of all with whom she may be associated. Ira P. Smith, M. D.,

A. A. Surgeon, United States Army.

Hospital for Colored Troops, Army of the Potomac, Oct. 11th, 1864. The bearer of this, Miss S. E. Bucklin, has been nurse in Depot Field Hospital, First Division, Second Corps, for the past three months under my charge. She has been faithful, efficient and competent—a good nurse, and I cheerfully recommend her as such.

F. M. Hammond,

Surg., One-Hundred-and-Twenty-Sixth New York Vols.

POINT OF ROCKS, VA., May 30th, 1865. **HOSPITAL STEWARD THOMAS POWELL,**

Miss S. E. Bucklin having been nurse for three months in the ward under my charge at Point of Rocks, I take pleasure in recommending her as a faithful, kind and industrious woman. I always found her attentive to the wants of the afflicted, and an upright and moral young lady.

A. C. Fox,

A. A. Surgeon, United States Army.

THE END.

Get more great reading from BIG BYTE BOOKS

Made in the USA
San Bernardino, CA
12 July 2018